A Lifting of the Veil

A Lifting of
the Veil

. . .

Betty Andreasson Luca and Bob Luca

ISBN: 1539345734
ISBN 13: 9781539345732
Library of Congress Control Number: 2016916970
CreateSpace Independent Publishing Platform
North Charleston, South Carolina

In loving memory of
Rebecca Andreasson Smallwood

Daughter of
Betty Andreasson Luca
James Andreasson

Stepdaughter of
Robert Luca

Wife of
Rick Smallwood

Sister of
Mark Andreasson
Scott Andreasson
Bonnie Andreasson
Cindy Andreasson

We all love and miss you, Becky.

Contents

Foreword

· · ·

THE BOOK YOU ARE HOLDING in your hand may be one of the most important you've ever read. It is the continuing saga of an often beautiful contact between certain chosen human beings and an alien presence that is more ancient than we can know. This alien presence can be traced back to a period before the beginning of recorded time, farther back than the limited understanding offered by our paleoanthropologists with fossils and skeletons and the vagaries of human science. Perhaps our creator aliens are still with us, watching over life on Earth and guiding us in the directions that have been determined for us.

One of the most crucial arguments for this belief is found in the modern-day alien-abduction phenomenon, which involves an interaction with UFO occupants that goes well beyond sightings of lights in the night sky or finding landing traces in some backwater forest area. It is a form of direct contact with a hidden race that some call extraterrestrial, although, in truth, their time on our terrestrial Earth likely predates our own by unknowably vast eons.

The attempt to place the abductors within a spiritual context is still a hotly debated one. Are aliens something we have historically called demons? Or should we—as Betty Andreasson Luca and her husband, Bob, do—understand them to be angels sent among us to do the will of a loving heavenly Father?

This heavenly take on alien abduction, a phenomenon admittedly fraught with many moral complexities, began for Betty on January 25,

1967. She was at home with her children on a typically cold New England winter night. She had fed and dressed the children, and they were watching *Bozo the Clown* on television. Betty was in the kitchen, finishing up a few remaining chores. Suddenly, the lights went out throughout the house, and a strange pink glow began to shine in through the kitchen window.

What followed is an alien-abduction story that never ceases to both amaze and comfort me. It involves the typical gray aliens, journeys to and from waiting UFOs, alien medical procedures, and frequent episodes of missing time. As with nearly all abduction accounts, Betty obtained most of the narrative information through careful use of regressive hypnosis. Another familiar element is that the aliens were obviously interested in Betty along with other members of her family, abducting not only Betty but also her daughter, Becky, and her second husband, Bob Luca.

But the amazing and comforting part is this: the aliens who spoke to Betty that January night spoke of Jesus as "coming soon." They also told Betty not to fear, because the Lord is with her. They warned her she would undergo many trials, but love would guide her and answer her throughout whatever she endured.

The aliens recounted in most abduction literature generally say very little to their abductees. This fact has been compared to a cat being treated by a veterinarian. What can a veterinarian actually *say* to a cat to explain the various medical processes being carried out in the cat's treatment, let alone their ultimate purpose? But in Betty's case, the aliens *did* speak to her—in terms of her Christian faith and with comforting promises that any believer would be glad to hear. Betty has never wavered in her belief that her gray abductors are angelic creatures preparing the way for the second coming of Christ.

I first heard of Betty and her angelic encounters when reading Whitley Strieber's *Transformation*, his first sequel to his groundbreaking alien-abduction bestseller *Communion*. Whitley wrote about "the stunning mystical and religious overtones" of Betty's experiences.

When I interviewed Whitley in 1993 for the now-defunct *UFO Magazine* and asked him about Betty, Whitley told me, "The number of us who are so spiritually superb as Betty Luca, who can really make this encounter experience fly, is tiny. Most of us are down here in the muck struggling with it. That's why Betty is such an inspiration to me. When I was at the depths of my depression, one of the things I did was read Betty's interviews and listen to her tapes, just to hear the sound of her voice when she was talking. I would look at the drawings she sent me. Betty's experiences are the thing you grab on to while you are sinking."

I also had the privilege of interviewing both Betty and the UFO researcher who told her story so capably, Raymond Fowler, many times. Betty and Raymond have been hugely important to my writing career, but even more crucially, they have helped shape my beliefs about UFOs and Christianity to a degree I cannot overstate.

In my first interview with Betty, again for *UFO Magazine*, I asked Betty if her abduction experiences were related to the popular Christian belief in the rapture.

"Quite possibly," she answered. "There is scripture to support the idea. In the book of Luke, chapter 17:34–36, Christ says, 'In that night, there shall be two men in one bed. One shall be taken, and the other shall be left. Two women shall be grinding together. The one shall be taken, and the other left. Two men shall be in the fields, and one shall be taken and the other left.'

"Further evidence that may support the rapture," Betty continued, "is verses thirty and thirty-one. 'Even thus shall it be in the day when the Son of Man shall be revealed. In that day, he which shall be upon the housetop and his stuff in the house, let him not come down to take it away. And he that is in the field, let him likewise not return back.' Doesn't it sound familiar? Of course, most Christians believe it will be one fell swoop of believers, starting first with those who are in the grave and have died in faith, and those believers that remain will be caught up in the air."

For me, what Betty is saying here is that the rapture is, in a sense, an ongoing event that happens all the time throughout the world. One can draw comfort, therefore, from knowing the mechanism for an ultimate rapture—involving the full body of believers being taken out of the world—is already in place, has been proven to work just fine, and is simply awaiting its time.

But in spite of the inspiring, faith-affirming story Betty and Bob Luca tell, there are certain elements of the shadow government on whom the Lucas' message is apparently lost. Over the years, the couple has been subjected to what has become the familiar pattern of surveillance and harassment by some element of the government that is hostile to even such mild-mannered folk as Betty and Bob. Troubling overflights by unmarked black helicopters; tapped phone lines; and being followed by suspicious-looking observers who fail to disappear completely into the background—their experiences with this kind of official but secretive scrutiny run the gamut.

Betty and Bob have responded to this challenge by trying valiantly to find a paper trail of documents that can prove somehow what they have been forced to endure. Their requests for specific documents, made through the auspices of the Freedom of Information Act, have been only partially successful, as is the case with most UFO researchers who pursue this method of investigating the phenomenon. It is always an effort fraught with uncertainty, perhaps even danger, but Betty and Bob unflinchingly discuss the situation in detail in this, their first book, offering a blow-by-blow account of their battle to make the government confess to its heavy-handed response to an alien presence the powers that be apparently have come to define as an enemy of the present world order.

When I was asked to write this foreword, Betty and Bob warned me that they are not professional writers and that their manuscript would require extensive editing by its eventual publisher. My first thought was that their amateur standing might be to their advantage—and ours—because it meant the book would have a purity of approach and execution, a guilelessness one could not easily find in the verbal flourishes and stylistic niceties of professional wordsmiths. In other words, it is the unvarnished truth as the Lucas see it, as plain and simple and yet as cosmically complicated as the alien-abduction phenomenon itself.

Please keep all this in mind as you read further. Betty and Bob Luca together constitute what may be, in spiritual terms, the most important case of ongoing alien contact in our world. If that is the case—and I, for one, believe it is—we don't want to miss a single word.

Sean Casteel

CHAPTER 1

Retrieval Begins

• • •

"THERE ARE MORE THINGS IN heaven and earth than man has ever dreamed of." Shakespeare used this thought-provoking phrase in his play *Hamlet*; however, today we've come full circle. Rather than hiding behind a veiled, phantomlike dream of reality, life speaks to humankind for itself. The strange truths and awesome realities that definitely exist within heaven and earth are no longer obscured; they are seen, felt, and experienced by many, as the veil of disbelief is lifted from the souls' eyes. And humankind begins to experience the profound and phenomenal existence of extraterrestrial life that, for some unknown reason, tends to draw ever closer to us. This awesome otherworldly realm cannot stay hidden forever in order to exist. It is here for a purpose: UFOs are real. The beings flying these craft are real.

The series of Andreasson Affair books have recorded the strange and awesome phenomena of this otherworldly presence. As you read this book, some of you might say, "Well, I know a lot about this information from Raymond E. Fowler's five books on the Betty Andreasson Luca case." As a matter of fact, during the investigation of this long-standing case of high strangeness, a top-notch team of intelligent researchers and a doctor were gathered carefully to test her claims of strange beings who entered her home, took her away temporarily in one of their crafts, put her through tests, and returned her home, leaving her with just enough memory to seek help. She spent countless hours retrieving unbelievable material through extensive hypnosis sessions, follow-up interrogations, and character references. She employed weather reports and background checks. Betty even took a psychological stress evaluator (PSE), which is a type of lie-detector test, and she passed.

Dr. Kornburg, a psychiatrist who had examined Betty previously, came for a follow-up visit and spent many hours at Betty's home with both Betty and her husband, Bob. The psychiatrist found Betty to be completely normal. While he was visiting, the psychiatrist heard a loud crash in the kitchen. He verified no one else was up, and there was no obvious cause for the noise, as nothing had fallen or was out of place. Around five thirty in the morning, Dr. Kornburg, Bob, and Betty were outside talking in the yard when Dr. Kornburg looked up and asked if either of the other two had noticed the huge, unusually shaped, lengthy cloud stationed directly over their house and not moving. They could see the rest of the sky was very clear except for scattered stars, including those that twinkled and shone through the thinner mist surrounding the outer edge of this peculiar stationary form. Bob replied that he had seen the shape, but he hadn't planned to mention it unless the doctor saw it first. To Betty, it looked like an enormous, cigar-shaped, solid white form, surrounded by a thin outer layer of mist, which stars blinked through.

Many years after this silent yet obvious visit, Betty was taken aboard one of these gigantic mother ships that had the ability to create a stealth effect, possibly through natural means, by cloaking its shell with a cloud that clung over the surface of its body, which was very much like what they had seen over the house. But for now, we shall return to the rest of the information concerning the activity of the UFO phenomenon in Betty's life, which was being recorded during the hypnosis sessions. All the findings helped to reveal what had happened to her and what she had lived through. This information includes unusual-looking beings, many odd machines that she described seeing and later drew, and information concerning strange examinations and implants from the different UFO abductions she went through.

There are many who have never heard about her unusual life and personal struggle to understand and live with the multiple, continued UFO encounters she has gone through and survived. The UFO phenomena embody spirit, psychic, and paranormal realms that surround and influence the physical presence of soul and spirit to awaken to the total reality of the unknown. This reality often will place an enormous trial within the heart and mind concerning faith. When faced with ongoing spiritual and physical UFO experiences, which at times seem to have no rhyme or reason, it becomes a hard pill to swallow. What do you do? Especially since the phenomenon is so difficult to understand and at times impossible to explain away. But during Betty's UFO experiences, there was always a light within, giving her strength. For she believes the beings she has been involved with are angels, or messengers sent by our Creator, the One who wants us to embrace who we are and connect to the divine plan that has been in place since the beginning of time.

Included in this book will be a preliminary summary of what has happened from the beginning, which will allow the reader to walk through and absorb several of the earlier encounters with an open mind, and come to the most recent experience, which contains new and continued information. Besides this new encounter, the book will reveal other unusual happenings that both Betty and Bob have seen and experienced, which may or may not be associated with the UFO phenomenon.

But first, let's go way back to the beginning. This has nothing to do with the UFO phenomenon, except for an odd and hidden circumstance concerning the Andreasson name. It was in the early eighteenth century that this happened. Betty's ex-husband's Swedish grandparents and their four children were trying to come to America as immigrants. Wanting to move the family to the land of opportunity, his grandparents tried to get tickets for the last and only ship at that time that was leaving England for America. But there was no more room, and it would be many months of waiting before any tickets would become available again. The grandmother was a small, blind woman, yet she was determined to get her family to America. While at the dock, she kept asking around if anyone had, or knew of, any tickets she could purchase. By an odd stroke of luck, she heard of a family of five who had tickets to sail that day but could not use them because their children had taken sick with chicken pox. Because of this unfortunate situation, the woman sold her family's five tickets to the grandmother, and the grandmother and her children boarded the ship. The grandfather had to stay behind until many months later, when another transport to America became available. So the grandmother and her four children were on their way to their new home. As the ship docked at the New York Harbor entrance in Ellis Island, each boarder had to present his or her ticket to enter the country. Not one of them, mother nor child, could speak English. The passports that the blind grandmother had bought were already stamped with the original owner's family name, which was Andreasson. That is how they became the Andreasson family. It was not until many years later, when their children learned English, that they realized what had happened. Evidently, their parents felt it was too late to change the name, so the family name remained Andreasson...even though their true family name was Jamesson.

It is so strange how heritage or, for that matter, hidden things will somehow find a way to surface and reveal the truth. Betty did not learn about the Jamesson family name for many years after her marriage, after her seven children had been born. Her father-in-law and his family kept the Andreasson name; however, she sometimes wondered if he consciously or subconsciously decided to name his only son James to keep his family's identity and true name alive. Then, when James and Betty's first son was born, they automatically named *him* James as well. As the years passed, the couple had three more sons, and Betty's first husband, James, insisted that each of their middle names was to be James. So, indirectly, their four sons, in a hidden way, still carry the Jamesson family name. Thus ends the mystery involved with the name.

Evidently there are many peculiarities in man's ancestry. The names of Betty's ancestors also carried some strange scratch-your-head questions. For example, her father's last name is Aho. Today, a person possessing that last name is allowed to claim it only if he or she is born with it or marries into it. It's against the law to carry it in any other way. Like the Jamessons or Andreassons, Betty's grandparents and their family also came to America from their homeland, which was Finland. The Finns at one time were called the Pics and lived on the coast of England long ago. This artistic race used to draw pictures on their bodies. To Betty's knowledge, there have been three generations with artistic abilities in her family line.

Her grandfather was Elias, and her grandmother was Esther. They were hard workers and bought, owned, and produced the largest dairy farm in the Fitchburg, Massachusetts, area, where they sold milk to the local communities. Many years later, they were sued. Back then, they could not speak English and did not understand what the court system was all about; nor were they aware they needed legal counsel to represent them. When they went to court without counsel, they lost their entire farm, their cows, and their thriving business. The sad story is, unable to speak English, they had trusted one of their hired employees to deliver their milk. Unknown to them, however, their farmhand, Willard, while delivering their milk door-to-door, was skimming the cream off the tops of the bottles and adding water to bring it up to the cap, so people were not receiving whole milk. Because of Willard's thievery, Betty's grandparents lost everything.

As for the ancestry on Betty's mother's side, it was English and Spanish. Betty's grandfather came from Spain or Portugal, though she isn't sure which one exactly. His last name was Belyeah. He was much older than her grandmother, Emma, and had served in the Civil War for the North; at one time, he was stationed in the exact area of Virginia where Betty's daughter Rebecca lived many years later. Betty's grandparents had four daughters named Katharine, Mabel, Eva, and Lulu. Her mother was the second youngest girl. When she was little, her father sold her beloved horse, and she cried and carried on so much that he gave in and had to buy the horse back for more money than he had sold it for. As for Betty, her mother said she was originally named after her grandmother's middle name, Elizabeth, but became Betty to shorten her name for records. Betty's grandmother told Mabel, the second oldest of the four daughters, that there was royalty in their family lines. Her grandmother had lived in England, and her last name was Lucius. A long time ago, Betty read somewhere that there was a King Lucius, who was the first English king to become a Christian, and she often wondered if the family's last name had anything to do with what her grandmother had told Mabel.

On January 7, 1937, Betty entered this world like most babies, with a cry of "I've arrived." She would have been her parents' fifth child but became the fourth, as her mother had given birth to twins before her, one of whom was stillborn. After Betty, her baby sister was born. Betty's first peculiar experience and memory as a child of something odd happening was when she was only seven years old and living on Howard Street in Leominster, Massachusetts. Her brother had built a little lean-to hut in the lower part of the front yard, and Betty was sitting in it all alone, eating some crackers and waiting for her friend Deedee to come over to play dolls. A small insect the size of a bumblebee flew into the hut, circled Betty, and began to fly around her head. It made a dull buzzing sound, and Betty remembers thinking it was after the cracker she was eating, so she threw the cracker down. The unusual bee looked like a small marble or ball of white light as it slowed down, and suddenly it landed on her forehead. It bit Betty and stuck to her forehead between her eyes. She felt a soft, wiggly vibration from it as the marble-like ball stuck to her head. She fell backward to the ground, felt drowsy and cold, and started to hear talking, with more than one voice going on in her head. She heard the multiple voices say, "The wee little one is coming along fine."

They called her name, and because Betty couldn't see anyone, she asked, "Where are you?"

"We are here," they assured her, but she couldn't see them. And they said, "We can see you." Again she wondered where they were, and they said that very soon she was going to be very, very happy—that she would see them in time and that she should not be afraid, for they would never hurt her, but for now she must not remember, except that the bee had stung her. *She must not remember.*

Deedee came into the little hut and saw Betty crying. Betty told her a bee had stung her on the forehead, but Deedee felt the area and said there was no mark or bump. At that time, all Betty remembered was that the bee had stung her.

Many years later, on the morning of May 25, 2013, while living in Virginia, Betty experienced another voice; however, this time it was the voice of a woman. Bob had gone to the automotive store for some truck parts, and while he was gone, Betty was out in the backyard, doing some weeding in the garden. Suddenly, she heard a gentle female voice call her name. Betty continued weeding, because as far as she could see, there was no one near. The same gentle, almost erythematic voice called her name again. Betty kept weeding, because she knew and could see there was no one close by. Once again, for the third time, she heard, "Betty."

This time, she stood up to look. Bob and Betty's next-door neighbor was not at home; his car was not there, so it couldn't be him. Besides, it was a woman's voice. For a fourth time, Betty heard the voice call her name. No one else in their area knew Betty by her first name, as she keeps a low profile due to her connection to the UFO phenomenon. She quietly stood there and looked all around. There was definitely no human, nor a physical angel, present. Betty was dumbfounded. For a fifth time, the same voice clearly and calmly called her name again.

Betty said, "What? Where are you?" After she answered, the voice stopped. Shortly thereafter, Bob arrived home and came out to where Betty was. She immediately told him what had just happened.

"Five times the voice called out 'Betty,'" she said.

Bob replied, "Have you forgotten how you sometimes receive messages from five stations back?"

"Oh, yes, you're right." Betty answered. "But this was spoken audibly to me, so it was a little different. It's been years since I received those messages."

That is what happened that morning, but it did not end there. The next night, Bob and Betty stayed up to watch the news before retiring to bed. It was past midnight when they were finally quietly drifting off to sleep. Suddenly, Betty was wide awake and saw a vision appear. A woman's bare upper shoulder, arm, and hand were outstretched and facing downward about a foot above Betty's chest. There were no other parts of the vision: only the bare shoulder, arm, and hand, which were draped over Betty's body as if to shield her. The vision disappeared, and Betty shook Bob awake and quickly told him what had happened.

The two both fell back to sleep, and in the morning, Bob asked, "What was that arm and hand all about last night?" Betty was surprised, because she didn't remember telling him about it. She didn't know if the vision had materialized because of the invisible woman calling her name five times the day before or what else could have caused it. Besides her encounters and receiving UFO messages, this was slightly different. Betty was moved to find out what this unusual vision might mean and remembered that, long ago, a friend had given her a small, thin booklet called *Types and Symbols of the Bible* by George Kirkpatrick. After locating it, Betty turned to the booklet's third chapter, which was titled "Parts of the Body." She learned that shoulders represent the seat of God's government, eldership, and strength; arms mean "strength of the body" and "enabler of ministry"; and hands exemplify tools of ministry and giving.

Betty was seventy-seven years old when this strange vision occurred. And because of what happened during her last encounter with the One, she believes she will do something for him to show the world in the near future. In addition to the unusual vision she experienced, Betty has had other peculiar things happen to her throughout her life, including occasional contact from the UFO messengers. But for now, let's return to 1944, when she was seven years old. The odd visitation of the tiny ball of light and the words Betty heard back then stated that something in the future was going to happen that would make her very happy. Evidently, time with them is nothing like it is with us humans. We seem to have to have everything now, immediately, to be happy—shame on us for being so impatient. Betty thinks when humans stop to consider time, however, it seems that the simple things in life are the ones they can count on to really bring them joy and happiness.

When Betty's family moved to the country, she was seven, and she definitely was happy, at least for five years. At that time, she was not aware that, at twelve years old, she would have another unusual visit from an otherworldly presence. Her parents had purchased an old farmhouse in the countryside of Westminster, Massachusetts. The property boasted a pond with an incoming and outgoing brook. Betty felt it was the most wonderful place that anyone who loved nature could ever live. The bottom piece of land where the house stood was a large flat yard that stretched outward to an old stone wall that bordered the woods. Two large raised levels of hills stood in the back of the yard by the barn. The first level held three medium-size, twelve-by-twelve-foot chicken coops in a row, the last of which Betty's father used to raise chickens and one mean rooster. The second hill led to the top-level field, where her father had a large vegetable garden. The hardest part was climbing the hills, for there were no stairs, and it was difficult stabilizing oneself while trudging up a hill of loose soil and sand. Betty's father finally built stairs for the first level.

A deep forest bordered all three sides of the cleared land, and way to the left in the woods was a huge lake called Crockers Pond, where Betty fished all the time. For a tomboy like Betty, it was a paradise. A stream on the opposite side of the main country road ran through a large underground pipe that stretched underneath the road and emptied into the family's pond. Betty's friend Eddie would stand at the end of the pipe where the water emptied into the pond holding a bagged wire hoop as Betty walked through the tunnel wearing rubber boots, carrying a stick to ward off the occasional snake swimming toward her, and dragging along another burlap-bagged hoop. They caught many beautiful large trout in each sack.

The whole area was wonderful, and Betty loved it. There were blueberries, blackberries, and concord grapes growing wild on the land. Along the roadside, hazelnuts, black raspberries, elderberries, and wild plums sprouted. The smell of pine trees, woods, and different wildflowers was intoxicating. Today, as Betty thinks back to what the ball of white light told her at age seven, she realizes how very, very happy she had been since her family had moved to the countryside of New England. However, when she was twelve years old, her perfect world was about to come to a screeching halt. Once again, an undeniable energy was drawing her away from a normal life and into a hidden and mysterious realm. As much as she loved nature's woods, chickadees, polliwogs, and frogs, she was about to have another close encounter of the third kind.

When her parents bought the old house in Westminster, there was an old shed down by the pond. The shed housed old tools, nails, horseshoes, other rusty metal rims, and two traps hanging on the wall. As Betty rummaged through the junk and brushed away cobwebs, her interest suddenly focused on the odd foot traps, which she wanted to try, to see if they worked or not. She remembered seeing a large hole in the ground in the woods by the mountain laurel and decided to set one of the traps at the entrance. The next day after school, she was excited and quickly rushed up the back hill. She passed the chicken coops and picked up a few small stones along the way. She continued moving toward the woods and mountain laurel, hoping to see if she'd caught anything with the old foot trap. As she drew closer, she could see the stick she'd used to hold the trap's chain was pulled out and lying down on the ground. The trap was gone.

Betty leaned over toward the large hole, somewhat startled to see something round coming out; it looked like a big, gray bee nest. Betty squinted to see what the peculiar thing was as it continued to emerge. She could not believe her eyes at what was now standing before her. She was very afraid. To defend herself, Betty stepped backward and threw some stones at the creature, which mysteriously stopped in midair and fell to the ground. The strange-looking, very small person had somehow come out of the large animal hole and was standing before Betty. It was short. It had a large head with no hair; gray skin; and big, wide-open, scary black eyes. Its clothing was a tight-fitted, brown suit with six flat, shiny, black, oval-shaped badges with small colored buttons inside them positioned in the center of its chest. This vertical egg-shaped patch also had some odd writing in the center of it. The creature pressed one of the lower buttons, and suddenly a tiny ball of light shot out of the vertical patch and hit Betty between her eyes. It was the same kind of thing that had happened to her when she was seven.

As an adult, Betty attended regressive hypnosis sessions concerning her childhood and early years, which helped her retrieve many major and minor details. Interested readers can find more details about this process in the book *The Andreasson Affair, Phase Two*, by Raymond E. Fowler. After the first investigative research team had gathered most of the information concerning the primary 1967 close-encounter experience, the team decided to try to go back to capture any possible earlier abductions. One might wonder how the team retrieved so many details from Betty's memory; as a child, her curiosity was such that when she beheld something, she made sure to pay close attention to what it was, so she could easily recognize it. She always tried to examine an object's characteristics fully, for everything that is had to be created by the wonderful Creator. When she held a flower, a leaf, or even an insect, she felt joy from truly checking its lines, shapes, sizes, and colors, observing every amazing detail of its being. Betty just loved—and still loves—nature. That is probably one of the reasons she became an artist: she enjoyed the unique beauty and original details that a physical living creature or object possessed.

But now it is time to return to her 1949 encounter. The little being standing before Betty suddenly touched his chest, and a ball of light shot out, which quickly struck her forehead. She fell backward and felt cold and sleepy. The little person stood over Betty as she lay silently on the ground. She began to hear multiple voices talking to her in her head. They said, "The time has come. Just be still." She felt a squiggly sound in her mind and some odd speaking, but this time she heard a second voice speaking as well. She glanced up at the small being standing next to her, but she could not see its mouth moving. She heard the voice say, "She's not ready yet. She has another year to go."

She tried not to respond to the inner voice and turned her attention toward the small being. Out of curiosity, she asked, "How were you able to come out of that hole?"

Instead of replying, the other voice coming from the ball of light asked, "Why did you put a trap there for an animal?"

Hearing the words made Betty feel ashamed of herself, and she dumbly replied, "I don't know."

The voice immediately informed her, "You will soon learn of the One. There are things in the future to see that will help you and others to understand. It is time for you to awaken and forget."

Betty automatically stood up and had no memory of what had just happened until many years had passed. Through regressive hypnosis, the memories of her childhood experience flooded her mind.

CHAPTER 2

Taken before the One

• • •

I CONTINUED TO ENJOY EACH and every day and had no idea what would soon happen to me. Time passed quickly, and it was not long before the appointed year arrived, and I was thirteen years old. Not much had changed. I still did things I had done before, such as going fishing; catching night crawlers and shiners for bait; and picking lady's slippers, trillions, and jacks-in-the-pulpit—oh yes, and going to school. We still had chickens and a mean old rooster that didn't like me. My father and I were the two who had to collect the eggs, and that rooster would often attempt to attack me. Each time I tried to enter the coop, he would strut around in a circle, like he was ready to strike. He hated me, and I didn't like him much either. I had to carry a big stick when I entered the coop, and a couple of times, I had to knock him out cold before I could collect the eggs. Conking that rooster out may sound cruel, but I was just trying to defend myself. His sharp spurs and beak drew blood, and I was tired of bleeding each time it was my turn to collect the eggs. Thank God he always quickly recovered; they're pretty tough birds.

One morning, I awakened to the rooster's crow without knowing what an eventful day it would be. I got dressed, ate a quick breakfast, walked out the front screened door, and was ready for a day of discovery. I decided to go see how the blackberries were coming along; they grew next to the woods, at the edge of the vegetable garden on the second-level field and hill. My father had made stairs and a railing for the first-level hill, but he had not yet built stairs for the second level. It was very hard to climb up the sandy hillside to get to the field. I started up the first-level stairs near the barn, and as I got halfway up, I stopped and turned. Something to the right had caught my attention. I looked skyward and could see the moon; it was very bright, and I wondered what was it doing out at this time of day. It seemed to be moving my way and was becoming larger, as if it had started to grow. I couldn't move as I was suddenly enveloped by its light. Then I was inside it.

Oh, I felt very relaxed, and I realized I was standing in a brightly lit white room. I wondered what happened. I caught my breath, for there were three funny-looking little people gliding toward me, but they finally stopped. I felt afraid and thought, *What are they planning to do to me?*

"You try to hurt me, and my father will grab hold of you," I threatened.

I heard them say, "Don't be afraid. We won't hurt you." Suddenly, for some reason, I felt relaxed, as if I had the upper hand. Then one said, "Your father knows all about it."

I thought, *I don't think Daddy knows these funny-looking little people.*

They kept telling me they wouldn't hurt me and that my father knew all about it. They were very small and were wearing white clothing, which made it hard to see them, except for their gray skin and black eyes. They were standing there looking at me and said, "We're going to take you someplace; we're going to take you home."

I said, "I am home."

They said, "Don't be afraid," and one put his hand up.

I felt very relaxed, almost sleepy. I didn't seem to know what was happening, as I voluntarily followed them through misty white light. We went into another room, and I seemed to be floating along across a floor with them. It was so cold there. They went off to the side, and somehow I just kept moving closer to what looked like a long white box. I was automatically lifted up in the air and moved over to a box that was now beneath me, and another box came down over me. I just lay there, in midair, between these two white boxes, and couldn't move. I could feel someone taking off my saddle shoes and bobby socks and sticking something to the bottoms of my heels. I was able to watch most of what was happening but could not move. Two balls of light hung in midair and were placed above my head and down by my feet. The bright white boxes now turned to a pale green color from blinking lights, and the three-foot-tall beings left me there all alone.

It seemed as if the movement of mist within this area was being disturbed by oddly shaped machines. Something big appeared to be surrounding me; it looked like double metal barrels coming out of the mist on all four sides, and I was still lying between these two boxes where I couldn't move. I heard humming, and suddenly, two steady streams of broken white light bars shot out of the barrels. Then, a purple and blue beam of light shot out, along with the other white broken lights. Between the low humming sound, the flashing green light, and being cold, I began to get a headache. The lights kept shooting out from each barrel, causing the machine to hum, and I heard some thunder. After a while, the lights from the machines stopped, and the barrels pulled back out of sight, disappearing in the misty light. The small beings came in, and the green, blinking light stopped as they removed the two balls of light that were hanging in midair. Somehow, I floated off the middle area and stood upright, as the top box disappeared above and the small beings removed something from the bottoms of my feet. I was then led barefoot through some very heavy mist. We stopped briefly at a door to wait, and the small beings just left me there.

Another door opened, and I entered a very dark room. There were two other beings in this dark area that looked like the small ones, except that they appeared to be about five feet tall. They must have been expecting me, for they knew my name and said, "Hello, Betty. You're going for a ride."

The beings took me into another room, and I floated onto a big circular tube. As I was lowered down upon it, I could feel how smooth it was, but it was also rubbery. And then they wanted to put something in my mouth. I didn't want them to and started to cry as they quickly put it in my mouth, around my tongue, and over my ears; it seemed to hold my head down. They said they had to do it because I was going for a ride, but

I should not be afraid. The wheel I was on began to turn, and I could see a large glass window overhead. Suddenly, water began to sprinkle down upon me. I was sinking deeper and deeper into the spinning wheel and could see through the large window above me that we were headed toward a dark body of water and waves below. It appeared as if we stopped and entered the water. I could see white bubbles of water rushing away from the glass, and it suddenly stopped. The craft lifted out of the water, briefly hovered above, and moved downward into a cavern of ice. Within this cavern, there were large icicles hanging downward from its ceiling, and others grew upward from the ground below. As we continued to move down the tunnel, it seemed to be lit. I could see a cluster of odd, tall, elongated boxes of ice or crystal glass gathered by the left side of the slanted walls in this area. The craft continued onward, and up ahead there were more boxes, some short and others tall.

As we passed them, I looked closer at the blocks of ice and was shocked at what I saw. There were what looked like frozen humans inside some of the elongated boxes. As we moved along, I could see men and woman and even a child. In the background of each person was a pale scenic view within the box. As we passed the clustered glass-like containers holding varied people, children, and animals, large spots of heavy mist began to hit against the window above, blocking out whatever was close by. It became very heavy with mist and fog and grew very dark. The wheel I was on began to slow down and finally came to a stop.

One of the beings came in and said, "See? You're all right." He lifted my hand and checked my fingers and hands, then took off that awful thing they had put around my ears and in my mouth. Suddenly, I was floating up and standing, and the being said, "We are leaving now." I floated along, following him out of the room into the misty darkness outside. My body felt funny, as though I had pins and needles in my skin, and we moved into a larger area of heavy fog and darkness. I didn't like this place and wanted to go home. It was dark and gray, with some kind of metal machines hanging in midair. It was difficult to see because of the heavy fog, but I felt afraid of this place as the being went off to the side, leaving me there alone.

I was moving along without even using my legs, and I came up to three shadowy beings who were just standing there. It was scary; I couldn't see any faces—they were just standing there in the fog, like solid black shadows. Behind them were some big, dark, metallic machines just hanging in the air with heavy pockets of mist all around them.

As I automatically drew closer to them, the beings could tell I was afraid, because I heard one tell my mind to be calm and relaxed, as they would not hurt me. The middle form came over to me and uttered some strange language about going home and where I was, but I couldn't understand what he was telling me. He raised and lowered his hand, and I automatically followed him. We were going off to the side through the heavy fog. It was damp and dark in here. The being stopped and began to tell me with his mind, "You're getting closer now."

I thought, *Closer to what?* Again with his mind, he revealed I was getting "closer to home." Finally, I thought, *I can understand; I'm going back home.* We kept moving and approached something on the ground that looked like an opened long shell, completely lined with differently size mirrors on the inside. The being floated me into it, and as I lay down, the top closed me inside. It sprung open again immediately, and I was in a different place, where there was bright light. Oh, it was so beautiful there, and a little being stood by, as if expecting my arrival. He floated me out of the mirrored machine and over to the side, where there were these clear, glass, blocklike shoes. Somehow the being lifted me up and lowered me over the shoes; as soon as my soles made contact, the shoes stuck to the bottoms of my feet, and a small light appeared in the glass below.

The being was also wearing the shoes and said, "Follow me." This time, my legs were moving, and I was actually walking on my own with him. We traveled over a beautiful sea of glass, and there were sparkling crystal trees, bushes, and grass. It was like a crystal forest of glistening glass or ice, and as we continued along the path, everything seemed to be so absolutely beautiful. The only thing odd was that nothing was moving but us. Even crystal birds in the air were still, and next to the path, there was a delicate glass butterfly in midair. As we moved closer, I felt drawn to its delicate structure, reached out to touch it, and caught my breath in disbelief. I couldn't believe my eyes. It was fantastically beautiful. Colors began to appear in its wings and body as the butterfly came to life and fluttered about. Within seconds, the butterfly stopped, its colors beginning to fade. A tiny drop of water appeared, followed by a quick flash of blue-white light. Once again, the butterfly had returned to a form of clear crystalline glass. I briefly touched some crystal leaves, which temporarily turned green and quickly returned to a crystal form. I asked the being what was happening.

He spoke to me through my mind, saying, "This is for you to remember, so humankind shall understand." Just now, writing down their message in this book, I paused briefly to consider, what was so important for us to remember or understand concerning this unusual butterfly experience? Was there a spiritual message connected to this wonder? Could it be referring in some way to our beings, bodies, souls, and spirits? Like the crystal butterfly form, could it be about how short and fragile our physical lives really are? Perhaps the likeness of crystal represents the earthly beauty of form, like our bodies, while its color represents the living soul that fills the body, and movement might represent the spirit. All three are in one, when together and alive.

Somehow, because I'd chosen to touch it, color had filled its body, and I said to the being, "Why did it turn color and fly away when I touched it?"

He told me, "You will see when you get home. Home is where the One is, and we are drawing closer to home." Seeing he did not give me an answer that I could understand, my attention turned to the shoes I was wearing.

"How come we have to have these funny glass shoes on our feet?" I asked.

He said, "They are necessary," but he never said why. We continued to walk along this path, and I could see the round top of a huge, clear ball close by, located way below the crystal garden. The little being led me to the edge of the garden and told me to lean back as far as I could. As I did so, I tumbled into the ball below, and it began to move through a long tunnel, carrying me within it. It stopped up ahead, where everything was so bright and glass-like. There were other small beings standing there watching me, and I couldn't move until someone came to get me. My fingertips really hurt for some reason. Another little being appeared. He told me to come out of the orb and follow him. As I did, we moved a very short distance, and he told me to lift my foot. When I did, the glass shoe fell off my foot. I automatically lifted my other foot, and that glass shoe fell to the floor as well. I was now barefoot again. We were floating along, getting closer to an immense wall of crystal-like glass, which appeared to be above us and so long that I couldn't imagine seeing its glistening end. We moved closer to a magnificent crystal door of glowing white light that stretched upward. As we stood before the entrance to the world of light, the being said to me, "Now you shall enter the door to see the One. Fear not."

Somehow, I immediately stepped out of my physical body, so I was now in two places at the same time. My being suddenly moved into the magnificent door that appeared to be deeper, deeper, and deeper. There was so much light here that I didn't know where I was—but, oh, it was so overwhelmingly beautiful here. There was intense light all around and within me.

When I underwent hypnosis, the hypnotist pressed harder to retrieve any memories of what I was seeing at this point as I stood within the light or being told, including what happened before the One. The presence of immense joy and absolute wonder was taking place within my heart and mind, which made it impossible to express or share. For as I embraced the miracle of oneness, I did not want to leave such glorious truth. The hypnotist and researchers tried their best to draw the information of my time within the world of light forward. I was aware I had somehow entered the great door into light but didn't know how it had happened at the time. What I was allowed to hear, see, and learn was not ready to be revealed. The awesome experience and memories were beyond words, and they were blocked for a reason; however, I felt sorry I couldn't share the joy with the group at the time. In their research, they had worked so very hard to find the answers for humankind. All the information concerning the

One was not obtainable during my 1950 abduction, for time was involved, and there was more to come.

My experience with the oneness of life came through. Unfortunately, statements with religious undertones bother some people. This actually hurts people's opportunity to learn through spirit the truth about oneself. I'm amazed, because it concerns *love.* Who doesn't want and need love in his or her life? The hypnotist continued to ask, "Betty, can you explain this to me, so I can understand?"

This made me feel very sad, and I started to cry. "Father loves the world so very much, but so many reject him."

The hypnotist continued, "Can you explain more?"

I said, "The words will be felt by those who believe and have faith. They will feel love radiating from them."

"OK," he said. "Where are you now?"

"I'm where there is light," I replied.

"OK, when will I understand the words being said?" he asked. "Could you tell me?"

"When you allow the Spirit to come upon you, and you are filled with that love," I answered.

The conversation continued, and so much happened during each encounter that Raymond E. Fowler wrote five books that contain the entire account of what my husband, daughter, family, and I experienced within the realm of the UFO phenomenon. Included in the books are the names, credentials, and questions asked by each participating researcher; the excellent hypnotists involved; and many other cases, including that of Mr. Fowler, that were compared with similar experiences. And now this book, which my husband and I are writing and bringing to the reader, contains information of most of our life story as it happened, along with the most recent encounter I've had with the One. But rather than jump ahead, it is time to get back to the world of light.

The hypnotist once again probed for information concerning the One. "OK," he said, "relax. You've been to see the One, and everything is a little nicer, right?"

"Yes," I answered. "I now understand that everything is one."

"What do you mean?" he asked.

"I mean that everything fits together. Everything is one. It's beautiful, no matter what it is."

While I was still under a deep hypnotic trance, the hypnotist, thinking we were not making much progress in discovering who the One was, decided to withdraw me from the world of light and bring me back outside of the door once again. Standing by the door was a tall, white-haired person waiting for me with two similar tall beings. The hypnotist asked, "Do they look like people?"

I said, "Yes, but they are very tall, and he's motioning for me to come over to him." The being's robe was white and glowing, and as I looked at his face, I noticed his eyes were really blue. He put me inside the same shell-like machine again. The inside was lined with mirrors on the top and the bottom. The door closed and quickly opened to another foggy and damp place. Another large-headed, gray-skinned being was standing close by to greet me as I climbed out of the machine into the surrounding area of misty, dim darkness. I could see many of those rounded, metallic-looking machines in the air again. The top of one of them was lit and silently revolving, while its reddish-orange lights bounced off the heavy mist and fog within the space. The being motioned for me to follow, and we moved past them through some heavy mist. Up ahead, I could see light coming from a rounded blocklike structure with three open windows. The being said for me to follow, just as we both, one after the other, swooped through the first window into a tunnel that looked like ice. There was a smaller being there using a long, thin, rodlike tool that shot out a blue-white light toward some beautiful blue stones that either were growing or embedded in the icy cavern walls. Three other beings standing by began to pick up and carry chunks of the blue material to a pile next to one side of the cavern wall.

The being I was with moved past the work going on; I followed close behind him, and we headed up the long tunnel toward a lit area. We entered into a rounded room where the walls looked like black, cut coal that had amazing reflections of sparkling colored lights within it. In the middle of the floor there was a metal machine. Suddenly, one of the small workers entered, carrying a blue stone. He hurriedly placed the stone, along with a gray, jellylike substance from a triangular cup, on the glass center of the metallic machine. At that point, a large upper glass tube came quickly down and connected to the raised lower glass tube that held both the blue stone and the jelly. As soon as it connected, a thin, bright, purple light shot upward from the machine, causing both stone and jelly to catch fire and burn. Odd feathery things floated upward from the burning material. The being informed me it was time for us to go, and we headed out of the unusual room, back through the tunnel, to where the small beings were. We easily lifted up and out of the window once again into the misty gray atmosphere and stopped by the large floating machines hovering in the fog. One of the little beings was following us. I could see him from the blue light of the stone he was carrying. We boarded the odd metallic craft.

CHAPTER 3

An Unexpected Implant

• • •

THERE IS BRIGHT LIGHT IN here, and I can see a shiny black thing near the wall. The gray being I am with told me to go to it. He said he was going to give me something. I asked what, but he said, "First you must do something to see what it is." He told me to sit in something like a long glass chair in front of the black, shiny box. Below the box on a narrow shelf were ten colored buttons. He directed me to put each one of my fingers on top of each button. When I did, the buttons lit up, and a small ball of light popped out of the square glass frame before me. The ball automatically turned every which way in circles, changed color, and stopped. It turned back to white light and continued to revolve in a back-and-forth circular motion, changing to a new color each time.

He told me to continue to watch the white ball as it became a different color. It began to hurt my eyes, and my fingers felt like they were stuck to the colored buttons. I guess I passed the test, for after a while, he said, "Now I am going to give you something." I lifted myself off the long chair, and he brought me over to the other side, where he showed me what looked like a magnified glass shelf with tiny beads and thin, short needles or slivers in it. The being said, "This is for you. This is what you're going to have."

I remember thinking, *I don't want those things. What good are they?*

He said to me, "You're ready now. Follow me."

My eyes felt tired and heavy because of the machine I had worked with. A door opened from the wall, and we went up into another brightly lit room. In the middle of this room was a long table-like box. The being turned toward me, and I felt myself lift off the floor and float to the box. As I lay on the table, I could see other beings coming in who were dressed in silver suits. The room was extremely bright, and I began to fear what was going on. One of the beings placed his hand on my forehead and said to relax. "It will only be awhile," he said. "We have something to give you."

I could see three of them around me. He told me to be still, but one of them was leaning over me and coming closer to my eyes.

"Oh no," I cried. "I don't want you to do that." I was afraid of what they were planning to do. "Please don't do that. I want to go home now."

During this time, the hypnotist, sensing I was experiencing something terrible, immediately pulled me away from the situation and kept repeating, "Betty, move out of it. Move yourself away from it." But my mind was reeling, and I didn't understand how I could move out or get away from what was happening. His commands continued to move me away from the terrifying situation taking place, which was the removal of my right eye. "Betty," he said. "I want you to imagine it is happening to someone else. Remember when you were standing before the great door, and your body separated and became two of you? Well, now I want you to calm down and see the other Betty receiving this, not you. Now, tell me what is happening to her—not to you."

"First, she was placed on a table and could not move," I said. "Then, the being used his fingers to remove her eye. After the eye removal, he used a long needle to release something deep inside the empty socket before replacing her eyeball. It was terrible."

The hypnotist, seeing my obvious reaction to the frightening discovery, decided to take me away from the situation and gently brought me out of hypnosis and back to our world. The next hypnosis session took place a few weeks after learning about the removal of my eye. The hypnotist and loyal researchers made every effort to ensure the submission of the account would be as painless as possible. The hypnotist began by progressing me beyond the point of the beings taking out my eye to when they had finished and put my eye back in. He said, "I will count from one to three, and you will be beyond what occurred. You will not be afraid, because you know you are OK, even though you went through what happened. There will be no discomfort, for you have gone through it nicely. You have been anesthetized and will be able to speak about it without any difficulty. OK, close your eyes. Deeper, deeper, deeper...one...two...three."

I was placed in a very deep relaxed state, so I would be able to handle what happened next concerning my eye. He continued to bring me closer to the experience. "I want you to now go back to where they have your eye out," he said. "What's going on, Betty?"

"It seems like the being used its fingers somehow to take out, and later put back, my right eyeball. He placed his hand on my head, and they're using some very long, thin needles of light, which are connected to long, thin, silver-colored tubing. At the end of the needle, there appears to be a very tiny glass ball. I think it was one of those bead-like balls that were on the shelf they showed me much earlier. They pushed the needle into my head through my eye socket. I could hear it break through tissue inside, and my head felt odd," I said. "I was helpless and shuddered at the thought of what was happening. I had a little pain from the strange operation as the needlelike tool moved way down and jiggled as if something moved or was released. It was so bright; all I could see was a bright white light everywhere. And once again I felt them pull the needle up to the inner area of my forehead. It jiggled again. At the same time he was doing this, I suddenly felt a feeling of comfort from his hand on my forehead. While they were working inside my eye socket with the needle, I started seeing all sorts of colors. He lifted his hand away from my forehead and waved it over my face. The other silver-suited beings had moved closer to me. They were holding long silver needles and briefly pointed them over and at my head. After a short while, they stopped and carried the other material away. The operating being came back to me, placed his hand on my head once again, and somehow put my eyeball back into its socket. My eye felt sort of dry, and my sight was blurry, but now I was able to see more of the room again. As soon as they finished, they floated me off the table and directed me to the side of the area, where a gray, padded pillow inside a slanted, glass-like basket stood. And at the end of the basket, there were short glass and silver stems, with tiny colored lights. The oddly shaped basket sat on top of a clear glass base, which had holes below on the floor, where a stream of waves suddenly appeared."

"What happened next?" the hypnotist asked.

"They took off my dungarees and put a small white skirt around me," I said. "They had me kneel on the basket's pillow. I was told I must sit very still and raise both my arms and hands straight up as far as possible. As I obeyed their command, the odd basket I was in gently separated from the base and rose upward. I could not move and was now stationary in midair. I could feel someone behind me separating the skirt and pulling down my underwear, and immediately I felt something sharp like a needle pierce my spine. My back felt like pins and needles, and a chilled feeling rushed through my body. I felt helpless and unable to move."

At the time, during the recall through regressive hypnosis, the hypnotist quickly moved in, not knowing what was going to happen next, and assured me they were just anesthetizing me so I wouldn't feel any pain. The basket came down, and someone pulled up my underpants and fixed the white skirt. Suddenly, my arms came down, and I was lifted off the basket and floated back to the table. I was now lying on my stomach. The hypnotist broke through and repeated, "That is the most pain you should have felt. They've anesthetized you, so the following procedure will not be uncomfortable. OK, go on."

"I remained very still, as five beings now stood over and around me with tools in their hands and began to wave the silver instruments up and down the center of my back," I said. "At first, my whole back felt extremely cold. And then, suddenly, it felt like tiny crawling things were moving inside my skin along my spine. Something very white was briefly brushed against my head, and it seemed to burn. The beings were holding some long needles that had whitish-silver handles with tiny blinking lights and odd writing on them. These particular tools did not touch me. They were held over and away from my body at first. All they did was point them at me, while the other tool that had been used earlier had made something inside me move. Whatever it was, I felt it slowly move in my back and head, and then it stopped. Once again, something sharp was applied to my heels. Then, all of the beings holding the long, silver needles moved toward me and held them over my head. Although they did not touch me, it felt as though it was causing something to move into place. They were looking at the handles of those long needles as if they were reading them. Two of them went to the side of the room, and it seemed like they may have been conversing through the mind about the results. They came back, looked at me, floated me up, and turned me around, so I was now lying flat on my back. I was tired and wanted to go home, so I briefly closed my eyes to rest, hoping they were done. They quickly lifted my eyelids once again to check my eyes.

"Shortly after, I was off the table and in my dungarees, and the small white skirt was removed. I was then returned to the other room, where the black box was, and they told me to sit in the long chair once again and put my fingers on the white lights, where there were colored buttons before. The colored buttons were no longer there. But the white light popped on to the black box and went around one way, then the other, and a purple light showed up and returned to the white light again. This occurred over and over again, changing into the colors of white-blue-white, to white-green, and so on. As I sat in front of the black screen, staring at the moving lights, my eyes started to hurt. The motion of changing white to color to white continued until it turned to white-red-white and stopped. The being standing by told me to press hard with my thumb. As I pressed down hard on the white lights, a purple light appeared and covered the black glass. Then there were odd purple writings and symbols as the black color returned. He told me to keep looking at the things, which suddenly appeared and quickly disappeared. All sorts of things were popping out in midair before me. Suddenly, there were dots and dashes and weird symbols. Pictures of storms; people; and three jagged rounds of whirling light, stars, mountains, and much more were instantly flashing before my eyes. I was tired and wanted to go home, but he told me to keep looking at them. I thought maybe since they took my eyeball out and put it back in, they were just making sure my eyes were OK. I just wanted to go home. The pictures finally stopped, and I was able to take both thumbs off the lights.

"I knew they were reading or hearing my thoughts, because the being said, 'Very soon you will go home.' I floated up out of the chair and followed him out of the room and into another, where there was a tall, glasslike container, like a bottle. The being led me to it. A part of the container opened upward like a door. The being put a rounded, glass-like helmet mask on me that had tiny lights and other small things stuck in the center of it. Once they placed me inside the container, the door closed. Grayish water began to fill the tall glass container. I was wet, but it felt comfortable, and as it rose higher, it completely filled the container. I was OK, because I could easily breathe, and none of the gray, jellylike water was able to get inside the mask they had put on me. After a short while, the gray water began to get lower and lower as if the beings were draining it away. I started to feel warm air blowing down on me. The air felt comfortable, and it was quickly drying my clothes, but my hands and feet started to feel very heavy, and they hurt for some reason. I heard a high-pitched noise as the air stopped blowing.

"The glass door opened, and I stepped out just as one of the beings came in for the mask, took it off my head, and laid it down. Then he said for me to follow him. We moved along and entered a dark room. I knew where we were right away. Inside was the same rubbery wheel they had put me on before. He knew I was wary of this thing, for the last time it had caused me to sink deeper and deeper inside it, and I'd felt an intense pressure on my body. It whirled round and round at an extreme and frightening rate of speed. Once again he lifted me upon the wheel and began to put the same mouthpiece on my tongue and around my ears. I was going for another ride on this thing, whether I wanted to or not. It started to cycle round and round, and water lightly sprinkled down upon me as the wheel moved faster and faster. At that point, I must have blacked out."

Raymond Fowler published all the details and much more of what happened to me at age thirteen in *The Andreasson Affair, Phase Two*, which may be found at most local libraries. Off and on, I will bring forth a few more of the details of what happened, though I don't remember how I got back home. I do remember a further experience, however, but I'm not sure if this happened after I had been on that wheel or not. I remember being with one of the taller gray beings and two small ones. We were outside of a silver, orb-like craft. The shell of the orb had almost a mirrorlike finish, which reflected the surrounding trees and bushes. At the top center of this craft was a circular area, where thin and thicker glowing blue lights were sticking out and up. There was a large hill with many trees to the right of where it had landed. The large orb was parked in a partially wooded field and was bordering what looked like a lake a short distance away. I could also see some kind of markings on the orb's exterior by its door.

I remember walking through the dense field with three beings, one taller, large-headed being and two smaller ones who were both carrying glowing balls of light. All of a sudden, we heard a loud boom close by. The beings stopped, and we all stood motionlessly. The noise had been caused by a pheasant that had been scared up as we moved through the heavy underbrush. As we drew closer to the water, I realized where we were. We were not very far away from my house, which was over the two huge hills, dotted with mountain laurel, and a large forest, which would eventually bring me to the last chicken coop on the first hill in our yard. Crocker Pond was very close to where we were. The pond in our yard empties into the very stream weaving in and out through the lower wooded ground that spills into Crocker Pond. I felt relieved to know I was so close to home. We began moving again, closer to the water's edge, where I used to go fishing.

The little beings, each holding a ball of glowing light, continued to follow us as we all moved closer to the lake's edge. The taller being stopped and said, "You will not remember this. We will be watching you." He told me to go to the water; as I did, the two small beings moved toward me with their glowing orbs. I was told to sit next to the water and take off my shoes and socks. The small beings raised their orbs of light, and I immediately stuck my feet into the water, splashed them back and forth, stopped, and watched some small sunfish—kivers—swimming close by. I could hear the sound of a train in the distance. There was a track that bordered the back of the large lake. My pants were rolled up, and my saddle shoes and stockings were sitting on the ground next to me. To this day, I think that may be how and where they took me back home after my 1950 UFO experience, but I'm not sure. I've also had other small encounters that have been recorded in *The Andreasson Affair, Phase Two*. Mr. Fowler is an excellent author of the five books and has included these experiences, along with many comparative encounters and explanations that help the reader to see the similarities of what happened to me, as well as to others whose lives have been involved with the high strangeness of the UFO phenomenon.

CHAPTER 4

School, Friends, and Changes

• • •

ALTHOUGH CHILDHOOD MEMORIES OF BEING taken aboard a UFO were temporarily removed, I began to feel a haunting presence while in the woods. But as long as my friends Eddy or Lorraine Andreasson were with me, I was fine. Lorraine lived across the street, up on a very steep hill, and Eddy lived to the right of her house at the bottom of the hill. Lorraine was Swedish and had pretty, thick blond braids. Many years later, she became my sister-in-law. But while we were young, Lorraine and I were very close friends and often played together.

One summer, Lorraine's father stored his rowboat in a small pond at the bottom of their land, close to the woods. We just happened to see the boat and decided to climb aboard. The two of us spent all day trying to get the heavy boat upstream, until we finally learned to push the two paddles deep into the water, mud, and rocks below to force it to move. That way, we were able to work our way up the narrow, rushing stream, which wove in and out as it flowed down the hill to the small pond. The hardest part was trying to turn the heavy boat around to head back. After securing the paddles inside, we got ready for our voyage. The ride down was delightful, as we swooshed in and out, bouncing wildly up and down, back and forth. And then, in less than a few minutes, the ride was over, and we were back at the pond once again. As kids, we had no idea what we were doing to her father's boat. I now wonder what he thought when it came time for fishing, and he examined the condition of the bottom of his rowboat. During our sailing days, there were sounds of loud bangs and scrapes, which must have left marks from each trip we took.

Things began to change for me at fourteen and fifteen. I still loved the woods, but I started to shy away from being alone there and became more interested in school activities and friends. I was very interested in art and often won first prize in competitive school projects and art contests. My interest in art continued, but drawing was quiet time, and my mind and energy needed to be more active. I loved basketball, baseball, and cheer-leading at school, but I participated only if I had a ride home, as the walk was quite a distance to my house from school. I often went swimming, ice skating, fishing, and rowing, for the lake was close by. Lorraine and I would go to the youth center's Friday dances in town, where we learned to jitterbug and waltz. Occasionally, my sister Violet would take me and my youngest sister, Carol, to the movies. I loved Bud Abbot and Lou Costello. Off and on I was able to attend the Baptist church in town. My brother went into the army, and my eldest sister, Shirley, was married and living in Fitchburg, Massachusetts. She started to attend a small Pentecostal church and enjoyed the service so much that she invited my mother and father to come, and I decided to tag along with them. I was happy to be there; it was such a joyful church with singing and giving praise and testimonies to the Lord. The pastors were called Brother Johnson and his wife, Sister Johnson. In those days, they used to call people who attended a Pentecostal church Holy Rollers. I didn't mind, because you could sure see they loved God and were happy. Off and on I would go there or to the Baptist church in Westminster. During one of the Pentecostal services when I first turned sixteen, I gave my heart over to the Lord's care and felt so much joy and happiness because of it.

At sixteen, things started to change for me; I was now old enough to date, but I had no interest in dating. I was not interested in boys as a boyfriend- or sweetheart-type friendship. I just enjoyed being with my friends, male or female. The strange thing was that I developed a terrible phobia to needles when I was young, and I think it had something to do with my hidden UFO encounters. I don't remember being vaccinated, and I felt faint and sick at the thought of having any kind of school shots. When I went to the dentist, my father had to literally hold me down if I needed a shot to pull a tooth or have any drilling done. The phobia continued into adulthood. I've been married twice, where of course you have to have a blood test, and each time, the needle phobia was so bad that I honestly considered not getting married. But I succumbed to love, knew it was time to grow up, and took the needle like a crybaby, though that was much later in my life.

It is time to backtrack to when I started high school. After graduating junior high in Westminster, I would soon be faced with another disappointment. For years, the Westminster students from the tenth to twelfth grades had finished their schooling in a nearby city's high school. Every year, we were bused to the city's school, where students were used to new students from another town; however, the city's high-school population had grown so large they could no longer accommodate any other small-town students. This meant my graduating class would be shipped to a new and different city's high school. So Westminster students were bused for the first time to the new school, which meant we who were out-of-towners were strangers walking their halls, where we were not wanted in the first place and were definitely not well received. We tried to support the school's football team by attending and cheering for the players, but the female populace of the school was not happy with the Westminster girls being there, because some of their male students were interested in the new girls.

When I was younger, people thought I looked like a young Elizabeth Taylor. Because of it, I went through some very difficult times. Girls snubbed me and gave me dirty looks. When the school had a dance at the auditorium, most of the kids from Westminster tried to attend, hoping the city students would be able to accept them, want to get to know one another, and try to get along. A young man in the twelfth grade came over to talk with me. His name was Jerry. After we stood around talking, he asked if I would like to dance. It was a slow waltz, so I agreed; while we were on the floor dancing, three couples purposely moved around us and pushed us off to the side. We continued to dance as one of the couples came close to us again, and the girl actually poked me very hard on my back. Jerry pulled me away from them, and as we kept dancing, another couple moved closer to us, and a second girl struck me on my back. Jerry saw what they were doing, felt bad, and asked if I wanted to get some air. I could see the two couples off to the side glaring at me and laughing, so we went outside, were talking, and started to walk up the sidewalk. Two girls came toward us. I thought they were going to the dance when they passed, but instead, one of the girls yelled to Jerry, "How can you be with a—like her?"

The girl called me a bad name. Jerry was mad and upset and started to chase them, but I said, "Don't bother. They don't know what I'm like." I was really hurt. We went back to the dance, and when I got home, I dreaded the thought of returning to that school, for there had been a couple of other uncalled-for incidents, where I'd felt like I was being put through a wringer by the girls. All my Westminster friends were in different classes and probably going through similar things. When the bell rang to change classes, we were all on our own.

But something was about to happen to me that would change my life. The classroom entrances were scattered along both sides of a long hallway. In between these classroom doors were row after row of metal lockers that stretched down the lengthy hallway, where students were assigned a locker so they could store their books, papers, or gym clothes. As the bell rang, I gathered my books and started to walk down the hallway toward my next class. Up ahead I could see two separate clusters of several boys, standing by the lockers, watching and waiting for me. As I approached, they began to whistle, and as I tried to quickly pass, they pounded on their metal lockers with their fists and repeatedly panted while they stuck out their tongues like mad dogs. I had to pass by both groups of thoughtless boys and felt so humiliated by their mean and aggressive behavior I wanted to cry. Because of the vulgar treatment and disgusting display of harassment from people who did not know me and did not want me there, I could no longer take it. Being sixteen was terrible. I was so embarrassed and ashamed of such treatment that I walked out of that high school, never to return again. Because of it, my education was cut short, and it would be many, many years later that I went to get a GED. After what I went through at the city high school, my parents were upset as well and were trying to figure out what to do, for they knew I would not go back to that school.

I was still very interested in art, and my father and mother, believing in me and seeing my drawing ability, contacted a well-known art institute to speak with one of their representatives. The man came to our home to test my talent and talked with my parents about costs and supplies. He told us what kind of help I would receive and what material would be provided through my correspondence art course. I was enrolled, excited, and wanted to study my courses as soon as possible. Most children don't know how much their parents do for them. Daddy had to pay each month for the course, and as time went by between mailings, the course was so very slow that I began to lose interest. I still was seeing many of my friends at the Friday night youth-center dances, but it just didn't seem the same anymore. Without the daily presence of friends and a school curriculum, it felt like there were no challenges left for me. I missed being around people my age; however, after what I had been put through, I knew I would not go back to what was the only available high school for me. So at sixteen, while staying home, drawing was to be my main outlet.

When I was a child, it had seemed as if there were always things to do, and my interests were in nature; my beagle, Pal; and my two cats, Blacky and Red. We got Pal from my aunt and uncle, who could no longer keep him in the city where they lived. They said he barked too much, and he had to live in their cellar. They actually brought Pal to our house for my father to put him to sleep, and he had an open wound on his neck from being tied up. I begged and pleaded with my father to let me keep Pal, insisting that I would take good care of him. I loved that dear little dog. I'm extremely sensitive and emotional over any mistreated or abandoned animals. Even today, every time I see a commercial on TV about animal abuse, abandonment, or mistreatment, I can't help it: I start to cry and get all choked up. Those poor little animals are innocent. As for Pal, I was so happy to be able to keep him. His neck healed quickly with my father's help. He was always with me, and during my early grade-school years, he'd wait for the school bus that brought me home. As I got off the bus, he would patiently stand halfway up the stairs in the yard wagging his tail, always excited and ready to greet me. One day, as I started up the stairs, Pal opened his mouth in a yawn, and I definitely heard him say, "Hello, Betty." I was stunned, for that was the first and only time he ever did that.

Bob and I, at a much later time in our life, had Becky's dog, Brutus, for many years, as Becky and my granddaughters were living in Massachusetts in an apartment where dogs were not allowed. Brutus was a wonderful, well-behaved Belgian shepherd and came to live with us in Cheshire. A couple of times he was funny, such as the time he had a look of "Huh? What happened?" when he was sprayed by a skunk. Another time, during the Christmas season, Bob brought a large box of stored decorations for the tree into the garage from the shed. Brutus stuck his head into the box and discovered a mouse, which he tried to catch. When he had finished, the mouse escaped, but Brutus looked like a decorated Christmas tree, with silver tinsel, sparkling trim, and a colorful bulb somehow stuck to his ear.

As time moved on, we sold our ranch-style home and moved from Cheshire to Bob's mother's two-story apartment house, which he had inherited, in Meriden, Connecticut. We were thinking of purchasing a travel trailer to eventually go to Florida. After we had moved from Cheshire to Meriden, Brutus, who didn't know the area, suddenly disappeared from our new backyard. I was heartsick, and for days, I searched the neighborhood for him. Even while driving, I called his name from the car window, hoping he might hear me. I called the pound, animal control, and other places that might have picked him up. He was not at any of them. I kept praying he was all right, and we would somehow find him. Three days later, while rechecking the telephone directory, I noticed that, because I had been so upset, I had called Wallingford's dog pound rather than the one in Meriden. Immediately, I called the right ASCPA and found out he was there. I rushed down to pick him up. They said he'd been there for three days. I paid them to get him out of there and put Brutus in the back of my car. As we rode away, I was talking to him, saying, "I was so worried about you. Brutus, where were you?"

Once again I was stunned, for like Pal, Brutus yawned, and it sounded like he plainly said, "I-don-no." As a kid I loved all sorts of animals, and later, when I had children, they loved animals as well. However, sometimes, as a child, I was not so kind and did not think of the animal's freedom. I used to try to catch chickadees but was never successful. Becky loved birds as well and for many years had different kinds of them in cages. Once, when Bob and I were in Florida and planning to come back north to see Becky around her birthday, I happened to see the most beautiful, expensive, red bird in a pet shop. I was sure Becky would absolutely love to have the bird for her birthday, so I bought it. Becky was thrilled, but many weeks later, she had an insight and a moment of empathy concerning all her caged birds, and she let every one of the birds go free. I was shocked, but I understood how much she truly loved them to give them their freedom.

Bob and I had a number of funny things happen in our lives concerning birds. One time, we were in a pet shop and decided to buy a green and yellow Amazon parrot that we later named Gabby. I knew this was going to be interesting, because even the clerk did not dare to take the bird out of his cage in front of us and brought the cage into the backroom to box him. I had never heard so much screeching, and I think part of it was coming from the clerk, who was wearing long, strong gloves when he came back out with the caged bird. We were in Florida at the time on a vacation and staying in Bob's small trailer when he decided to take Gaby out to get used to him. He lifted the parrot out of the cage and set him down on his arm and hand. Thank God Bob had patience and rugged hands from working on cars, for Gaby bit him time and time again while getting used to being our pet. Time went by, and the parrot began to occasionally perch on Bob's shoulder. Gaby was doing better, but he still bit Bob's earlobe every chance he got—yet Bob had the patience to keep trying to tame and train him. Whenever the telephone would ring, Gabby would start squawking, making it impossible to hear anything.

I thought maybe he was sad or needed a friend to help calm him down, so I bought another gray parrot that we called Ollie (and to quote a well-known phrase: "Nothing like asking for more trouble."). However, this bird was less noisy, so I assumed it was a female. Every night we covered their cages and enjoyed the peace and quiet. One summer, we put both cages outdoors in the backyard on the grass, and I moved the cages close together, hoping they would finally get along. To my surprise, they both moved sideways along their perches toward each other. I was excited and thought, *Yea. They are finally trying to become friends.* But as they drew closer and closer, both of them suddenly thrust their clawed feet between the bars of the cages and tried to grab each other around the neck. To my astonishment, they were trying to strangle each other. I was so upset that, for me, it was the last straw. I realized then that both birds were males, and I quickly separated the cages. That ended our fascination with parrots. It wasn't long after their choking duel that we decided it was enough, and Gaby and Ollie went to separate new homes.

Large birds and Bob just don't seem to get along. While in a Florida campground, he was feeding some wild ducks when one overanxious duck bit him but good. This happened with a squirrel as well. While Bob fed the squirrel some peanuts, the squirrel bit his thumb, held on, and would not let go. Of course Bob got shots for that one. Another time, at Sea World, there were a couple of tall crane-like birds with long, thin beaks standing by. Bob thought their narrow beaks would not have much biting power, so he poked his finger at one. *Chomp.* The pressure was unbearable. Bob was wrong again, and it hurt. That bird held on to his finger for dear life. But there was one more unforgettable time that Bob had an altercation with a large bird. We were once again in a Florida pet store when we came upon a large black myna bird and stopped to say hello. The bird was trained to talk and responded with a hello. Bob asked, "What kind of bird are you?"

To our surprise, the bird said, "I'm a myna bird."

Bob was not able to resist the bird's talking ability and wanted to see what he would say next. Bob said, "You're not a myna bird; you're a turkey." The bird kept insisting he was a myna bird, and Bob kept telling him he was a turkey. To Bob's surprise, the bird was evidently unimpressed by Bob's insistence that the bird was a turkey, and he inched his way over to the very edge of the cage, cocked its head toward Bob, and said, "You're full of shit."

We were stunned and stood there in disbelief with our eyes and mouths wide open, wondering if the bird actually had told Bob off. I thought, *Who's the turkey now?* We called the owners, who were standing in the aisle listening and laughing. Today, I think they were deliberately waiting for someone like Bob. Bob asked if the bird was for sale, but the owners said his extensive vocabulary had taken many, many years of training, and they would never sell him. As for us, we will never forget that fearless myna bird that stood up for itself against Bob.

But now it's time to get back to a much earlier time in my life. When I was a youngster of about nine or ten years old, I remember having a strange thing happen. My cousins were visiting when, out of the blue, I nonchalantly told my cousin Billy, "I'm going to marry Jimmy Andreasson." Billy, who was a few years older than I, thought it was a funny joke and laughed. I, on the other hand, changed the subject but wondered, *Why did I ever say that?* I was not much older than eight when my family had first moved to Westminster. While growing up, I had not seen, heard, or thought of Lorraine's brother Jim. He was much older than Lorraine and I and hung out with the older teenage kids, including my brother. I had no interest in him, except that many years later, my best friend, Lorraine, would once in a while mention she missed her big brother, who was in the navy. Evidently my odd statement, blurted out long ago to my cousin, was a future projection, which meant Providence had my life worked out way before I knew it.

After leaving school at sixteen, I continued with the art course, but it seemed to go so slowly. Each month I was supposed to mail my work into the school, and I had to wait for their slow reply. So far I was doing well, but I was quickly losing interest. After Lorraine was home from school,

I went up to visit her. While there, I met her brother, who was home on leave from the navy. Jim had his motorcycle out and asked if I would like a ride. I had never been on a motorcycle, so I was a little hesitant, but Lorraine said, "Go ahead. It's fun. I've been on it." So I got on the back, and we went up the road. I couldn't believe I was on a motorcycle. We rode back up the hill, and I thought, *Wow, that was fun.* I thanked him for the ride, but I felt a little nervous around him, because he was about my sister Violet's age. I was still just sixteen and hadn't dated anyone, so it felt strange to be around an older man. As for Jim, while he'd been in high school, he had been dating a girl, and everyone in his family thought he would probably end up marrying her. As for me, I was still sort of a tomboy, and the only boy I felt comfortable around was my buddy Eddie. He treated me as an equal, and I could be myself.

CHAPTER 5

Marriage, Troubles, and Unseen Woes

• • •

Being home and away from school was not what I expected it to be. I realized I was not learning anything new; there was little challenge and less discovery going on. I understood sooner or later I would have to grow up, but I was not ready for a sweeping change as yet. While at home, I was bored and decided to try to get a job. It seemed as if the art course was too easy and was taking too long for my lessons to get back to me.

I applied at a local factory that made plastic spoons, forks, and knives, along with other plastic items. I got a temporary job sorting and packing plastic picnic ware. It was in West Fitchburg, which meant I had a ride to and from the factory, because when my father went to and came home from his work, he stopped to pick me up. I started to feel pretty good. The job was easy and sort of boring, but I was now in the workforce, meeting and talking to other people while making some money. There was a party going on uptown. Lorraine and I decided to go, as there were a lot of people there whom we knew. A couple of times, I finally did decide to go out on dates, but though the young men were very thoughtful, there was no one in particular I was interested in.

Lorraine's brother completed his four-year hitch in the navy and came home. To my surprise, he asked me once again if I would like a motorcycle ride. His older sister and her husband were going on their motorcycle to an aunt's house in New Hampshire to get a promised kitten for their daughter, and Jim was going with them on his bike. So he asked if I would like to go. It made me feel pretty special. The ride had been fun the last time, so I said yes, why not? Many of the back roads in New Hampshire were narrow and winding, and as we went around a sharp corner in a wooded country area, the tires slipped on sand and gravel leftover from winter. My head bounced against Jim's back and leather jacket as we went down. I was fine, but Jim hurt his leg. Once we got home, he had to have his leg in a cast and was walking around with crutches.

Meanwhile, my temporary job had ended; I was home and bored, so I went up to see how he was doing. His mother was home and was grateful that I visited once in a while to give her son some company while he was healing. As we talked, I began to feel very comfortable around Jim, and it helped me to get over my shyness. He was a tall, handsome, wavy-haired blond Swede about four years older than me and seemed to be pleased with my company. When I visited Lorraine, we'd sit and chat with him as well. I was surprised he was interested in hearing what I had to say, seeing as I was just the kid next door. Of course, my parents knew about the accident, which meant they didn't want me on the motorcycle again. Jim's injury healed well, and a few months later, he was riding his bike to work. He was working at a lumber mill close by and once again asked if I wanted to go for a ride to New Hampshire with his older sister, her husband, and two other friends with bikes. I thought maybe he was inviting me so his sister Ginger would not be the only female in the group, and my mind went to how my parents felt, for since the accident they didn't want me on a motorcycle again. I was going on seventeen and had enjoyed the bike rides and being with Jim. He was always thoughtful and kind. So against my parents' better judgment, I was on his bike, riding along with the group, headed into the state of New Hampshire once again.

We got a third of the way into the state when, while riding through a small town, we were stopped by the police and arrested. To this day, I don't know why or how it happened. It did not seem as if we were speeding. For some reason, the officers put planks down leading to the courthouse doorway and confiscated one of the bikes—the officer literally rolled one of the motorcycles into the small courtroom and parked it there. And all six of us were put into jail. All I could think was that, if we had to stay there, my mother and father wouldn't know where I was and would be upset and calling the police looking for me. Not only that, it was the wrong thing for me to do without telling them, but I had also gone against their wishes. There was a fine from the court, and what money we all had was not enough to pay for it. Ginger was going to put her diamond ring and watch up as collateral, but they would not accept them. Jim called his work and fortunately got his boss and friend, who wired the fine, and we were able to leave. We were all starved, so we pooled what change we had left after the partial cash payment used for the fine and got three quarts of soda, two loaves of bread, and a pound of bologna to eat. I was never so happy to get back home.

As for Jim, we started to see each other off and on, but there was nothing serious going on, for I was still afraid to come out of my safety zone. Ever since the degrading high-school episode I'd been put through, I felt emotionally scarred and very guarded around the male populace; however, it seemed as if the more time I was spending with Jim, conversing and enjoying his company, the more I trusted him and realized I was growing up and might be falling in love. He had not even attempted to kiss me as yet. I was truly happy that he didn't push the relationship, and I felt comfortable, because it automatically made me trust him all the more. I think he realized if our time together developed too quickly, my shyness would kick in and ruin the growing possibility of something real. As the days went by, I would think about him and want to see him again, and I could tell he felt the same way.

It wasn't long before he asked me to marry him. On June 13, 1954, we were married. I was seventeen, and he was twenty-one. We rented an apartment in Fitchburg. Jim was no longer working at the lumber mill in Westminster; he had gotten a job welding and was doing very well. His parents had given us a piece of land as a wedding gift, where we would eventually build a house. We rented the apartment for several months, and not long after we married, I became pregnant. On May 8, 1955, we were blessed with a baby girl on Mother's Day. We named her Rebecca Marie Andreasson. Now that we had started our family, we were hoping to save money to build our own home, so we bought a small trailer; temporarily parked it on Jim's father's land; and looked into designs of small homes, prices for lumber, and other costs for building materials.

After two months of living in the trailer, something odd happened. It was very late at night. Jim had quickly fallen to sleep from a hard day's work. Becky was sleeping in her bassinet, safe and sound, while I was in bed wide awake. As I lay there, I heard a man's gentle voice call my name. I glanced toward Jim and could tell he was in a deep and restful sleep, so I didn't want to wake him. But I thought, *What was that?* Then I heard the voice call me again. It sounded like it was outside by the locked door of our trailer, but no one knocked. I remained quiet and closed my eyes, as if to make it go away. I had no idea who or what had called me. Unable to recognize the voice, I became afraid as once again I heard him call my name, and it seemed like it was in the trailer. When he did, I quickly pulled the blanket over my head in fear and wondered if I should wake Jim. I lay under the blanket, not daring to breathe or move. I didn't know who it could be calling me, for it was very late, and we were living in the country, surrounded by many trees, in the woods. I thought about the baby and bravely pulled the blanket away from my face, took a deep breath, and got up to check Rebecca. She was fine, and there was no more voice calling me. I lay awake for some time, wondering who could have been calling my name, and I finally fell to sleep. Morning came, and I got Jim's breakfast, and he was off to work. I didn't tell him about the voice, for I thought he would worry about Rebecca and me all alone in the trailer.

As time went on, we finally decided on the house we would be building and went through a Fitchburg company to receive the plan, material, and mortgage. It wasn't long before construction began, and I found out I was pregnant again, which meant our little family was quickly growing in number. We immediately had the cellar hole dug, laid out, and cemented. My father had the ability to dowse for water and found exactly where our well would be. Jim installed trenches and pipes to the foundation. The work was exhausting, and although he was strong and healthy, working daily on the house and his welding job began to wear him down. A few months later, he capped the foundation, and the rest of the two-by-fours arrived for the shell and division of rooms. The house slowly came to life, and we moved in. It wasn't long before our first son, James, was born on April 25, 1956. We continued to complete the house; however, our finances were stretched to the limit. In order to get out of debt, we decided we'd have to sell the house. Right away, there was interest to buy, but we found out that some of the materials the company had provided were not up to code, so we had to invest more money to change the material that was unacceptable to the bank. It was heartbreaking, but we had to sell the house Jim had worked so hard to build for us, and we moved into a ground-floor apartment in Fitchburg on Summer Street. Six months later, I discovered I was pregnant again. This would be our third child.

Losing the house and knowing we had another baby on the way started to weigh heavily on Jim. He had been in the navy, and back then, he'd had a great deal of freedom to party with friends and come and go as he pleased. While carrying the responsibilities as the sole provider, he seemed discouraged and started to have a few beers to help him relax. His welding job was seeing us through these times, but I could tell he was very exhausted and disappointed about our loss, as was I. During this time, Becky's age was close to two and a half to three years old, and Jimmy Jr. was a year and two months. One day, while living in the ground-floor apartment, something mysterious occurred concerning Rebecca. It was early morning when I awoke to make Jim's breakfast and see him off to work. The entrance to the children's bedroom was located off the kitchen. After Jim had left, I once again went in to check them. They were both in their cribs fast asleep, so I decided to lie down until they awoke for breakfast. The windows were closed and locked, and I checked the kitchen and front-door entrance to make sure they were locked as well. Then I went into the bedroom to lie down. I must have fallen asleep, because I awoke with a start.

Someone was knocking on the front door. I went to the door, where a woman who evidently lived in one of the apartments nearby was standing.

She informed me that my daughter was up in the backyard sandbox, playing in the sand, and was naked. I was shocked and rushed to the backyard, where sure enough, Becky was sitting in the sandbox without any clothes on. I scooped her up and hurried back to the apartment. I immediately rushed into their bedroom to check on Jimmy Jr. He was standing up, holding on to the vertical crib bars. I couldn't understand how Becky got outdoors. It seemed impossible. At her age, she was neither tall nor old enough to open the securely locked doors. We had two large wooden cribs for them, and they never tried to climb out of them to my knowledge. The children always had diapers, a night shirt, and a nightgown on when I put them to bed. I was so shaken that I couldn't remember if her clothes were still in her crib or not. It would be many years later that the mysterious circumstances surrounding my daughter's obvious abduction would come to light. Once again, the helpful tool of hypnotic regression would open Becky's subconscious to release information stored in her memory of what had happened to her as a child.

The mystery turned out to be a UFO-related experience. *The Andreasson Legacy*, written by Raymond E. Fowler, reveals what happened to Becky then, as well as other UFO encounters she's been through since. It appears a close encounter with the UFO phenomenon will often follow through family lines, where some of the children experience the unknown factor as well. It was 1967. I was thirty years old when I had my first adult encounter. Beings landed their craft in the backyard. The house lights went out, and strange beings with large heads and big, scary black eyes entered my home. My husband was in the hospital due to a car accident, and my parents were staying with me and my seven children to help out at this time. Thinking there was a fire because of a pulsing red light streaming in through the pantry window, my father rushed into the pantry and was the first to see five unusual-looking beings outside, sort of hopping down the small hill toward our closed-in porch. They entered the house, passing right through our closed heavy wooden kitchen door. I was stunned and amazed at their strange appearance and their unbelievable ability. Scripture immediately came into my mind, and I realized they had to be angels. At the time it happened, I remembered their visitation and some things I was put through. However, as time passed, the strange experience began to fade. Anyway, there was not much I could do about it. Years later, all I remembered was that an odd-looking being had been in my home. At that particular time, I did not know why or how the memory was there. My earlier experiences remained safely stored away in my subconscious as well. The strange thing was that my memory had faded, and I had probably been programmed to forget.

Many years after the visitation, I saw a strange request from a Dr. Hynek in a small local paper and decided to send a letter and picture to him of what I recalled. Three years later, he asked me to undergo regressive hypnosis to find out why I saw the thing. After many sessions, I remembered a peculiar being that had been in my house, handing me a little blue book to look at. I remembered this odd-looking being telling me to keep the book safe for ten days, so I had stored it in my bedroom closet on the top shelf and had looked through it for three days. At that time, Becky was about twelve years old when she came to me, very upset. She said, "Momma, I've been having an awful scary dream over and over again at night that seems so real. There were funny-looking, big-headed people with large scary black eyes in our house." I immediately whispered to her to be quiet. I told her it was real, but I didn't want her to frighten her brothers and little sisters over it. I knew right away she had to have seen the same beings and that they had briefly taken her out of suspended animation at the time to show me my family was all right. I told her not to be afraid because Jesus was with us. It was then I decided to show her the book, and I brought her into my room. She placed her hand on its surface and must have felt something, for when she lifted her hand away, there were sparkles of light on her palm. The peculiar thing was that, later in life, Becky received the innate ability to handwrite their strange symbolic language. When I showed her the book, she promised she would not say anything about it or tell the other kids about the odd people who had been in our house. The days passed quickly since I'd received the book. I continued to study the strange drawings and writing within it, and after the ninth day, it disappeared.

Many people don't believe in hypnosis, but hypnosis helped me to slowly and safely realize the awesome reality of my encounters, even those that were frightening. Once the shield or veil covering my memories broke free and revealed the hidden knowledge of my multiple UFO experiences, my mind was wide open, and a plethora of details from each and every personal encounter flooded my being. I was grateful to learn the truth and handle the strange existence of these remarkable things, such as the peculiar-looking beings, their amazing abilities, and their wondrous craft. On January 25, 1967, beings entered my home, but it would be many years before I learned who they were. At the time, I was unaware of my strange encounters, for my interests were in my husband and children, in trying to get by, and in clinging to my faith in God. Of course, now, decades later, I know what happened to Becky at three years old, when she was taken out of our rented apartment on Summer Street. So what was happening? The beings were following through not only with me, but with my daughter as well.

As if I didn't have enough stress at the time, it was a long, hot summer, and within a few more months, I would be giving birth to our third child. Jim was starting to come home later and later in the evening after work, and he was not in a very good mood or good shape to be driving. One night, he just didn't come home at all. Weeks went by with no word of where he was. He evidently had deserted us and taken off to places unknown. My parents came to get me and the children, and we stayed with them at their house. While there, I wondered how I was going to be able to support my children. I had no idea where Jim was and no income, and I was getting closer to the birth of the baby. I kept praying to the Lord to straighten things out, to help Jim see that family is what's important. Finally, I could tell by the onset of pain that it was time to go. I was taken to the hospital, where I delivered my second son, whom I named Mark James. After a few days, my sister Shirley came to the hospital to get the baby and me, and she brought a whole layette for him. Shirley was my eldest sister and was like a rock. She loved the Lord and gave her all to family and God. My parents had five children, and each of us had large families. Shirley had eight children, Wayne had five, Violet had five, I had seven, and Carol had seven, so my parents had thirty-two grandchildren. This was wonderful when we all got together on holidays, but that was later in life.

At this time, I had the baby and was two days home from the hospital when Jim showed up at my parents' door. He begged for forgiveness, pleading with me to take him back. He said he couldn't live without me and the children and was so sorry he had left. I was still in love with him. He looked so tired and sad, as if he, too, had been put through a time of hell. He told me where he'd been and what had happened; because he had been in the navy and on a ship, he knew what to expect at sea, so after he left, he went to Pensacola, Florida, and got a job on a ship. He did his work, but the older seamen knew something was wrong for such a young man to be working there. A terrible tropical storm arose while the ship was out at sea, and the captain called Jim to his cabin for a talk. He asked Jim what had happened for him to choose to be out to sea. Jim told him how he'd lost the house and left his wife and children behind and that I was probably just about ready to have his third child. The captain said, "Jim, you don't belong here. You should go home to your family. They need you." After Jim told me what the captain said, I cried, for I knew God had heard my prayers, and the manifestation of the Holy Spirit's love was at work.

Jim had made money while on the ship, so once again we rented another apartment in Fitchburg. A couple of months went by, and Jim was unable to find work. Our finances were getting slim, so I got a job as the candy girl at Kreskies. At this time, we had no car, so I had to walk home after work, which was from the city to the town's outskirts. My parents watched the children while Jim tried to find work. He was an ace welder and finally landed a job with the General Electric Company. We finally were able to start saving for a house. Jim's father, who loved to fish and hunt, had bought a cabin in South Ashburnham next to a lake for his retirement and was thinking of selling the large two-story family home in Westminster, as he lived there all alone. After he retired, he spent most of his time at his cabin, leaving the large house empty except to come by to feed or take out his hunting dogs. Seeing that his father wanted to sell, Jim spoke with him about an option to buy the family home. His father approved, and we moved into the large house. We occupied the house from 1959 to 1963. During that time, we were blessed with four more children, two more boys and two girls. Their names were Scott James, Todd James, Bonnie Beth, and Cindy Dawn.

We began to refurbish the interior of the house and also had a bulldozer level the steep dirt road from the bottom to the top flat area, and we had the road tarred. While fixing the house, Jim had taken down a quarter of the cellar wall to put in a garage door. While waiting, he framed it and made a narrow roof above to keep the rain out until the garage door was ready. Within the cellar were many expensive tools and summer things packed away. Jim was working nights at General Electric, which gave him the opportunity to work on the house during the day. My mother and father still lived down the hill and across the street from us, so it was pretty safe, even though there was now an exposed area down in the cellar. Jim was working the late-night shift until midnight when, for reasons unknown to me, I spent three days fasting. On my third evening of fasting, the children were watching the last cartoon show before bed while I read. The show ended, and I put the children to bed. I went into the kitchen to check the entrance door, which was locked; however, the kitchen door that led down wooden stairs to the cellar had no lock on it. I walked back and forth in the long kitchen, thinking about what I should do, because I had an odd feeling that something was wrong. The cellar wall had been open for more than a week now, and it had never bothered me before. But this particular night it did. It was hot and muggy outside, and some windows were open with screens in place. Rather than worry, I decided to take the tall, metal garage chair we used at times at the table for my younger children and forcefully wedge it beneath the cellar doorknob.

I returned to the living room, shut off the television that sat under a window with white nylon curtains, and began to read again, but my eyes were drawn back to the window, where I was shocked to see a face outside staring in at me. I quickly got up, went into the kitchen, and wondered whether I was seeing things. I went back to the seat and lifted my Bible, and as soon as I did, my eyes were drawn back to the living-room window, which was located just above the open cellar area, and there was the same face. A man with auburn hair; thick, dark eyebrows; and menacing, dark eyes was outside the window, perched on the small rooftop, glaring at me. The face quickly disappeared, and suddenly I heard movement in the cellar. Someone was trying to open the kitchen's cellar door. It kept jiggling against the wedged metal chair. I held my breath and prayed. Suddenly, I heard something like wood falling down the stairs. There was a brief silence, followed quickly by wet, heavy footsteps running down our long, steep driveway. I quickly moved to an open screened window to try to see who or where the man was. In the darkness and mist, I could not see anyone, but I heard the sound of a car door suddenly slamming shut. There were no car lights as a vehicle sped away, as if someone other than the trespasser had been driving.

The front of our house was very high off the edge of a deep bank. There was a front screened door in the living room that had no steps as yet, for it was too high up off the ground for stairs. I quickly opened the door and screamed down for my parents. My mother pulled in with the car just as my father woke up and came to the door, and he said she was just coming in from an evening prayer service. I told her someone had just tried to break in, and she started walking up the driveway while I pulled the chair away from the doorknob and went down into the cellar to investigate what the burglar was after. Some heavy wooden stakes and twine lay on the cellar stairs. Whoever it was must have brushed against the stored material we had used to protect our newly grown grass seed and when it fell, the noise and the intruder's inability to open the door must have scared him away.

While I was in the cellar with a flashlight, I unknowingly frightened my mother. When she rounded the corner to the cellar, she saw the light and cried out, "Ba...ba...Betty, is...is that you?" She was relieved to hear my voice and stayed with me until Jim got home later that night from work. I told him exactly what had happened. In the morning, he called the police, and an officer came to write down the report. I told him every-thing that had taken place as well and that they must have been after tools in the cellar. The police officer wanted to speak privately to Jim. Later, Jim told me what the officer said to him, which was, "The person who tried to break in was not after anything that was in your cellar. He was after your wife." I was shocked. What did he mean? What was the man planning to do to me? So that was why I had fasted for three days—evidently it was for protection. Jim immediately boarded the cellar, put a heavy lock on the door, and bought a gun.

As time went by, we continued to work on the house, and Jim joined the pipefitters and welders union, which meant we would now be able to really save, for his wages dramatically increased. One morning, I was sur-prised to see some very tall trees on the edge of the property bent over, along with a few that had been knocked down next to the pines, which were located near the entrance of the house. I wondered, *How could that have happened?* We'd had no storm to cause it. Also, we were having some odd things happening in the house. One night I awoke from sleep and could not move. It felt like something was holding my whole body down. I couldn't speak or even move to awaken Jim. I then thought maybe I had done or said something that was displeasing to God, so I prayed for for-giveness. Finally, the pressure was released, and I could move. It would be a long time before I learned I had experienced what is now known as sleep paralysis.

But there was more to come. One night, Becky, still a young child, experienced a frightening encounter in her bedroom. Thankfully, she was protected. A large beam of light lifted her in the air and protected her from a strange, growling animal that appeared in the corner of her room. The experience is recorded within the book *The Andreasson Legacy*. The location of her bedroom was upstairs, next to ours, on the same side of the house where I had seen the broken and bent trees. Another strange event occurred around 1963 or '64, while Becky and Jimmy Jr. were at school. I would make sure my rather rambunctious children, meaning the three boys, Bonnie, and the baby, had a nap. During this particular day, while they were sleeping, I had more time to clean, so I decided to mop the kitchen floor.

But for some reason, while in the mopping process, I automatically put up the mop and walked outside, as if being drawn someplace. I could hear some kind of vibrating noise. Without thinking, I headed out the door toward the back woods. I crossed over the stone wall and was drawn next to the huge rock at the edge of the forest. There was someone or something standing by the rock. It was staring at me, and I felt afraid, because it didn't look like a normal human being. It seemed like I couldn't run away from this, so I asked the Lord to be with me. The unusual-looking being had a large head and big, black eyes and was a little taller than I was. I couldn't see its small mouth move, but I could hear its multiple voices talking to me through my mind; it was telling me that I would go through many things, to keep my faith, and fear not. It was telling me about certain things that would happen. It said I was not to be anxious and that I would understand in time. I just did not understand what he meant or what he was telling me, so he placed his hands on my head by my temples, then touched my forehead between my eyes. He said I was blessed, and he was talking in an unusual language. But then he said, "You will forget all that was spoken and will not remember. You must now go back to the house. You will not remember any of this at the sound of the ring. Peace be with you, as it is."

I automatically turned around and headed back to the house. Once I was home again, I continued mopping the kitchen floor, oblivious to what had just happened. Little did I know what was waiting up ahead for our family. As a family, including Jim, we were all attending the Baptist church in Westminster. I, like most people reading the Bible, was into the milk of the Word, which is the Gospels, but I felt like I was being led to the meat of the Word, which included the prophetic books of Ezekiel, Isaiah, and Daniel. The book of Revelation was fascinating, and I wanted to know what it meant. At that time, in the fifties and sixties, most people shied away from the prophetic works, for they were hard to understand. However, I was in love with the whole Word of God. Jim enjoyed the services at the church and was doing much better as a father and husband,

and our children attended Sunday school. The Baptist church was very supportive, and the dear ladies gave me such a wonderful surprise—an unexpected first and second baby shower. For as time went by, our seventh child, Cindy Dawn, was born. A year later, we had saved up enough money to finally purchase the family home, and Jim approached his father with the good news. But his dad did not want to sell the house now. Jim was devastated, for we had put so much work and money into the building and property. Jim's dad while living in Ashburnham had befriended some Canadian French people at the lake. Later, he decided to sell his cabin and move back in with us, which he did. But the people he was involved with visited often, and there was drinking involved. I do not drink, and Jim was trying not to, but it was a difficult time. Meanwhile, rather than harbor hurt feelings about the house and situation, Jim and I decided to hunt for another place for our family. For we remembered and were grateful that when we were having it rough, his father offered us a place to live with option to buy.

CHAPTER 6

Surprise, Surprise

• • •

RIGHT AWAY WE MANAGED TO find an old colonial-type, two-story dwelling, which was sort of a historical house in South Ashburnham. It was called a halfway house, where in the late seventeenth and eighteenth centuries, people stopped by for food and lodging while in transit. At this time, it was owned by an elderly lady wanting to sell, for it was too much for her to keep up. It was reasonably priced and needed work. It had a fireplace in each bedroom, with wide, heavy, plank floors and a wraparound porch with a lengthy shedlike addition. When we were moved into the house for a while, much to our surprise, we heard that the young French couple moved in with Jim's father. But something very strange happened in the bedroom Jim and I had used while living there. It was evening, and evidently the three of them—Jim's father; the young, dark-haired female; and her blond husband—were drinking through the night and later went to bed. During the night, the young woman died while sleeping in that room. We never did find out the reason she died.

As for us, it was about 1964 or 1965 when we first moved to the South Ashburnham residence and got the children registered for school. The kids loved it, as they had plenty of friends in the neighborhood. Because I was such a mother hen, wanting to know where my children were at all times, there was always a large number of children in the yard. Other parents knew where their kids were as well, for I would often receive a call to please send their son or daughter home for supper. However, once we began to fix up the house, we started to have some very unusual things happen, like the time I saw something peculiar upstairs. During the day while Jim was away working at his job, I rented a floor sander and sanded the living room, hallway, and our bedroom floors, located downstairs. The next day we polyurethaned them in the evening before bed. This meant that we had to sleep upstairs in the girls' bedroom on our mattress so the downstairs floors could dry overnight. There was a lower hallway with a twelve-step winding stairwell going up to a six-foot hallway, which led into the boys' room to the left and the girls' room to the right. Our mattress was positioned in the girls' room on the floor, so I could easily see the hall and into the boys' room. Everyone was fast asleep, or so I thought, when I suddenly heard very loud noises coming from the boys' room. I looked that way and thought the boys were up horsing around. It sounded like someone was aggressively pulling out and pushing in bureau drawers, and by the loud sound was doing it recklessly. Suddenly, I saw a five-foot being of light coming out of their room rushing toward me across the hallway, and it turned and leaped down the stairs. The form looked like a person of light, but it had no eyes, nose, or mouth. I was shocked and mentioned to Becky what I had seen through the night. Unknown to me at the time many years later, I would briefly become a being of light exactly as what I had seen in the house. Evidently, Becky told her friend Kathy about what I had seen. Kathy was amazed, because she had seen something similar. She told Becky that she and a friend had been staying at the church campground. It was dark and late at night when they both had to go to the bathroom, but they were afraid to go alone, for the temporary outhouse was located way down next to the large lake. As they rushed down the hill and drew closer to the lake, they both saw a being of light leap into the water. This same young girl told Becky of another odd experience she had with a little person as well.

At this time, the strange things we were experiencing in this house started to escalate. There were noises, small sparkling colored lights floating around, the attic door was popping open on its own even though it was securely closed, and Becky was being plagued with something bothering her while in bed. I would lay down with her at times so she wouldn't be so afraid. Jim would get mad at me, and he said I was not helping her and that she needed to grow up. I knew someone or something was breathing very heavily next to her bed. As I lay on her bed with her, I could hear a rocking chair moving or something that sounded like a creaking boat, as well as the strange breathing sounds. There was definitely some kind of spirit activity going on, for while our whole family went to Horseneck Beach on a weekend vacation, neighborhood children upon our return reported seeing lights go on in our attic and a man's shadow walking back and forth in front of the widow. The neighborhood kids felt the house was spooky.

Another unusual thing happened to me one evening when I attended a church meeting with my mother and father. We went to a Pentecostal meeting that was taking place in the basement area of the large church located on the Main Street of Ashburnham. There were quite a few people attending the service. The minister asked for testimonials of what the Lord had done for them. And many stood up, thanked God for his love, and gave a tithe. I stood and thanked God for all his blessings and all he had done for me, and because of my love for him, my emotions welled up within me, and I began to cry. I wanted to give something back to him and said, "I don't have much money, but I will use the gift of art he has given me for his glory." The minister's wife sitting behind her husband, who was at the pulpit, was led by the Spirit; she quickly stood up and rushed down the stairs to me. She immediately placed her hand on top of my head and started to talk in the unknown tongues as tears rolled down my face. After the tongues were finished, the minister through the Spirit gave the interpretation and said I would be "blessed above woman." Of course, in my mind, whatever was given for me to do would not be compared to me as a woman, but perhaps an unusual job that is done. It was many years later, while under hypnosis, the memory of this experience returned. Unknown to me, there were two of the tall, white-haired elder angels present, standing by in the church at that time.

While under hypnosis, I experienced the recollection of the event, when one elder asked me, "Do you now remember what was spoken to you?" I remembered what was said but not the reason behind the words.

I'm beginning to think my 1994 encounter, which you will read about, has something to do with it. But right now, it is time to return to South Ashburnham. After moving into the colonial house, my children joined the People's Church, and each one was given a King James Bible. The church was located just up the street from our new residence. My children would often come home after church and say they saw either a red or white light surrounding some of the parishioners. Once in a while, I was able to attend the Pentecostal church with my sister Shirley, but there was so much work to be done on this house that I was at home quite a bit. It was at the Pentecostal church that I received the gift of tongues. And much later, while we were in prayer at home, my daughter Becky received the tongues of fire as well. It was at this time I once again started to draw and paint some pictures of the book of Daniel and Revelation to help me understand what was being said in these unusual scriptural prophesies.

The family seemed pretty happy in this old house we had purchased. The children had plenty of playmates and got along very well with these friends. Becky and I just love animals, and she had a black-and-white kitty named Boots. There were a couple of boys in the neighborhood who were bullies and were known to hurt defenseless animals. This story of my daughter and Boots is a great example of what faith can do. Boots had been missing for over a week, and every day Becky was searching for her. A friend told my son Mark that he saw Boots hanging from a tree up in the back woods. Mark and Becky rushed up to check out the story. Sure enough, a poor, helpless black kitty with white feet was dead and hanging in the tree. When the children came home and told me, I called the police, and they came and saw what someone had done to Boots. Becky was in hysterics over her cat. No matter what I said, I could not stop her from crying over her pet. This went on constantly for three days. I was worried she would become ill, as I did not know what to do to stop her tears. Of course, Becky knew about Jesus's death and resurrection from the Bible and church services. To comfort her, I told her all things are possible, and even Boots could come back. I knew I was placing a heavy burden of proof upon the Spirit and realized it could be a risky statement for me to make concerning Becky's future faith and her ability to handle disappointment. But I was fearful of Becky ending up in the hospital because of her continued oppressive sorrow, so I reminded her about the resurrection and said if she would truly believe, God could bring Boots back to life as well. She immediately stopped crying, for in faith, she believed it without a doubt.

Another week went by, and it was a hot, damp, and misty evening when I was upstairs in Becky's bedroom with her. The screen was in, and the window was wide open when we heard some noise on the rooftop below her window, which is the roof extension that jutted out over the kitchen below. We looked out the window and saw a bright white light about the size of a nickel fly into the air and off the roof. Right away, I thought someone had been on the roof with a lit cigarette and tossed it over so the light landed and glowed briefly on the small sloping ground below. We both ran downstairs and out the door to look for the light or discarded cigarette butt. There was none. At the same time, about fifty feet away, a neighborhood boy named Craig was heading home on the sidewalk. It was dark, and he was below the streetlight when we saw and heard him say, "Hey, where did this cat come from?" A cat walked up to him from off the road. Becky raced to the sidewalk, believing it had to be Boots. Sure enough, it was. It was a black cat with four white feet. Faith can move mountains and certainly did by bringing back her cat.

Years earlier, I was put through the wringer of sorrow and grief once again, an occurrence I caused with my own negligence. I was in the living room polishing the furniture and end tables and had the cover off the Old English bottle. I was going to go out to get the white doilies from the clothesline, but first I quickly glanced at the bottle, then over by the hallway, where my two younger daughters, Bonnie and Cindy, were busy playing with their dolls. I should have put the cap on the bottle. To this very day, I regret the decision I made to go out to the line. I quickly grabbed the doilies and rushed back into the house, just in time to hear my two-year-old choking from drinking the red polish. I was frantic and called our doctor. She wasn't home, but her maid said to force Cindy to vomit. I gave her some milk, hoping she would vomit, but it was the worst thing I could have done. While Cindy vomited, the oil rushed back into her lungs, and she ended up with aspirated pneumonia. Jim and I rushed her to the hospital, where a specialist for children put her in an oxygen tent. I thought I was going to have a nervous breakdown, for all I could do was lie on the bed and cry, as it was my fault my baby was so dangerously ill and close to death. After the second day, the doctor talked to Jim and me, saying, "She might not make it through the night."

I lay on the bed, grief-stricken, asking God to please save her and take me instead. *Just save my child, please, Lord.* My whole family was praying for her. The next day at the hospital, Cindy had an intravenous needle at the top of her forehead and her hands tied down so she wouldn't pull it out. Hot air was blowing in on her body, she was beet red, and the tent should have had ice in the back that would make it cooler for her. The nurse saw to it. I could see Cindy wanted to put her thumb into her mouth, which was why she was struggling to pull her hand up to her mouth area. I told the nurse she sometimes sucked her thumb, so the nurse loosened one arm, and immediately Cindy put her thumb in her mouth, which gave her some comfort. A few days later, when we came to see her, someone had put new ice in the back of the tent, but the cold water from the ice was leaking down around her back. I was so upset; I wanted to stay there with her, to make sure she was all right, but I couldn't. A few days later, she started getting better, and the doctor said he was amazed. I knew it was due to prayer. He also said he would never take on another case like that again. Instead, he would ship the child to a Boston hospital, where they are better equipped to handle such emergencies. The following day, thank God, Cindy was sitting up and was hungry. I brought her some spaghetti, and she used her hands to shovel it into her mouth. She had spaghetti all over her, but she was well on the way to recovery.

Before she came home, Jim insisted he was taking me to see our family doctor to make sure I was all right after such a traumatic ordeal of almost losing Cindy. She checked me thoroughly, and everything seemed to be OK; because I was already there, though, she decided to do a Pap smear and appeared somewhat upset when she did. I did not realize why until a few days later, when the test revealed I had cancer of the cervix. I thought it must have happened because I was so busy—I'd failed to go back for a checkup after Cindy was born. It turns out today they know it is caused by a virus. Our doctor sat me down to have a very serious conversation concerning my condition and situation. She told me, "Your test not only reveals the presence of cancer, but you are almost two months pregnant." I was shocked. She said, "When pregnant, the inside of a woman's body is so clean that cancer could spread like wildfire."

I caught my breath. "Oh no. What about the baby?" I cried.

She knew I was shaken from the news, and as she continued, she said, "Betty, I want you to seriously think about what this means and understand what will happen if you don't have an operation." She knew, seeing I was pregnant, that I wouldn't want one. "You have seven children who need their mother," she pointed out.

A thousand things went through my mind as I prayed to God. When Jim was informed of the dire consequences, he insisted I had to have the operation. My doctor referred me to an excellent doctor at the Burbank hospital. The operation was successful. He removed the tiny fetus and the cancer, and I had a complete hysterectomy. I was sad and cried and prayed over the loss, but I believe I will see this little one someday in heaven. Meanwhile, unknown to me, my mother had a heart attack while attending a prayer service for me. Many family members came to see me. Even my sister Violet flew up from Pennsylvania and came in to my room. I knew something else was wrong, and I begged Jim to tell me what was going on. Was I dying? Were the kids all right? My mother quickly improved, so Jim was able to tell me what had happened and that my mom was all right. Time passed, and Cindy's birthday was December 9. Jim was working as a pipefitter for a large Leominster company at the time; it was his payday, so I drove our Volkswagen bus down to the shop to pick up some extra cash to get a few more things for her birthday party. It was a bright and sunny winter day, and Bonnie and Cindy, who were now three and four years old, were fast asleep in the back of the bus. At Jim's work, the shop had a long, high fence surrounding the grounds. I pulled down the road and parked across the street from the shop's road entrance. I was waiting there when a car with two men inside passed and slowly stopped on the road about twenty feet up ahead, backed up into the entrance, and banged into the open gate. I looked away as not to embarrass the driver and thought it must be two bosses, for they both had hard hats on. I thought they must have had too much to drink for lunch. The driver pulled the car away from the gate, and they stayed in the driveway talking. I pretended not to notice what was going on when the passenger got out of the car, walked a few steps, and quickly returned to the car. As an artist, however, I was picking up details of what they looked like, what they were wearing, and what the interior of the car looked like when the passenger once again got out of the car and quickly walked up the driveway. After a very brief time, the passenger came running down the slightly slanted driveway with something in his hand. He flung off his hard hat, which bounced against the gate, then pulled down a green scarf from his face and jumped into the car. The driver took off, and I could see a reddish sticker on the back of the window as I glanced down and got the license-plate number. It dawned on me it was a robbery, and there might be guns involved, so I quickly ducked down in the seat. Jim came out to the car and said, "There was a robbery."

I said, "I know. I got all the information."

He turned white as a sheet and said, "You didn't say anything, did you?"

I told him, "Yes, I did."

It was not very long after that the police picked the two men up. We went to the police station, and I was given a bunch of mug shots to look through. I immediately picked out and identified the men. It was then I learned that the evening before, an FBI agent had been at a local hotel watching them and knew they were planning something. Apparently, they somehow had given the agent the slip. This story did not end there. I had to appear in court twice concerning the case. The first time, they were convicted. The second time, which was months later, they tried to get out through a much higher court. The police were sending an officer to pick me up for court and said I needed to make sure my driver was an officer—*before* I got in the car. The police arrived, and I went to the car. When I looked at the officer's name tag, it was incorrect, so I rushed back to the house and called the station. They were apologetic and said that while the officer had been en route, there had been a bad accident, and he'd had to respond, as he was so close to incident. They gave me the correct name of the new officer. In court, the detective and state attorney were with me and were totally surprised that the two incarcerated subjects were able to go through to a higher court. While on the stand, I told everything I saw. Once again, someone handed me a group of pictures, and I shuffled through them and picked the same two men.

After court was over, the attorney said the judge wanted to speak to me. Earlier, the attorney and detective had been telling me that a judge's word was like God's. The judge came over to where we were standing and said hello. Then he looked at me and said, "You lied to the court."

I kind of caught my breath and said, "What? No, I didn't. I told exactly what I saw happen."

He said, "No, you lied. Nobody, and I mean nobody, could ever believe you have seven children." He smiled, and a feeling of relief came over me.

The judge looked exactly like the comedian Flip Wilson, and one of Flip's famous sayings was, "Here come the judge; here come the judge."

The judge, who was very kind, could have been his twin.

CHAPTER 7

What Next? Enough Is Enough

• • •

IN LATE 1966, LIFE WAS once again about to deliver another devastating whiplash to our family. Jim was on his way home from work when a car came rushing down a hillside road into traffic and smashed directly into the side of Jim's Volkswagen sedan. The small car was completely demolished, and Jim was rushed to the Fitchburg hospital with serious injuries from the accident. He was immediately operated on, as his legs and feet had been terribly crushed and mangled. He also suffered a number of broken bones. Surgeons put metal pins in his hip and ankles, which meant it would be some time before he could come home. My mother and father came to stay with us to watch the children, so I could visit Jim while he was healing. A month went by, and Jim was still very much incapacitated and in need of constant hospital care, but because the hospital costs were becoming overwhelming, he was moved to the veterans' hospital in the Worcester, Boston, area. This meant that, because of the distance and snow, I was only able to visit him occasionally.

On the evening of January 25, 1967, my mother and father were in the living room while the kids watched *Bozo the Clown* on television after dinner. Suddenly, the power, the TV, and all the lights went out, and a reddish-orange pulsing light came streaming through the back kitchen window into the opening to the living room. I thought it was the police or fire department lights flashing away in the back of the house and told the children to sit still and be quiet until we found out. Unknown to me at the time, my father had passed me. He went into the kitchen area to look out the front pantry window. The house seemed eerily quiet as I went into the kitchen to check what was going on, and I saw five strange-looking beings coming into my kitchen, right through the heavy wooden door. They stood before me silently. They seemed to be almost as tall as I was, and they were wearing tightly fitted blue suits, each with a band across his chest and around his waist. I also saw that each had an eagle-like patch on one arm, and they were wearing some sort of odd boots. At first I felt afraid, for their physical appearance was so strange and alarming; they all had bulbous gray-skinned heads that seemed too large for their bodies, and they had no hair. Plus they had large black eyes that seemed never to blink. Their mouths were thin and did not move, and their noses and ears were just like two small holes.

I was afraid and asked God to be with us. A sort of peaceful feeling of love swept over me, and I heard scripture come to my mind: "Entertain the stranger, for it may be angels unaware." My mind tried to reason with my eyesight, and I thought, *Where are their wings? These beings don't look like any angel pictures I've ever seen. But then, who am I to say what God's myriad of angels are supposed to look like?* My mind questioned how they had come through that door without opening it, and I wondered why this was happening to me. The leader began to communicate with me, but not audibly; he was communicating through my mind. I thought he was saying they wanted something to eat, so I quickly got some meat from the refrigerator, put it in a frying pan, and started to cook for them. The leader quickly jumped backward as some smoke rose from the meat in the pan. Once again, he spoke to me through my mind. He wanted "knowledge tried by fire," so as I put the pan to the side, and I thought of the Bible lying on the end table in the living room. They followed as I moved into the room. I was astonished, because I saw my mother and children sitting very quietly and still. It was as if they were held in a state of suspended animation. I reached down for the Bible, wondering what was going on. The leader, who said his name was Quazgar, put his hand out to receive the book. When he did, I could see only three fingers on his hand. He waved his hand over the Bible, and three other thin books appeared. He passed one to each being standing by. Immediately, the beings, without physically turning them, made page after page turn; on each page, I could see no print—only white, shining light appeared as the pages flipped by. It seemed as if they were consuming the content of light with their eyes. Once again, I turned to see my family just quietly sitting on the couch, as if time had somehow stopped. I was concerned as to why my family could not move, and Quazgar briefly took Becky out of her suspended state to show me they were all fine.

The leader then passed me a thin blue book. He told me it was for my initiation and said I was to grasp as much as possible from the book within ten days. Then the book would be gone. I placed it on the end table. Becky was now standing very still as the four beings once again moved out to the kitchen area, with me trailing behind the leader. We continued to move right through the wooden door with no problem, to the side of the house, where a metallic craft was parked on the small incline in the backyard. The beings took me aboard, and at the climax to my encounter, I was informed by the One that I had been "chosen to show the world." The entire experience with every detail is recorded in *The Andreasson Affair*, which adequately covers so much more information than I can include at this writing. I was taken aboard their craft and put through an examination where beings dressed in silver suits probed me with a needle inserted into my left nostril. They withdrew a Beebe-like device. At the same time, they inserted another thin, tubelike needle into my navel to check for procreation. The being was surprised and said something was missing. How could he have known something was missing? I told the leader that I'd had to have a hysterectomy, as the doctor's Pap smear had revealed cancer of the cervix, and I'd been carrying a two- to three-month-old fetus. My doctor, who knew I had seven children, was concerned and believed I was very much at risk and should have a hysterectomy as soon as possible.

At this writing, I am wondering if Quazgar was referring to the missing fetus I'd been carrying. They were looking for something they thought was supposed to be there, though it's possible they were referring to the missing womb or uterus taken during my hysterectomy. This must have been revealed to them during their procreation examination.

As stated earlier, as the years went by, all I consciously remembered about the weird 1967 experience was a strange being in the house. As I also mentioned earlier, in the early seventies, I happened to see a small newspaper article placed by Dr. J. Allen Hynek requesting that any strange or unusual sightings be sent to the Center for UFO Studies (CUFOS). I sent a letter and drew a picture of what the odd being looked like that had been in my house. When I sent the letter, I felt relieved, for maybe this learned man might know what it was. Instead, Dr. Hynek filed the letter away for almost three years until some Massachusetts researchers interested in humanoids asked if he had any such cases they could look into.

But now to get back to South Ashburnham and what was happening at the time. It was many months before Jim was back on his feet and working as a pipefitter again. I was still reading, drawing, and painting pictures of some prophetic scriptures in the Bible, trying to understand what they meant. Time passed. Jim was now much stronger and had healed very well, so we began to work on the house again, planning to put it up for sale. Jim took down some walls, which enlarged the kitchen and dining area, and he built some cabinets and rearranged the kitchen and bathroom plumbing. The changes were more modern, and the interior began to look great. He and the boys also tore down the long extension of rooms connected to the left side of the main house, and I planted flowers and made a rock garden in the cleared space. The whole house and grounds were looking good. The children were doing well in school, and they had many friends in the neighborhood. We had a large Halloween party in the garage for everyone. The kids loved it. Then during the next summer, a television show called *Boomtown* asked children to help with a charity drive for muscular dystrophy. My children and their friends decided to have a fair with baked goods, games, and a circus to make money for the drive. The children did so well financially for the charity that they were invited to appear on the television show with host Rex Trailer. My sister-in-law Agnes and I piled the children in her station wagon and headed for the Boston studio. The children were so excited. Along the way, they sang songs and played guessing games, and poor little Johnny lost his breakfast from motion sickness. After cleaning up, we entered the busy city and were lost. I was worried we'd be too late for the show.

Agnes pulled the car to the side, and I shouted from the window to a lady waiting to cross the street. "Miss…Miss…oh, Miss," I called, but the person did not respond and did not turn toward us. Once again I called out in desperation even louder, "Miss…Miss…*Miss*, can you please help us? We're lost."

The person turned toward me, and my mouth dropped open, for it wasn't a woman but a man with long, long hair. I dared not apologize, which would have made the situation more embarrassing for both of us. He kindly gave us directions, and we arrived at the studio on time. Becky was given a cowboy hat to wear and was made the *Boomtown* storekeeper. All the kids had a great time during their TV debut.

Because of Jim's accident and his body's occasional aches and pains, we decided it would be far better to live in a much warmer climate, so we decided California would be the place to go. We purchased a brand-new and exceptionally large Ford van to carry the family across the country. Jim bought it without any paneling on the inside and removed the back seats, so there would be enough room to make bunk beds for the children, where they could comfortably rest or sleep along the way. We put the house up for sale and immediately got an interested buyer. We sold the house and were on our way.

Our country is so beautiful; however, it was tough and slow climbing the Rocky Mountains, though we finally made it to the coast of California. We thought we'd purchase a house with some land—ha. The prices for a place there were ridiculously high. It was getting late, and my map reading was terrible. Because of me, my family was moving on Route 1 bordering the Pacific Ocean. The kids were thrilled to see the open water and lights from faraway ships; I, on the other hand, felt like I was going to lose it, as I had never before been on a road that was built on the side of a mountain, with nothing but miles of endless water below. We passed a beach with some buildings that looked like a bar. I searched for a route to get back to an area with some land on both sides of the road, but there didn't seem to be any; at least, there were none I could see on the map. Also, there were no camping areas where we could pull off to rest, like there are on the East Coast. Route 1, in my opinion, was a cliffside secondary road (and to my knowledge may still be). As we passed the beach bar, there were people walking in the middle of the road in the dark, like they were bombed or on something. They seemed like zombies. It was getting darker outside as we continued to slowly weave our way upward. This road was terrible, and deer darted out in front of us and then stood still from the van's lights, making us stop in the middle of the road until they moved on. As we moved slowly upward, there was a large sign that read Beware of Falling Rocks, and on the right-hand side of the bank were some extremely large boulders sitting on the sand, while on the left was the cliff with the ocean way below. There were no guardrails on either side of the road. We continued to climb, and as we went higher and higher, in and out of this trail, it began to get foggy.

We started to see a beam of light, like a lighthouse beacon coming our way. It appeared, disappeared, and appeared again, then disappeared again, until we finally realized they were the car lights of a crazy driver speeding down this hazardous narrow road in a small Volkswagen bug, with very little room to get by us. The sedan shot past us, just as Jim barely pulled off to the extreme right into some sand. I thought of Jim's accident in his little sedan and how much that must have shaken him. It was now dark, and a foggy mist surrounded us, which made it next to impossible to see what was up ahead. Jim was really tired. We kept trying to find a right turnoff, but there was none. We continued up this risky, winding, foggy road. Tired, Jim slowly pulled on to what looked like a different road. My mind was telling me we were going to die, and I started to scream, "Stop, stop, stop." Jim immediately stopped the van. I got out to check where we were and started to cry—if we had gone less than three feet more, we would have automatically rolled over the cliff into the sea. Between the fog and his exhaustion, thinking it was just part of the main road, Jim had turned on to a foggy lookout point that tourists used to view the Pacific Ocean. Jim slowly backed the van out to the main road again, and we continued to travel upward. It was very late. A few miles ahead, the heavy fog began to lift, and we could finally see land on both sides of the road, which was very comforting. As we continued onward, large trees appeared, and a sign for Taylor Park came into view.

We pulled into the empty park and got out of the van. When we stepped outside, a wonderful smell of evergreen trees permeated the evening air. It felt like every cell in my body was drinking in its wonderful fragrance. I thanked God that he got us safely through. After that terrifying ride along the California coast, we were ready to head for the sunshine state of Florida. Again, we traveled over the Rocky Mountains, and although there were excellent roads with guardrails, the trip was nerve-racking with its extremely high and very low terrains. We temporarily pulled off the road so the children could stretch their legs and see the mountains. This also gave Jim and me a chance to rest from the tedious travel. Becky came running to the van, all excited over an unusual stone she'd found among some rocks in the area. It was a whitish-yellow, partially clear stone about the size of a large walnut. She was excited and said, "Look. Look what I found. I think it's a diamond."

It was an unusual-looking stone, but I said to her, "Let me see." As I held it up to examine it, I said to her, "If this is a real diamond, it should be able to cut through glass." To prove to her that it was *not* a diamond, I pulled out a glass soda bottle and dragged the edge of the stone across the glass. To my amazement, it left a deep mark etched in the bottle's glass. I told her to hold on to the stone, and we'd see what kind of stone it was later. She stored it in the hollow metal door of the vehicle, which was the main door to the back that the children used to get in and out of the van. Unfortunately, the stone must have popped out with the constant opening and closing of the hollow door.

As we continued our travel either up a hill or down one in the van, it just seemed as though the vehicle didn't have much power while in the mountains. As we passed through Colorado, it was very late. Both Jim and I were concerned about the van, for besides the loss of power we'd experienced while in the mountains, we were now beginning to hear a loud noise off and on beneath the vehicle. We were exhausted and looking for a place to stop when we saw a small store and garage up ahead. As we pulled off the highway, we once again heard the loud noise beneath the van. I thought, *Oh no, don't tell me we bought a lemon. This is supposed to be a new automobile.* The garage was closed, so we decided to park the van near the garage, go to sleep, and check what was wrong in the morning. We all hunkered down until morning and awoke to bright sunshine. The family piled out to use the garage's bathroom, and Jim spoke to the mechanic. He did not know what was wrong, because the van checked out fine.

At this writing, I finally found out what was happening. We purchased this van in the late sixties or early seventies, so the van was not equipped with a high-altitude compensator. This meant lower oxygen levels in the higher altitudes of the mountains caused the van to react that way. However, we were so tired at the time that we didn't realize the other noise was *supposed* to be there; its sole purpose is to wake up the driver—we'd been driving over rumble strips embedded in certain areas of the road. Not only that, but in the store out West, the clerks must have had a good laugh at gullible me. When I picked up some postcards to mail back home, I was amazed over the picture of a huge rabbit with horns, which they called a jackalope. They claimed the creature was real and roamed the Western Plains.

After the experiences in California, I was happy to see Florida. We arrived in Fort Lauderdale and stayed in the guest side of a house my sister Shirley and her husband, Bob, had purchased. My niece Kitty was living on the other side and redoing the floors with new carpets for her parents, who were still in Massachusetts. After a few days of recuperation, Jim began to look for work. We were there more than a month, but Jim couldn't find suitable work that would pay what we were used to, so we packed up and headed back to Massachusetts, where he was still in the local union that paid very well.

We ended up in Ashby, renting an apartment. It was then that Jim's Aunt Edith, who'd never had children, lived alone, and was in her seventies, offered us five acres of land to build next to her house. She was getting older, and I think she wanted someone in the family close by who could be there for her if she needed help. We accepted her gracious gift, and I began to design the house we would build. It wasn't long before we obtained electricity, dug the large cellar hole, and poured the cement foundation. We had an artesian well put in, and Jim installed a bathroom and large furnace. This meant we could move into the cellar, where we had a few odd things happen. Several separate times, large balls of white light the size of melons would quickly pop out of the cement floor with a bang and disappear. We had a kitchen area with a sink, a stove, and a table, and I sectioned off the bedrooms with sheets hanging from the rafters. But one day, the children came to me and said that during the night they'd gotten up to go to the bathroom and had found a stranger sitting in the living-room area. They did not know who it was. The man was just sitting there quietly and then disappeared.

That was the beginning of peculiar things happening in our new home. While Jim was at work, I took our floor plans and house design to a home-improvement store in Gardner, Massachusetts, and spoke to a manager about the cost to build it. He gave me an estimate, which I brought home for Jim to see. The store gave us a good price for the lumber, windows, and doors we needed. I happened to see some builders working on the new Fitchburg Civic Center going up off the John Fitch Highway, so I stopped to ask if they would be interested in framing our house. I learned they were French Canadians working down here in the States; however, before they could finish all the Civic Center's framework, they had to wait until other types of jobs were completed at the Center, which meant there was a chance they could do the framing for us, as the other additional work was holding them up from finishing the project. The foreman considered my request and came to our place to speak to Jim. After seeing the framing plans, they decided they could do it for $2,000. Thus, the work to frame the large twelve-room house began, along with the installation of windows and doors. The framing went well and was accomplished in no time, as the leader had all his men working on it. Once the builders completed the framing, we walled each interior room downstairs. Jim and the boys set to work shingling the roof and putting clapboard siding on the walls. All that was left on the outside to finish was paint and landscaping. Upstairs, Jim installed the plumbing, electricity, and heating. On the second floor, we still needed insulation, wallboard, plaster, and other finishing materials that we would obtain a little later. We moved into the first floor of our new home.

Time moved on, and as a family, we began to expand the use of our property. Jim built a chicken coop, and we raised a couple dozen chickens and two roosters; every egg we collected had a double yolk. The two roosters were weird, because the first rooster would chase the second all the way around the outside of the house, then stop, only for the second rooster to turn and chase the first back around the house again. They did this almost every day. It was during this year that Jim's father, while living alone in Westminster, suffered a stroke and could no longer be by himself. Of course we took him home to live with us, and we helped him to finally sell his house. Dad did well, but I had to take him down to the Fitchburg hospital for therapy every week. After the stroke, he had a difficult time swallowing, so his food had to be ground. Jim and our sons built a medium-size barn, and we raised four pigs in the bottom area. The country road where we lived had many large oak trees, so the children and I carried a paper shopping bag and collected the fallen acorns for the pigs. Besides the acorns, we fed them grain; table scraps; unused garden greens; and whey, when I made cheese or butter. It was a good, healthy diet, which made them pretty healthy animals. We purchased a black and white Holstein cow and named her Molly. She provided us with plenty of milk, cream, and butter, and we housed her in the barn's second level. Then we purchased two young heifers for beef and fenced off some land for them. We had two dogs; one, Lady, was a small collie, while the other, Kirby, was a mixed-breed cockapoo.

Dad bought us a small tractor, and Jim plowed one field. I became the keeper of the garden and planted, weeded, and watered many kinds of vegetables. The garden produced bumper crops, and I believe still that it was because of prayer, for I would stand in the center of the garden and pray to God to bless the plants. We had a large, clean, empty oil barrel next to the garden, which I used to put some of Molly's cow manure in. I filled the barrel with water and stirred it every day. The sun heated the soup, and I faithfully watered the plants with it every morning after the children went to school. I canned tomatoes, beets, carrots, and string beans. We also had lettuce, Swiss chard, and all sorts of greens. One weekend, the children and I stayed up until two o'clock in the morning shucking corn and scraping off kernels. We filled two freezers with frozen vegetables. The bottled carrots were the sweetest I have ever tasted, and we often had an overflowing wheelbarrow of cucumbers. Many of our relatives enjoyed the veggies as well. Between the garden produce, ham steaks, pork chops, and sausage, we were well prepared with healthy food. In addition to fresh eggs, we had plenty of milk, cream, cheese, and real butter from Molly. Farming was a lot of work, but it was well worth its price in sweat and energy.

Off and on, however, there were some peculiar things taking place in and around the house. One day, as I worked in the garden, a helicopter showed up over our field. It flew very low over the garden, stopped, and hovered above me for a while, then lifted upward and flew off. I never found out why. I now wonder if it was because of the picture and letter I had sent to Dr. Hynek about the memory of a strange being that had been in my house when I lived in South Ashburnham in 1967. I had sent the information when we were building our house in Ashburnham, and we were so busy with the house and farm that I forgot about it. We were still building, and the interior parts of the house were not finished entirely. We had three bedrooms that bordered the hallway. The first bedroom at the front was Jim's and my room; the middle bedroom was Rebecca's; and the third bedroom was Jimmy Junior's, though it later became Jim's dad's room when Jimmy joined the service. The rest of the children's rooms were still in the cellar area until we could start on the second-floor rooms upstairs.

One late evening, while everyone was fast asleep, Becky started to scream "Mar. Mar." Suddenly, I heard a loud bang. I jumped out of bed to rush to her side and found myself trying to get past hanging clothes and shoes on the floor. In my haste, I headed in the wrong direction and was in my closet trying to get to her room. Realizing my mistake, I quickly turned and went out the right door into the hall to my daughter's room. Becky seemed afraid, and as I felt her forehead, she was wet from profuse sweat. She told me she'd seen an identical form of herself smiling. It rushed toward her as she lay in bed half-awake, and she heard a loud bang as if it had entered her. Years later, I learned she must have had an out-of-body experience.

I remember that one day I was all alone in the house when I felt fear for some unknown reason. Jim was working and all the kids were in school, but I heard some loud banging upstairs. The second floor was not finished; it was wide open, with only bare two-by-fours dividing the many rooms. We hadn't put up any sheetrock or plaster as yet. I decided to go upstairs to check what was going on and found that several windows were wide open and a strong wind was blowing through the entire upstairs, even though it didn't seem as if it was windy outside. I thought one of the kids must have opened the windows and forgotten to close them. I quickly closed each window and went back downstairs. As soon as I got to the bottom step, it happened again, and I heard the same noises going on. I went back to check again, and lo and behold, the wind was gone, but all the windows I had closed were wide open. Whatever it was, I thought something must be trying to play games with me. This time I made it a point to securely close and lock each window, and I prayed that whatever was going on would stop. I waited on the bottom step to listen and was relieved; it seemed that whatever the game was that kept me going up and down the stairway was finally over. The noises were gone, and the windows remained shut.

As for the members of the family, Becky was the first to get married, and she and her husband lived for a while in an apartment in town. Jimmy and Mark, our two eldest sons, joined the navy after listening to their father's talk about what the naval branch of our country's armed forces had to offer. Scott married his high-school sweetheart and moved into an apartment in Gardner. Only Todd, Bonnie, Cindy, Dad, Jim, and I were at home then. Of course, this didn't happen all at once; there were many months and some years before the older children began to make their own choices. But before then, back at the farm, when all the children were still living at home, unusual things were taking place.

CHAPTER 8

Not Again

• • •

Unusual things started to happen in 1973. One night, the telephone rang, and I got up to answer it. It was a woman with an odd foreign accent. She said, "Eez...Jeemee...they-are?"

I said, "Junior or senior?" And the line went blank.

But I'm getting ahead of the experience of 1973 and 1975 telephone calls. We had two telephones; one was still on the cellar post next to the downstairs carrying beam, and the other was upstairs in the hall next to our bedroom. Once, the downstairs phone rang, and when I went to answer it, there was a noise that sounded peculiar, like it was out in space, and then it stopped. Later in the week, something else happened where late at night I saw bright lights that appeared in the driveway at the front of the house. I felt something unusual was about to happen, for someone had driven in and around to the right side of our building, where our bedroom was located. There was no road there, only piles of dirt, large stones, and holes, which we had not touched as yet, as we'd been too busy working to complete the inside of the house. I tried and tried to wake Jim without result. I was scared because the lights were so bright, and Jim wouldn't wake up for me, no matter how hard I shook him.

I covered my head with the blanket, and suddenly someone grabbed my arm, which was sticking out from the covers, and pulled on it. I said, "Go away. Go away. Please, Lord, make it go away. Whatever it is, please make it go away." As it kept pulling on me, it felt like it was pinching me and wanted me to get up. The blanket seemed to pull away from my head, and there were some strange beings in our bedroom. I knew I had seen them before, but I did not remember when. Their big gray heads and large dark eyes were too scary to forget. One of them communicated to me through my mind that I would be all right, but I must get up. I could feel myself being lifted up, and I floated along with the four beings as they moved into the hallway, to the cellar door, and down the stairs. One of the beings touched the telephone at the bottom of the stairs, and I heard it quickly make a dull ping noise as we moved to the back cellar door, which automatically opened as the leader raised his hand. We were now outside and moving down toward the garden.

I saw something brightly lit, big, and metallic with a rounded bottom above us. Then we were standing in the light and being raised upward into a room. They quickly escorted me into another room, where they put me into an odd chair. I felt sick and dizzy, as though I could vomit, because it felt like I was being squashed somehow. A great deal of the information was extracted and recorded from my memory through hypnosis. Once I was placed under a hypnotic state, my mind became very active, allowing many of the things that had happened, which had been conveniently hidden from me, to flood my memory. While sitting in that peculiar chair, I felt dizzy, and one of the beings came over to me and placed his fingers on my ears. My back started to feel odd, like it was vibrating or pulsing, as though a form of energy had been activated up and down my spine. I tried to get up off the chair, and the two beings had to help me. One moved in front of me and the other got behind me. I could feel the top of my body, but the bottom felt like stone, like it was still so heavy.

They brought me into another room, where another human, a woman like me, lay on a table. They led me over to her. She looked terrified. Her long, dark hair hung over the edge of the table. I felt sad for her and couldn't help but wonder if that was what they had planned to do to me as well. She was naked, with a small cover draped over the lower part of her body. Her eyebrows and dark brown eyes twitched as she looked up at me, as if to say, "Help me." She knew there was nothing I could do, but she appeared to be thankful I was there. She opened her mouth wide as if in pain, and I could see a space between her front teeth. Two beings were down by her feet, where her legs were bent upward. She was so afraid, and all I could do to help was put my forehead down on her forehead, hoping it would get her mind off what was going on. I gently whispered, "Sh... sh...sh." I think she realized there was not much I could do about what was happening. I started to softly rub both her temples to help calm her down. It seemed to be working, for she gently closed her eyes, as if to rest in my care. It seemed as if she suddenly fell asleep. I looked down to see what the gray beings were doing and was shocked, for there was a small fetus in one of the being's hands. They must have just removed it from the woman's womb. I tried to hold back my emotions so I wouldn't wake the woman and force her to sense the gravity of the horrendous situation. I could feel tears slowly rolling down my cheeks as the beings cut away the fetus's eyelids, exposing large black eyes.

I didn't know if the fetus was alive or dead, as it made no noise and did not cry. The beings knew what I was thinking and informed me through my mind that they could not allow the fetus to breathe the air. After placing something like a small, tight cloth mask on the lower part of its face, they quickly immersed the little body in a cylinder of grayish water and pushed a long, thin, silver needle down into the top, soft part of that baby's head. They could tell I didn't like what they were doing to that helpless fetus. The mask they had put into place covered its mouth and nose area, which was extended up toward the ears. They lowered the small body a little deeper into the water. The outside of the glass tank had two small holes; they inserted needles into these openings and into the fetus's ears. Somehow, they finished by filling the glass canister with more liquid. On the canister's top, they placed a kind of cup, with hairlike fibers that sparkled and quickly disappeared. They were pleased with the results and tried to assure my mind that the fetus belonged to them, that it was all right, and that in time it would become one of them. They explained the whole process of why and how it was being done. The beings said they had finished with its twin earlier, and it was also doing very well.

Sometime, many years later, I wanted to know why they were taking the fetus at three months. It appeared that some women, not even realizing it, had been artificially inseminated, and the fetuses were retrieved during the second or third months. One wonders if this is because of the enormous amount of electrical connections or synapses formed within the brain at that particular time. The more synapses within the head of the fetal being may be why the ET head becomes enlarged, to encase the brain's capacity to expand and activate supernatural functions. It is probably why their species has so much kinetic energy to move and control objects, why they are mysteriously endowed with powers to read thoughts, and how they converse through extra opened channels of the mind. The grays' abilities far exceed ours. They have the knowledge and power of invisibility, the ability to pass through solid material, and possibly immortality as well. The fetus I saw was not allowed to breathe any air, which may be the reason their skin is gray—without oxygen and blood, the skin color is gone. This must mean they have a very different internal source of life than does a human, as to be human, we need oxygen and iron-rich blood to survive. Within the brain development of a human fetus, a great cell death of electrical connective synapses takes place after three months. When the human infant is born, it breathes in air and usually makes an outward announcement of "I am" through a cry. So humans need air to live, while this other species of beings deliberately prevented the fetus's consumption of air. This may be why there is very little physical protrusion around the nose and ear cavities of a hybrid being: they don't depend on the constant intake of air to survive as we do. Perhaps breathing oxygen at birth shuts down a prospective ET fetus and limits its power. Perhaps an oxygenated being might override the ET blueprint and become a hybrid, or earthly human, in need of the breath of life as we know it. Whatever their life span is, they are another part of the Creator's creation, which means they are part of us as well. Much earlier, when I was taken into this craft, I saw where they were housing the first infant. Its eyes were different from those of the second fetus I saw later.

After seeing that the canister holding the second fetus had been placed between some odd flashing lights, we moved on. Once again I was taken from the craft into a heavily wooded area, next to water. It appeared to be dark, but I could see the same woman who much earlier had been on the table where the beings had taken twin infants from her. She was now dressed in a faded man's plaid shirt, and she sat there as if in a daze. Two beings carrying balls of white light came out of the craft and stood by us. I could see this area was a field surrounded by woods and a big lake. Much to my surprise, there was another craft beside the one we came out of. The craft we had been in had what looked like differently colored hoses on the ground underneath it, and a being was working with them while they were in the water. Somehow, the two other beings that had been beside the woman now flung the two balls of light over the edge of the lake. The lights hung in midair and were able to light the whole area. I heard a loud bang and saw a flash of intense light everywhere. It felt as though I could see through my hands, and my right eye and head began to ache. Then there were tiny lights floating all over the place, rushing around. Also, there was something like streams of electricity. It was so bright; it caused everything I was seeing to turn red. I kept asking the being what had happened. Within my mind he said something about a transversal shock. I briefly rubbed my eyes, which helped to make them feel better, but I was seeing a bright, solitary light in the sky way across the water, over by the distant woods. It is way on the other side of this large lake. It's big and very bright, and as its light came closer toward us, I could hear a loud whirring sound coming from it. My head and right eye began to hurt again as the sound drew closer still. The being with a ball of light came out to get the young woman and me and floated us into the craft once again, past the same place they had taken the fetus. We continued moving toward the cleared area when suddenly they lifted the woman onto a table again, separated her legs, and sprayed her inside and outer lower body with some kind of solution. She looked over at me to make sure I was still there with her as they floated her off the table.

Another being moved both of us into the area where I had been earlier. This was the same place where I had briefly seen the first small twin fetus they had taken from this woman. At this writing, I think I may have discovered a possible connection and answer to how the beings may have cared for and fed those healthy plants that were growing in a large water container aboard the craft. I have since learned of a possible source that could feed and take care of these plants. I was taken to a wooded area where there was a pond, and water was full of fish that were being released. The beings said they were just replenishing as the water and fish were dropped downward and disappeared. I now believe I know why I saw both plants and fish in water on this same ship. Today, people growing hydroponic gardens will often use fish to create an excellent balance for the plants above. The fish droppings can be a source of vital nutrients for the plants I had seen earlier. So ends the mystery concerning living plants, water, and fish that I witnessed while aboard their ship.

But now back to the being that ushered us into this now empty room. He took the shirt from the woman once again, and they wanted me to take off my nightgown. I refused. Again they asked me to take off my nightgown, and again I refused. They said I needed to take off my clothes for my protection. "Please take the nightgown off," they repeated to me. "It is necessary for your protection." I would not, so they moved me over beside the girl, who was now naked and standing on a metallic circular floor, which had small holes in it. As we stood there, a large clear tube slowly rose upward around us, and I could see something large and round on the ceiling come down to connect to the raised, glassy, cylindrical tube. Then we were being showered from above with a thick jelly liquid that felt like heavy raindrops. My hair and nightgown were drenched from the liquid jelly. It felt like it stuck to me, but it didn't feel sticky; it felt like water, but it was a jelly. The water stopped as the sprayer pulled back into the ceiling above, while the tube receded back into the floor below. As we stepped off to the side, the being floated us to him. He said to me, "We must have your nightgown now."

Once again I shook my head and said, "No, I don't want to."

Now he said, "You must, because of static electricity. The charge would be very high on nylon." I had no idea what he was talking about or what was going to happen. His answer frightened me, and I realized, to be safe, I'd better take off my nightgown, which was very embarrassing. They were moving us outside with no clothes on, and the watery stuff on us was extremely shiny. There was no one there but the beings and the large ship that had been coming closer to us earlier, which was now hovering above the second craft, parked beside the ship we came from. The being led the young woman and me away, toward the edge of the woods. We sat down by a large rock as the door on the smaller craft suddenly opened up, and some beings came out carrying objects that looked like jacks. They began placing them in the ground around the smaller craft. They had pointed bottoms that stuck into the ground. The beings went back inside. This time, they came out with a man, who was also naked and shiny. He was moving his legs as though walking, while they floated him above the ground. He was also embarrassed. As he sat down, he bowed his legs, placed his elbows on his knees, and reached up to his lowered head with both hands, as if to shut out what was happening. Meanwhile, two of the beings were placing silver balls on top of the jacks. The large hovering ship lowered its landing legs and attached them to the rim of the outer circumference of the smaller craft. Shortly after, something circular at the bottom of the larger craft came down, and the smaller craft's central upper section came up, made a connection, and began to spin in a counterclockwise motion. It kept spinning faster and faster.

As I watched, I was wondering what was happening. One of the beings spoke to me, again through my mind, and said, "They are purging and relining the cyclonetic trowel." At first it looked like water was spinning around and within it, and then it looked like a spinning watery vapor was smoothing out as it continued spinning around and around. I could see the silver balls were starting to lift off of the small jacks and turn into white orbs of light. As they moved above the jacks, they hovered in midair. The spinning trowel seemed to rotate faster, causing an abundance of mist and steam to appear. White puffy clouds were forming. It became very warm as this cyclonetic trowel continued to spin. It got warmer and warmer, and a lot of clouds began to form. The being told me they were balancing and relining the wheels. The being was telling me more things, but what he was saying was beyond my comprehension. At that point, bright light appeared right in the center, just as more steam was released. Clouds started to form all around the crafts, while light caused rainbows to appear. It was awesomely beautiful. I could also see the balls of light over the jacks that had now changed color to a beautiful vibrant blue. It was breathtaking, with the rainbows in the white clouds almost covering the two craft below. It was so magnificent that I almost forgot about the frightening situation I was in. As the clamor continued, there was so much fog in the atmosphere and it was so hot that I was becoming uncomfortable. Thunder and lightning started, which was scary. The lightning was streaming in different directions, and the noise of booming thunder was spreading everywhere. The lightning continued to crackle, and I was very much afraid, for it felt like it was very close; even though we were seated far away from the craft by the woods, the lightning seemed strange like it was all over the whole area. I was really scared, as it seemed dangerous to me. There was lightning coming out of the whirling center of the joined crafts, and it spread out into the surrounding atmosphere of the ships and clouds. Rainbows were forming within the clouds and appeared around the ships, which was beautiful, but it was too close, and I felt much fear with its multiple electrical and static strikes and charges.

To think about it now, I am glad they insisted I give them my nightgown; otherwise, I don't think I would have lived through it. Even though there was a mist and slight rain happening, the shiny jelly covering our bodies protected us by clinging to our skin and hair. The severe strikes of lightning seemed strange and frightful, for it was even hitting the blue balls over the jacks and seemed to bounce in a wild fashion all around the small orbs. The middle of the whirling trowel seemed to be slowing down and finally stopped creating the enormous strikes of lightning. But there were still scattered cracks of thunder and lightning coming from the massive clouds now around the craft. The crackling and booms began to finally subside, but it was still so very warm that it started to rain again. The revolving center was slowing down and almost coming to a stop. It was now raining very heavily. I felt drenched from the heavy rush of rain-water. It started to cool the area. The heavy downfall seemed as if it some-how was washing the jelly from my body, and it looked like bubbles of gel below me were quickly disappearing into the ground, as though being ab-sorbed. At first, the large ship's internal trowel stopped and turned clock-wise, then stopped and revolved counterclockwise as if winding down. It swung slowly back and forth and finally stopped. The upper body of the craft began to slowly withdraw its trowel within the craft, and the lower craft did the same. When it stopped, my entire body felt prickly, like it was asleep. I glanced over toward the being and lady standing by and won-dered what was happening. The beings from the lower craft moved over to where the jacks were and collected the hovering orbs that were no longer blue but appeared to be white light. They also pulled the jacks from the ground. One being brought a jack over by us and sat it on the ground.

Another being went into our craft and came out with my nightgown, the woman's shirt, and a round flat thing that looked like a record. We quickly put on our clothes, while the being was putting together the record with the upside-down jack, for some reason. The man from the smaller craft was escorted back into the lower craft, and one of the be-ings from that craft came over where we were, spoke to one of our beings, and checked the jack and record down on the ground. He held one of the glowing white orbs, and the woman I had tried to comfort suddenly stood, looked at me (as if to ask if I was coming), turned to follow him over to their smaller craft, and went in. The trowel cylinders, in both the big and smaller craft, had already pulled back into their individual ships. The large craft disconnected its landing-gear grip from the circumference of the lower ship's rim. Its legs receded back into the large craft as it hovered above the smaller craft. I stood there wondering, *Why didn't they take me aboard the other craft with the woman?* The hovering ship shot a powerful light directly over the lower craft. I quickly rubbed my eyes, and again, a second extremely intensified light was shot across the craft's frame.

I was amazed and could hardly believe what was happening, for the very bottom craft appeared to be shrinking. It continued to shrink into the size of a car. At first, I was concerned about the welfare of the other humans and the beings inside the shrunken craft. But then I remembered what the beings had told me before—that they could opulate and deopulate, which meant they could increase or decrease to whatever size was convenient. The large craft shot a light at the jack close by, which was sitting upside down on the round disk below it. It caused streams of sparkling, colored lights to appear and flow outward from the machine into the surrounding air. The large hovering ship lifted up as their lower lights went out, and they swiftly moved across the water and woods, followed by the smaller craft. The being picked up the record and jack, as two other beings came out to collect the orbs of light over the water, which were used to light the area. The door opened, and the tiny, multicolored lights rushed through and entered the craft. Once again I floated up and back into the craft that was preparing to leave the area as well. Once inside, a being got in front of me, and one moved to the back, and I was told to follow them.

We floated along and entered another door that automatically opened up in the wall. The room was large and round and looked like it was ribbed. In the center, from floor to ceiling, there was an enormous vertical cylinder of flowing water and light. Around this stationary towering waterfall, there were surges of energy moving within and around an unusual stream of white light. The energy kept circling within and around what looked like the shape of a doughnut or a huge round tube. I felt a tingling go through my body. We stood there watching as the vibrating streams of light and water began to blend and settle down into a huge, smooth form, like a glowing doughnut-shaped ring of vibrating misty light. According to the being, it was working as a shield for us. We began to move through the circle. It felt like a path had been formed for us to pass through. We entered the vertical waterfall light, which turned out to be hollow inside. The tiny, colored lights were moving along with us, and I could feel we were traveling upward. We stopped and moved out of the lighted cylinder into another area, which was even more difficult to explain. Unable to explain what this area was, we continued on. My body and mind were feeling disoriented for some reason. The atmosphere felt strange. My arms and neck seemed lame, and my hands and lower body felt lifeless. It felt like a heavy pressure was pushing against me. I was glad I didn't have to use my energy while floating along, because I was feeling very sore. As we moved forward, we passed through an odd curved area, where every five feet or more, I saw circular covers on the floor. And there were pipes on the walls, along with other odd things. I could see a large indented area, with a big window that had odd bars that looked like glass tubes with some peculiar objects running through them. There were three clear vertical capsules in front of it. Within the large capsules, there was a stationary rounded glass that might have been a screen. There were also smaller screens showing different pictures. A long, tall, straight bar was in front of it. My eyes were sore from looking at these objects and some of the odd symbols. I saw lights and a glass-like floor beneath it, where these capsules were attached from below somehow. As we continued to move along, my eyes really started to hurt; it felt like I had something in them that was making them sting. Perhaps it was from the extreme light that had shrunk the smaller craft earlier. We were now moving through an opening.

Oh, it was beautiful there. We were in the woods, and it smelled so good, as though I could take a deep breath now that I was surrounded by nature rather than the strange, exotic machines I had seen moments before. Within this area was a crystal-clear pond of water, full of medium to small fish swimming around. I couldn't understand how I'd come to these woods so quickly, because I could see no door where we had come through—only a forest. But I certainly was happy to be here. The beings were still with me as the peculiar forest entrance opened once again, leading into the light of the visible room we had just come from. Two large floating balls of white light swiftly flew in, and one floated over to the pond and hovered in the air. The other flew toward the deeper part of the woods and briefly disappeared, only to quickly return and settle above the open forest area. Again the entrance closed as if there was only the forest there. I couldn't believe how great the air was, and the multicolored, little lights were now in here with us as well. They were gathering together, forming small orbs of light that circled the two stationary spheres. It was beautiful. The being told me to sit down upon the grass, and I watched the beautiful lights. I happened to look over at their reflection on the pond and could see that the water was getting low. There appeared to be more fish flipping around. In fact, the water seemed to be steadily receding, until there was not enough to support the many fish. Just then the pond's bottom opened up, and the fish fell way below into water. The beings just stood there next to it. For some reason, my legs felt cramped.

I asked the beings what was going on. At first, they would not bother to answer, but I insisted they tell me, and finally they said, "Just replenishing. We are just replenishing." The balls of multicolored lights began to separate and scatter and then settled on the trees and grass. The pond closed up and began to fill with water once again. The lights on the trees were beautiful, like colored fireflies. The two beings left me there and went out of the foliage door. I was all alone, still sitting on the grass, and my attention turned to the pond again. I decided to stand and go down closer to the edge to see what was happening. Now there was a flow of rushing water that was filling the drained space in the little pond. I tried to stand to see what was going on, but I couldn't seem to move. I felt a pressure on me, so I was unable to stand. I struggled again to get up on my feet and was finally able to stand, but the pressure did not allow me to go down by the water.

Again, I tried to move. As I attempted to take a step forward, strange ribbons of light began to encompass me and started to swirl around my body. The ribbons would not allow me to move. The being returned, holding something in his hand, which quickly retracted the powerful ribbons into a small hand tool. He insisted I must sit down, for there was something special I must see and do. As I sat on the ground, beautiful small beings started to come out of the woods. I was amazed and thrilled to see such fascinating childlike creatures walking around. They seemed to be as curious about me as I was about them. One came very close, touched my leg, and made me laugh. They seemed so tiny and special. Their heads and eyes were unusually wide, and their skin shades varied in color. They looked human, but it was hard to believe they were capable of walking, considering how small they were. They were beautiful but very little. One of the regular three- to four-foot gray beings came over to me, carrying a crystalline box. He opened the box, and there was something inside. It was like a stick, with an egg-shaped crystal on one end. He told me to take it. As I did, it appeared as if the little beings were aware that something exciting was about to take place. I noticed that they immediately began to rush down by the edge of the water and form a line. I stood there watching and waiting, wondering what I was supposed to do with this peculiar thing resting in my hand. A greater light sliced its way through the forest of trees, as if a glowing doorway of white light had opened. I stood there wondering what was going on.

The being spoke to me through my mind, saying, "Take the crystal tool in your right hand, and point it at the tiny colored lights resting in the trees." When I did so, the lights shimmered, as if they were alive. I pointed the odd crystal object at them again. This time they sparkled with excitement, flew off the trees, circled the area, and began to land and settle between the eyes of each and every childlike being joyfully waiting in line to receive the light. One by one, the excited little ones began to move toward the forest door's entrance of glowing white light. I was sad to see such beautiful little creatures leaving, for they seemed so lovely and unique. As the very last of them went into the light, it disappeared. It was like the door in the forest was closed. All the remaining colored lights on the grass and in the trees suddenly disappeared. The being came back with the crystal box, and I returned the stick to its resting place. After the being took the box away, I sat there wondering why the unusual children had gone and where they went. I started to see spurts of water pop up from the little pond. Then I noticed some scattered clumps of ferns and low bushes moving off and on, as if something invisible was affecting them. It was like air was being pumped in.

As I sat there, two beings returned for me. They floated me up between them, and we moved along, exiting through a door that was part of the forest. We were going back into that long room we had come out of earlier. The room with a window and the three capsules was just a short distance up ahead. It was then that I saw two beings inside these capsules at each end. The central capsule was empty. Both capsules were raised so the bottom was somehow connected to the top thing in the ceiling area. I could not see a door or how the two beings got in there, but they were standing against the tall, long stanchion, where clear glass plates securely held their chest and arms straight. Guards secured their legs to the stanchion. In front of them, within the capsule was a thin extension that came out and had revolving balls of light on a thin crossbar. A large containment screen with thick, bendable silver tubing connected to the back. Something inside the window and wall had clear tubes with moving things inside them. The large central screen was bordered by four smaller screens. It looked like there were various scenes of Earth's environment, with stars, planets, and space in them. It suddenly became extremely cold in this area. My two escorts and I moved past the third glass-like capsule holding the second being and down the odd hallway where pipes ran along the side.

We went through a door into a small room like an elevator and briefly waited, until we once again began to move slowly downward. My head ached, and my eyes started to hurt again. The elevator stopped, and the beings and I moved out of the small space, and the elevator lifted up and away, like it had never been there. We moved along the outer part of this room while something else was coming down from the ceiling. We continued to move and entered another door, which led to the room that housed the odd chair they had put me in when I'd first come here. They brought me over to it and put me in it once again. I was reminded of what an odd chair it was, requiring users to sit and stand at the same time. During this time, one of the beings left, and the other being started to communicate with me. He said they were grateful I was able to help calm the woman during the fetal removal. Seeing we had open communication through the mind, I asked the being who they were. He answered that they were caretakers of nature and all natural form. They loved humankind and planet

Earth and had been caring for it since humankind's beginning. They watched the spirit in all things and were curious about human's emotions.

The being said, "In many ways, humankind is destroying much of nature. We are the caretakers, who collect all kinds of seed, including male and female seed. We are called the watchers, who have collected every species and plants for hundreds and thousands of years." While sitting in the chair, I started to feel pressure in my hands, legs, and feet. They felt heavy. Then my whole body felt pressure as the being stood by watching. It felt like the pressure was coming on fast for a while, and suddenly it started to let up, but my legs and feet were still heavy. Another two beings came in and looked like they were conversing. I could not tell what they were saying, but I knew they were communicating about something. Another being came in, so there were three beings in addition to the first one that was still watching me. They began to communicate to me through my mind and tried to explain about the chair they put me in. They said it was the only provision for me in this particular type of carrier. It was difficult to understand them at times. They began to talk to me about my life, and they said I had been watched for a very long time. Things in my life were about to change, they told me, and during those changes, I would have to bear some very difficult and unavoidable times. Certain events were meant to happen, and these changes were put into motion long ago. The beings told me, "You will try to fix some of the changes, but it will not happen. It will be a period of hardship and loss. At first, you will not understand why."

They removed me from the seat and placed me behind one of the beings again. We floated to a door that quickly opened. It was dark out, but there appeared to be grass below us. We floated down to the grass. One being was in front of me, and three were behind me. We were moving above the grass, and I could see I was returning home. I could see the house. We floated across the backyard toward the cellar door, which was wide open. The beings brought me up the stairs and back to my bedroom quickly. Jim was still lying in the same position he'd been in when I had left. The beings put me back in my bed, and one communicated to me in my mind again. He said I would be used to carry information to the world, and they would clear the way, for when the time came for me to remember, the human race would accept, receive, and believe, though many would not understand. But I must not remember for a long time, they told me. I must not remember until the time was right...I must not...I must not remember this. I could see the beings' presence begin to fade away, and I settled into sleep. It was still night when the telephone rang. Thinking it would wake my family, I rushed downstairs and answered. An unusual, high-pitched woman's voice asked, "Eez...Jeemee...they-are?"

I asked, "Junior or senior?" She hung up. I walked up the cellar stairs, thinking, *Oh boy. Why would that strange woman call here this late at night?* I felt a deep, foreboding feeling come over me.

CHAPTER 9

When It All Began

• • •

THE BEINGS HAD SAID THEY were setting things in motion. At this time, our family was living in the large new house we'd designed and built in Ashburnham. It was around 1975. More than eight years had passed since the strange beings had mysteriously appeared in our old restored colonial home in South Ashburnham. The memory of a peculiar large-headed, bulging-black-eyed being was far from my thoughts until I read an article posted in a small local newspaper. A person named Dr. J. Allen Hynek requested anyone who'd sighted anything unusual to please contact him. It brought that old memory back of the unusual being I had seen in our old house. At the time, it disturbed me that I had no answer regarding its presence. I didn't know anything about UFOs, but the being was unusual. So after reading the article, I decided to send what I remembered, and I drew a picture of what the thing looked like, wrote a description, and mailed it to the posted address. I don't know why, but after I mailed it, I actually felt better and thought maybe this learned man might figure out what it was.

I didn't hear anything back about the information I mailed to Dr. Hynek until three years later, when I was contacted via telephone by researcher Jules Vaillancourt, who asked if I would be willing to undergo hypnosis concerning the strange being I had reported to the Center for UFO Studies. I agreed, first to find out what had happened, and second, for my own peace of mind. Every time there was a meeting, Jules and his wife, who also lived in Ashburnham, would drive Becky and me to the office of Dr. Edelstein, the delegated hypnotist, along with other gathered researchers who were able to ask questions while I was placed in a deep hypnotic trance. After many months of hypnosis and questions, it became obvious to those involved that the accumulated information of my strange abduction was definitely UFO related.

Well-known researcher and author Raymond E. Fowler asked if he could write a book about it. I agreed, and that is how *The Andreasson Affair* became available. During many more months to come, I would be asked to undergo more hypnosis, for it appeared that I may have had other possible childhood encounters and that I was being visited in different ways. Ray worked very hard putting together UFO information and research material for the public to understand and witness what was going on with the UFO phenomenon. Much later, I was told by the beings that Fowler had been spiritually groomed to report and write about this important material. Meanwhile, the prophetic words from the beings concerning my life were about to take place—a change was about to happen.

Jim and I had been invited to the home of some longtime friends for their anniversary party. Jim and his father were in the living room watching a cowboy movie on TV, while I was in the bedroom getting dressed. For some reason, like I was being controlled, I came out of our bedroom, went through the kitchen, walked up to the television in the living room, and changed the channel while they were watching it. Then I returned to the bedroom to continue dressing. I didn't think of what I had just done, why I did it, or how rude it was of me. I hadn't done anything like that ever before. As a Christian, I have always tried to show respect for others. To this very day, I don't know why I did it. Jim and I drove to the party, and there were quite a few people there. The hosts served food, coffee, and an anniversary cake. Everyone seemed to be having a nice time and visit, but I didn't know Jim had brought some alcohol with him to celebrate. As the evening wore on, he got very loud and obnoxious. He was still in the other area of the party drinking, and because of his condition, I was worried about him driving. So were others. Friends offered to give me a ride home, and I accepted.

When I came in the house, Scott, Todd, and Bonnie were still up. Jim's dad was out for the evening, and Cindy was staying overnight with Becky and my granddaughters. A few hours later, Jim pulled up and came storming into the house, angry I had left without him. I won't go into the horrendous details of what happened, for when a person is inebriated, he or she might do things he or she would never do while sober. But I had to call the police, and they took Jim for an overnight lockup. The next morning, he did not return home. I thought it was because he was ashamed of what happened, and once he sobered up, he'd come home. Because I loved him and had hoped he would eventually change, I had suffered through several very dangerous episodes while we were married, which were brought on by his irresponsible drinking. Instead, he disappeared without a word. His dad knew I was worried about Jim and said he'd be home soon, but it didn't happen. Months passed with no word. I was devastated, not knowing if he was alive or dead. This was around the time my son Scott got married, and he and his wife moved to a Gardner apartment. So now only Todd, Bonnie, Cindy, and Jim's dad were at home. My son Todd was like the rock of Gibraltar. He was only seventeen but strong as a bull. Every morning he had to feed the pigs and the two steers and feed and milk the cow. Then he showered, ate breakfast, and went to school, and he never once complained about it. After school, he went to his job at the lumber mill; when he got home, he had to milk the cow and feed all the animals all over again, then finish his homework for school. When he got paid at his job, he would insist on giving me his pay to see us through. His grandfather was in his late eighties and couldn't help because his legs, heart, and throat were bad.

As the days moved on, I had to do something, because the responsibility of everything was starting to become too much for me to handle. Throughout the day, I was picking, canning, and storing vegetables coming in from the garden. We had plenty of food, but the finances were almost down to nothing. I had to call Jim's sister and ask if she could please take her dad to live with them, as my days were so busy I couldn't bring him for his therapy every day. She did not give me an answer right away. I thought of selling some of the animals, so it wouldn't be so tough on

Todd and I'd have enough money to pay the power bills and buy feed for the animals we had left. There was no problem with a lack of food, as we had two freezers filled with meat and vegetables and plenty of fresh eggs, cheese, real butter, milk, and cream. Eventually, Jim junior and Mark were allowed to come home from the navy to assist and to help look for their father.

Jim finally called the house one night while he was drinking, and I found out that he was alive and working at a garage off Route 10 in Florida. Because the older boys were home to help, I sold our truck, and Todd and I flew down to Florida to hopefully convince him to come home. We got a hotel room in Jacksonville and rented a small convertible. Todd and I went to the garage where Jim had been working. We met Jim's boss, the garage's owner, but Jim was not at work. The owner and workers were Christians, and after they heard what had happened, we stood in a circle holding hands in prayer that God would work out what had to be done. Todd and I went across the street and got a room at a motel. Meanwhile, the boss had called Jim, and he was now at the garage. I went over with Todd, hoping to talk to him, but I could tell Jim was irritated we were there. Todd said, "Mom, let me talk to Dad." I agreed and went back to the motel while Todd spoke to his father.

Instead, Jim took Todd back to where he was now living with another woman. I was so upset, because now I didn't know where my son was, and it was getting late. I went back to the garage, but it was closed. The area did not seem safe, as there were different men outside just walking around, so I waited in the room, hoping Todd would return. The later it got, the more it seemed like an unsafe place to be. I decided to go back to the hotel in Jacksonville. Before I left, I wrote a letter for Todd to call me right away, and I would come get him. I left a note in the room, pinned another to the door, and left one with the proprietor of the motel, then went back to the hotel in Jacksonville. Right away I pulled out the Gideon Bible and prayed that Todd was all right. The telephone rang, and it was Jim. He said angrily, "Come get Todd." He gave me the address of a small restaurant. I raced down Route 10, thankful my son was OK. I stopped in front of the restaurant's full-size window and tooted the horn. Todd came out and said he'd just ordered a meal. I could see Jim and another woman sitting on stools at a bar. I finally knew my marriage was over, and I told Todd to give the meal to his father—we were going home. As we drove back to the hotel, Todd told me his father, after finding out where I was, had started walking to the motel alone. The woman Jim was living with had jumped into her truck and told Todd to get in, and they'd sped down the road to get Jim. From there, they stopped at the motel, got the number for the Jacksonville hotel, and called me to come pick up Todd. Todd and I went back to the hotel, returned the rented car, and flew back home. A few more months passed, and Jim's sister finally decided to take her father to live with her, as she must have finally realized Jim and I were finished as a married couple. Mark returned to the navy, but Jimmy, our eldest son, took leave of the service to help at home.

At that time, Becky and her children had separated from her husband, who would not hold a job, and she came home to live with us. As time passed, my sister Shirley, who lived in Florida, called and said, "Rather than stay up north for the winter, come down where it's warm, get a job, and look at some houses." Becky watched the kids for me. I got a loan on the house, which was too big for me to keep; flew down south; and purchased a small house in Pompano Beach, Florida. I got a temporary job as a waitress and started working at a restaurant called The Clock. It was here that I would meet my future husband. While there, I met all the help, including Katherine, the restaurant's cook. She was so nice to talk to that I confided in her that I'd had a UFO experience. During our conversation, she happened to mention that her brother-in-law and his friend Bob were coming to town to do some fishing and were going to stop at her house. That evening, Katherine must have mentioned me and my unusual UFO experience to them at the supper table, because she learned her brother-in-law's friend had also experienced an unusual UFO encounter and wanted to talk to me about it. He figured I was someone he could tell who would understand and who wouldn't think he was crazy. The next day, he came into the restaurant to ask which waitress was Betty. Katherine was not present that day, so he was unable to prove who he was to me. Ray Fowler had told me not to talk to any reporters, and at first, I thought he might possibly be one. He promised he wasn't a reporter and mentioned Katherine's name. He said he was Bob, her brother-in-law's friend. He seemed like a sincere young man, but I was unable to talk with him, as it was quite busy at the time. He asked if he could take me out for lunch so he could tell me what had happened to him. I finally agreed, and as Bob says today, he's "been buying me lunch ever since."

I gave him my sister's address, and he showed up and met my sister the next day before I went with him to the beach. He told me what had happened during his UFO experience. There were missing pieces that needed to be addressed, which meant he really needed to undergo hypnosis as well to find out the rest of the story. I spent time with him for the next week, and I learned he and his friend had traveled across the country, pulling a small trailer, to see if he or his friend might like to relocate from Connecticut. Becky had been watching the kids back home while I was working and waiting for the papers on the new house to go through, and she called to say she couldn't handle it all. At that point, I knew I had to go back home right away. Instead of flying, Bob offered to give me a ride back. I didn't know either Bob or his friend that well, but Becky was very upset, so I gratefully accepted his kind offer. Bob was a perfect gentleman, although I felt very nervous and upset at what people might think of me, accepting such a long ride with two strangers. Bob drove, his friend sat in the front passenger seat, and I sat in the back, as his car pulled a small house trailer behind. When we reached New York, I saw an unbelievable message on a large white billboard; in big black letters on a large white background, it read, "Betty, Jesus Loves You Anyway." And it ended with a big red heart with an exclamation mark. I took this as a sign not to worry what people thought, for I hadn't done anything wrong. I was amazed. I knew God moved in mysterious ways and was watching over me and my family. He had sent Bob to help me.

We reached Connecticut and brought Bob's friend home. It was morning, and Bob parked his trailer at his mother's house. I met his mother and could immediately see she was a wonderful person. After that, we drove to Bob's work, where we left his car, and Bob decided to use his motorcycle to take me home. Along the way, however, it started getting cold, so we turned back and used the car instead. When we pulled into my driveway, the kids were so happy to see me home. I think Bob was a little overwhelmed to meet my large family. I was glad to return home and clear things up concerning the house. Now that I had a house in Florida, I was going to put the big house up for sale. Bob returned to Connecticut and came up to see me on weekends. He is such a wonderful person and helped me in so many ways. My son Scott had been working on his car in front of the house and somehow had plowed into the front of the house, which made a hole and ruined some clapboards. Bob repaired the front so you couldn't tell there'd ever been an accident there. Each weekend, Bob would visit for two days and then return home for his job. Meanwhile, I set to work selling the animals and furniture and cleaning up the house and yard.

Our cow, Molly, stopped producing milk because of me. We were getting low on grain, and not realizing their effect, I gave her some of the cornstalks from the garden, which had fermented while in storage. She got drunk, became extremely frisky, and started kicking up her hooves and jumping up and down like a horse. I didn't know what to do until she settled down. This incident had stopped her ability to give milk, which meant she would have to be bred again, birth a calf, and nurse it in order to produce milk once more. So, sadly, I sold Molly to a farmer. As time went by, there was no more fresh milk, cream, or butter. I sold the chickens, along with the two full-grown steer and the pigs. I had to be the one who helped the buyer get the two huge pigs into his truck. He had me hold a pail over the pigs' heads so they couldn't see what was happening, and we somehow managed to get them up the hill and into his enclosed truck. Stripping both house and barn to get the property ready for sale was quite a job.

Meanwhile, I called Ray Fowler and told him about Bob, his UFO experience, and how I'd met him in Florida. Ray was very interested in meeting him. Throughout the week, I was at a flea market trying to sell furniture and household things we no longer needed, so we wouldn't have to carry so much to the new house in Florida. Most of the beds were in the large living room, where we were now sleeping. Since my beloved father had passed on from prostate cancer, my mother had sold her house and come to stay with us as well. Bob called me from Connecticut almost every night. He had just recently met with a MUFON investigator and told him what he remembered about his UFO encounter. One night, while we were talking on the phone, we heard some odd clicking and peculiar noises on the line. The beings broke into our conversation and started to communicate in an unusual language. At first, it sounded like they were mad, like irritated bees, with an odd buzzing noise. It sounded like they said, "It is finished. It is done." They seemed angry, and I could hear heavy machinery, like bangs, clunking sounds, and other noises. They said something about "the people."

I told them, "Speak up louder, so Bob can hear you better," and as I said it, the noises got louder, and there were more clicks and sounds.

Bob said, "We better get off the phone. I was told to report any strange thing that might happen."

I feel a little unnerved reporting this again, for the memories of that call still haunt and upset me. It was as if their communications were trying to tell me something bad was about to happen. Becky and Todd were in the doorway to her bedroom at the time and could see the call had rattled me. They came over to me, and I told them the beings had broken into Bob's and my conversation. Becky became frightened and said with alarm, "I'm not sleeping in my bedroom tonight. I'm sleeping in the living room."

Todd, not taking it seriously, started clowning around. Partially trying to ease the tense situation and comfort his sister, he said, "Come get me, UFOs. Come on; come get me."

I immediately said, "Cut that out, Toddy. You're not funny. This could be serious." It was evening when we all retired to bed. Todd slept in Becky's room, and all seven females slept in the living room. It was late and heading toward dawn, when everyone was fast asleep. Suddenly, within the living room, a huge ball of white light appeared; it was quickly moving around the room, leaving a bright trail of light behind it.

As it whirled around and around the room, Becky awoke, screaming, "Mar, Mar."

I immediately sat up in bed and said, "It's all right, Becky. It's all right. I know it's here. Don't be afraid. I know what it is." Within the light, there were all sorts of loud noises like moving trains and heavy machines. It was as if my soul knew something was about to happen. Again I tried to comfort her. "The Lord is with us, Becky. Don't be afraid." The light swirled around once more and swiftly swooped over my head and out the window. Becky said whatever it was, it had tried to take her breath away, and that was why she had screamed for me. What's strange is, except for the two of us, no one else in the room heard or saw it, and no one woke up during the strange experience. We looked out the window and were amazed, for the whole sky was now lit with beautiful multicolored lights, just before the arrival of dawn.

Later, I called Raymond Fowler and told him about it; because Bob was coming to my house from Connecticut, Ray wanted to meet and talk with him about the call as well. So Bob drove me and my two younger daughters, Bonnie and Cindy, to Raymond Fowler's house. When we arrived, I introduced Bob and my daughters to Ray and the other investigators present. We were not going to be able to stay very long, so Ray asked right away if it was OK for him to record my words of what had actually taken place. He and I went into another room to tape, while Bob and the girls were questioned about what they'd experienced. I was apprehensive and shaken from all the unbelievable activities occurring at my home in such a short period of time. I felt the two separate incidents were definitely associated with the UFO phenomenon, because I knew if the beings were trying to communicate to us, something devastating was going to happen. What were they trying to tell me? The unusual interception of Bob's and my earlier phone conversation, combined with the appearance of the peculiar white ball of light that whizzed around and around our large living room, was sorely unnerving. After such a frightening close experience,

I was completely unnerved by what might happen next. It seemed like a premonition of something unavoidable to come. I shivered as I related the entire mysterious telephone experience to Ray. It felt like something bad was going to happen, and there was nothing I could do to prevent it. All through the strange language spoken, clicking sounds, and loud clanking noises, the beings had sounded angry about something. I also told Ray about the ball of white light that had appeared later that evening and swooped over my head and out the window. It was getting dark when we headed back home from the Boston area to Ashburnham, so Bob stayed overnight and asked if I would like to meet his dad and see his mother again.

I said, "Yes, I would like that." My mother, Becky, and Todd were home and very capable of watching the younger ones, and my son Jimmy had rented a small house in Ashburnham and could be home to help in a matter of minutes if need be. Jimmy was trying to figure out what he wanted to do with his life and seemed very interested in the ministry and learning of the Word. He would exhaust me at times, playing the devil's advocate by dancing around questions about certain scriptures. I would say to him, "Jimmy, why don't you ask me outright about them, instead of me having to answer each and every question to prove to you what they mean?"

He laughed and said, "Mom, I learn more this way." I was proud of him. I learned later that he had arranged a come-together meeting with his younger brothers Scott and Todd, where all three were kneeling at his couch in prayer. As for Mark, at that time, he had already returned to the navy. The kids were OK about me being gone for the day to meet Bob's parents, and we were once again on the road headed to Connecticut, so I could finally meet his dad and uncle Anthony. I felt safe and comfortable with Bob and was happy to meet his family and learn more about the man I was falling in love with. Back home, Jimmy and Scott had been working on his car and must have finally fixed it, for he had picked up his girlfriend, Elaine, and Todd to join some friends for an evening out. Jimmy was twenty-one, and Todd was seventeen and soon to graduate, so any chance they had to get together with friends, they did. There was a party going on that evening. Meanwhile, Bob and I had been on the road for about two and a half hours when we finally pulled into his mom's driveway. His uncle met him at the door while I briefly waited in the car. Bob came quickly back to the car and said, "I have to take you back home."

I was shocked. "What happened I asked? Is everything all right?" Bob was quiet and said nothing as we drove along. I thought something must have happened to his mother or father, as Bob was very somber and said little. "What's wrong?" I asked. "Can't you tell me? Maybe I can help in some way.." He was still very quiet and seemed occupied with his thoughts. I sat back quietly and wondered what was wrong. I could sense Bob was trying to remain calm. I remained quiet as the car raced safely up the highway toward home. Miles went by, and Bob still seemed very somber and refused to talk or tell me what had happened. We were now very close to my home, and Bob pulled the car over to the side of the road and stopped. Again, I asked him, "What happened?"

He said the police had called his home, and his mother told her brother Anthony to go downstairs and tell Bob. Bob said, "There was an accident. Jimmy and Todd were in an accident."

"Oh...nooo, noo." I caught my breath and asked, "Are they all right?"

Bob said, "No, I'm sorry. They both died."

I went weak and started to sob. "Not my sons. Oh, dear God, nooo. Please, no." I was sobbing, and Bob held me. I couldn't believe it. "Why? Why?" I cried. "Haven't I gone through enough?" Bob started the car, and we slowly pulled into the driveway. All the children were at the door crying as we stopped. I was dazed as I climbed out of the car and saw the utter sorrow on my children's faces. Sadly, I told Bob I thought it would be best if he didn't come in, as I felt he shouldn't have to go through the grief and sorrow we now were faced with, and I certainly didn't want a problem with Jim if he showed up. Even though I knew Bob was willing to help in any way possible, I didn't want to lean on him or anyone. I needed to get through this and be strong for my children to carry through for my family. So Bob reluctantly pulled the car out of the yard and went back to

Connecticut. I knew there would be sobbing throughout the many weeks to come.

Bonnie recently told me something that surprised me, something I was not even aware of and have no memory of doing. I must have been angry toward the ETs' actions, even though they were probably trying to warn me of the impending death of my sons. I must have lost it. She said, because of my grief over the boys, I smashed a plaster-of-paris ET head into bits, thinking the beings who were now part of my life had caused the accident. I still have no memory of doing it, now or back when it evidently happened. The tragic loss of two of my sons left me feeling numb and helpless. At that time, knowing how emotional I am, I realized for the sake of my children that I must try to control my sorrow as much as possible, for at such a critical time, there would be much I would have to do for the funeral and my family. My mind thought of Jimmy and Todd.

The Lord had blessed me with seven children, and now two had returned home to the Eternal Father, where I knew they were resting safely in the arms of my Lord Jesus. To reveal this truth within me, I ordered an all-white floral arrangement to be placed over their caskets with blue flowers that read "LORD, my sons are thy sons." The funeral was held at the Baptist church in Westminster, which was the first place my little ones had learned of God's grace in Sunday school. My emotions started to weaken as I sat there, for not only was I grieving inside over the loss of Jimmy and Todd, but the sadness and suffering coming from my children weighed heavily on my heart as well. Mark was summoned home once again from the navy, and he stood by my side to comfort and strengthen me. My mother was there also, watching over her two younger great grandchildren. Becky was a tower of strength and comfort for the girls and Scott. At first, the reality and utter loss of our loved ones had not completely set in. My heart was broken, but I kept telling myself inside that I was strong and could handle this and overcome anything I had to do. Or so I thought. Because I was starting to look weak, like I was going to crumble or break down, a doctor prescribed a tranquilizer to calm me down. Today it is hard for me to remember how I ever got past the tragic episode that claimed my sons' lives. Within a few hours, I began to feel like a walking zombie, caught in a hazy gray twilight zone. During the funeral, the absolute reality swiftly and suddenly caught up with me. I could hear people talking to me but could not assimilate their words. My eyes were open, but I was dazed. I could not see the people, only forms of those around me. Wave after wave of sadness had taken over, and feelings of loss and emptiness rushed through my body, mind, and spirit. My boys' death and absence filled my heart and soul with lethal sorrow. Deep inside, a continual flood of silent nothingness filled my being. There were so many people who attended the funeral that the service had to be televised on three viewers outside, for the crowds stretched out to the road. In addition to relatives and friends, the whole high school attended. I was unaware, but at the time of this writing, Becky said that the dear and thoughtful minister took up a collection to help with the costs of the funeral. I never knew this until now, which means my thank-you notes of appreciation were left undone. I am sorry for that. Because I didn't know or wasn't aware of what was happening in the background at that time, I would like to take a moment to thank everyone who was there for me: Thank you for all your thoughtfulness, respect, and help during such a terrible hour of grief and need. To all those who came, passed by me, and gave of your time and prayers for my family and me, I love you. Thank you, dear ones, for your sympathy, kindness, and love. God bless and keep you in his care.

Looking back at the accident, I questioned what had happened. No police came to the house to speak to me about it and let me know what exactly had caused the accident. It seemed that there were many questions left unanswered, such as why there were lengthy dark tire tracks on the tar road where Jimmy had let off his girlfriend, which was a short distance to where the car had hit the tree. Another mystery was left behind during the impact. Embedded deep within the tree trunk was a symbol of salvation. A long silver cross was there, formed by the chrome trim from the front of the car. The car was called a Vega, and I have since been informed that there were many recalls for this automobile, because of a large number of reported deaths caused by this vehicle. Also at this writing, Bonnie recently revealed to me what the two girls, Elaine and Maria, had to say about the accident and what they remembered. After their evening out, Jimmy, Elaine, Todd, and Maria headed home. They pulled into Elaine's driveway, and after saying goodnight, Elaine went inside. Jimmy started the car and pulled out of the driveway to the main road. The car suddenly shot forward out of control at an extremely accelerated rate of speed. There were black skid marks starting from Elaine's road, and they continued all the way along a short span of road to the crash site. If I know my son, he must have been almost standing on the brakes to try to stop it. Maria said there were balls of light happening and that Todd quickly put his arm out to protect her, which saved her from serious injuries. Both Jimmy and Todd died instantly in the crash the evening of October 22, 1977. It was many days before I could pull myself together. Mark had to return to the navy once again, and I put the house up for sale.

Bob continued to call and eventually came up to see me again, and he began to visit each weekend. The house was finally sold, and Bob brought his trailer up to carry the few belongings the children, my mother, and I were taking down to Florida to the house I had purchased. Today, while writing about what happened and going over and over again in my mind how the accident came to be, it dawned on me. Jimmy must have either bought or borrowed this car from his brother Scott, since they were working on it together earlier that day before going out. I now believe this particular car may have been the same vehicle Scotty had once had, because I remembered something that occurred months earlier. Back then, Scotty was working on his car while parked in the yard in front of the house. When he got inside to start the engine, the automobile suddenly raced forward and smashed into the house, causing the big hole and broken clapboards on the face of the house that Bob later fixed for me. I now believe it's the very same car, which continued to have the same problem off and on, as it happened to do the day Jimmy used it. This proves to me that the particular car would work fine at times, for there was no problem at first when they were driving around with their dates during the boys' night out. It was much later when the unusual malfunction happened after

Jimmy entered the street to take Todd and Maria home. Some part of the car managed to go haywire, and the accident swiftly happened. I finally have some closure, an answer, and understanding concerning the accident. I also now understood that the beings had nothing to do with it and had tried to communicate or warn me that I was about to go through an earth-shattering ordeal.

Time had passed, and Bob called to see how I was doing and eventually came up to see me again. He began to visit each weekend. Once again, some strange things started to take place. We would see bright white balls of light the size of basketballs or grapefruit that would zip through the air past the first-floor windows. This event continued to occasionally happen either day or night. This same light-ball phenomenon also happened when Maria stopped by to talk with me about Todd. She was sitting at the table and suddenly turned her head to look at the stainless steel built-in oven by the cabinets, then quickly turned back the opposite way to look outside the window. She first thought the oven light had flashed on, but she'd turned just in time to see it was a reflection of one of the balls of light outside passing by the kitchen window. She looked so puzzled that I asked her what was the matter. She immediately told me she'd seen a moving ball of white light outside. Bob and I have seen these same bright balls of light traveling around the kitchen and living-room windows, as if they were checking what was going on inside the house. In the past, while we were living in the cellar, a similar type of bright light would occasionally show up. It looked like a glowing white energy ball that made a cracking sound as it popped out of the cement floor and quickly disappeared. It makes me wonder if, when we had the cellar dug up to build the house, we unknowingly might have disturbed an Indian burial ground.

Another odd thing happened to Bob while he was sitting in one of the ladder-back chairs at the harvest table while visiting me. The chair began to vibrate and shake with him sitting in it. He got up and sat in a second chair at the table, and as soon as he did, that chair started to move and vibrate with him on it. He thought there had to be a logical reason for the vibrating chairs. The location of the furnace was just below the harvest table, so he thought it must have gone on and somehow caused the chairs to shake. He went down to the cellar to check. The furnace was completely off, so the shaking and vibration could not have come from it. Bob and I were then sitting in the living room when I began receiving some telepathic messages. I was very tired and could tell the beings were trying to break through with a message. Bob was by my side and knew something unusual was happening. Realizing I was still quite exhausted since my two sons had died, he immediately used a mental command and clapped his hands very loudly between us, which temporarily shut off the communication. I immediately heard the messenger's voice come back and say, "He's got to go."

This startled me, and I told Bob what I'd heard. He said with authority, "No way." Thankfully, their open line to communicate with me had temporarily closed. But I felt troubled over what the beings' rash statement might mean. The following weekend, Bob came up again, this time to bring me to Connecticut to finally meet both his parents. As we were riding west toward Orange, Massachusetts, the sun was out and shining through some puffy white clouds when suddenly the whole sky lit up. The clouds turned into a beautiful blend of golden yellow and soft orange. Bob thought the colors seemed unusual, for the whole sky seemed to glow with awesome lights. Being an amateur artist, I felt overwhelming joy from its unbelievable presence and beauty. The awesome colors gave me a feeling of love and peace and at that moment, I heard in my mind the beings say, "He can stay." I was relieved and told Bob. It made me happy; for I was definitely in love with him and did not want to lose him. We finally pulled into his parents' driveway. I had met his mother much earlier when Bob had parked his trailer and taken me back to Massachusetts. In that short time, I could tell she was a loving and devoted mother. I was looking forward to meeting his dad as well and wanted to hear what Bob was like as a kid. We'd met because we both had unusual UFO encounters, which had begun for both of us at a very young age. The synchronicities between us are astonishing. We both had a childhood UFO experience in 1944 and another adult experience in 1967. And then once again, after we married, we were both taken up together in 1978. But at this time it would be much better to hear about it from Bob. Starting with his life as a young child, he will reveal what has happened to him up to now.

CHAPTER 10

Bob's Life in His Own Words

• • •

My OTHERWISE ORDINARY YOUNG LIFE was forever changed in 1944, when I was just five years old. At that time, the Second World War was raging, and my dad and five of my uncles were in the armed forces and fighting far from home. My mother, who was working at the local rationing board at the time, and I were living with my grandmother in a small home she owned in Meriden, Connecticut. As a small child, outside of knowing my dad had been gone for a long time, I was otherwise not much affected by the war. I played with the neighbor kids and enjoyed climbing the apple tree in the backyard; borrowing cherries from the next-door neighbor's tree that hung over the fence a bit into our backyard; sledding down a nearby street in the winter months; and during the summer months, I spent hours enjoying the swing set my uncles had installed in the backyard for me before they entered the service. Little did I realize as a child that a moment of time spent on my swings would change my life forever.

It would be decades before I realized that what happened on those swings would lead me into a life that included UFO spacecraft, other-worldly beings, and harassment by our own government or that eventually, it would be the catalyst that helped to bring my first marriage to an end and bring Betty and me together. All of this would be in my future at this time, and I had no idea that I would be in for a shocking awakening as the years moved along to 1967 and beyond. One of the surprising events that came out under hypnosis was the following. I had a memory of a light in the sky that even as a youngster I knew did not appear to be normal. During the course of my hypnosis session, this is what I described. In 1944, while five years old, I was in the backyard of my grandmother's house, enjoying my swing set on a warm, sunny summer day. Even as a child, I noticed a light in the western sky that seemed to be brighter or whiter than the sun, which of course was somewhat yellow, while this object looked like highly polished chrome. The object drew closer and closer until it finally stopped and hovered over the victory garden in our backyard. This object was now above and to the left of me. I was curious as to what this could be and looked directly at it, and a thin beam of white light came out of it and struck me in the center of my forehead, slightly above my eyes. It was at this point that I became paralyzed and fearful. The craft itself was round like a saucer, and the top was domed with a clear glass-like structure that allowed me to see inside when it tipped toward me. Inside I saw what I could only describe as strange little people, and they were talking to me not with a voice but inside of my head. They were telling me that people who had seen them would meet at a time in the future, and it would be regarding something that would be good for humankind. It was impressed upon me that I could not tell anybody about this talk, not even my mother. At this age, all of this really did not mean much to me, and I forgot the entire incident shortly after this day.

Bob's Confirmation

Years later, Betty and I met a well-known psychic who had often worked with police departments on difficult cases. She had no prior knowledge of my case or experience. She took my pocket knife and, through what is called psychometry, began to relate what had happened to me so many years ago as I sat on my swing. She had seemingly every detail right, down to the thin light striking me in the forehead. But she also described pipes and vines in the backyard as well. I had no recollection of this and thought surely she was mistaken or that maybe someone had told her of my experience earlier, but who? No one at this time knew of this, other than the hypnotist and the investigators, and it was doubtful any of them would have said anything. Sometime later, I was telling my mother of this, and she said, "Don't you remember? Your grandfather built a pipe arbor in the backyard and had grapevines there." This convinced me that the psychic was quite accurate, since I did not have any memory of this myself as an adult. Another interesting point is that for years after this incident, there was a circular area in the garden where nothing would grow. One of my cousins still remembers that to this day.

Bob, Possibly Mistaken

In *The Andreasson Affair, Phase Two*, there is a story about an abduction where I was way up above the earth, looking down on cloud tops and land. At the time, it was dark in Connecticut, but as I looked down, I could see there was still light on the ground. I apparently mistook this experience for a UFO abduction. It always bothered me that I did not remember seeing any craft or beings of any type. Later, I read a book by Robert Monroe titled *Journeys Out of the Body*. It was this book that finally led me to the realization that what I'd experienced in 1952 may have been an out-of-body experience (OBE) and not a UFO abduction, as I had erroneously thought. It seems that the buzzing noise I'd heard so clearly, leading to the feeling of weightlessness, is associated with the OBE; this fit well into my experience, as it would explain not only what I saw, such as the clouds and western states, but also would account for not seeing any UFO craft or beings. To this day, I cannot be 100 percent certain either way, but I think this is what happened.

Bob Growing Up

By the time I had reached the latter years of grade school and started junior high school, I was totally fascinated with how things worked. I had disassembled and reassembled my bicycle, as well as radios, toys, household items, and anything else I could get my hands on. At this young age, I was also keenly interested in airplanes and cars. While still too young to get involved with cars, I started building and flying model airplanes. I tried all categories of model airplanes, including control-line flying of stunt, combat, and speed planes. I also built free-flight and radio-controlled airplanes, and I got good enough to fly in contests in New England. I designed and built a number of my own airplanes from scratch.

There came a point where I saw plans for a disc-shaped model UFO. This was not a kit, but you could build it from the plans, which I did. It turned out to be a fantastic performer that flew at a high rate of speed and made ninety-degree turns almost effortlessly, as well as loops, figure eights, and inverted flying. I thought this would be a great model to use for combat flying. For those of you who are not familiar with this term, it simply means that two people fly together, and each airplane has a long streamer attached to the tail. The object here is to cut the other flier's streamer off as close to the tail as possible; whoever does that wins. Unfortunately for me, this aircraft was a bit *too* maneuverable, and as I tried to make tight turns or come up on my opponent from unusual altitudes, I quite often ended up cutting off my own streamer—so much for UFO combat flying.

As I grew older, the interest I had in cars, especially fast cars, began to peak. This carried on through high school, and when I landed a job at a gas station and repair shop, I had gained the experience I needed to make my cars go faster. My first car was a 1946 Chrysler coupé with fluid drive, and I quickly discovered that the acceleration from a dead stop was not much faster than a turtle's. At the age of sixteen, I completely rebuilt the V-8 engine in my mother's 1950 Oldsmobile. My dad was both surprised and glad the car actually ran when I got done with it, but he was not always that happy with me. When he got called out of state for his job, he left his 1949 Cadillac, a car I would later own, in the shop for repairs, since it was burning oil and needed new piston rings. He asked me to call the shop on Monday and tell them what needed to be done to the car, which I was more than happy to do. I called on Monday and told them my dad wanted the cylinders bored out and larger pistons put in and that he wanted the valves ground and the cylinder heads planed to raise the compression. Well, when my dad got the bill for this work, I think he wanted to disown me, at least for a short time; however, after driving the car for a few days, he said, "This thing goes like hell now," and it seemed he really liked it. In short, I was off the hook.

I worked and saved my money, and by my senior year in high school, 1956–1957, my dad gave me that 1949 Cadillac convertible. It already had the oversized pistons in it, as well as the higher than stock compression. So it didn't take too long for me to modify this vehicle a bit more, starting with dual exhaust and working up to a number of performance-enhancing modifications to the engine and transmission. This car, although not superfast on acceleration, was great for road racing and top speed. All through my senior year in high school, I never lost a road race to any challenger, as can still be witnessed by the signatures and writings of my classmates in my high-school yearbook, which I have to this day. My next car was a 1948 Ford coupé in which a modified Corvette engine was installed. This car was left entirely stock on the outside, and many times other racers would pull up next to me with either newer cars or their dads' muscle car of the day and make fun of me sitting at the light in my old car. That is, they made fun until they were looking at my back window through the dust and smoke from my rear tires, which happened more often than other racers liked. This vehicle provided me with many hours of enjoyable racing on the highways of Connecticut. Later on, I did belong to a hot-rod club in Wallingford, Connecticut, where the equipment was available to build pretty much anything you could imagine. Enter my friend Larry, who had a 1950 Ford coupé and wanted to make it much faster. It turned out the answer to that would be the installation of a 1955 Cadillac engine and transmission in this small Ford. It took a few serious modifications to accomplish this, such as welding in stronger motor mounts bracing the frame and cutting the drive shaft, but the car was pure brute power when done.

Most of my friends at this time were gearheads, and we all loved to street race. Besides, there was not yet a drag strip in Connecticut where we could test our projects. On one occasion, a police officer tried to pull me over for burning rubber. He decided to chase me with his cruiser while I was driving a modified Ford Model T with a 450-horsepower motor in it. Needless to say, he just couldn't keep up. At that point in my young life, I thought this was great fun. My days of street racing got me a few brushes with the law, but most times I was able to outrun the cruisers of the day. You may ask what this has got to do with UFO and government surveillance—the answer is, a little bit.

You will learn in the coming chapters how the experiences I've gained in the past from road racing and keeping a sharp eye focused on looking for the police would be a big help in both catching and getting behind those who were often following Betty and me. Since the information about our UFO experiences went public, we were literally being watched twenty-four seven. My earlier years of training gave me the ability to, on occasion, get behind the vehicles following us and get the license-plate numbers from them—and, whenever possible, embarrass them.

BOB AS A YOUNG ADULT

Nineteen sixty-seven rolled around, and I was now an adult. I had long ago forgotten about the mysterious light in the sky at my grandmother's house. It was a beautiful summer day without a cloud in the sky, and I was headed to Hammonasset Beach State Park in Branford, Connecticut. Around eleven that morning, I was nearing the area known as the trap rock, where there was a rock quarry. As I got closer to the quarry, I noticed five men working on a railroad track that went into the trap-rock area, presumably so crushed rock could be loaded into the railcars and transported to their destination. I could not help but notice that none of these men were working; rather, they were all looking up at the sky. Apparently something in the sky had caught their interest.

As I looked up, I could hardly believe my eyes, for there in the clear, blue morning sky were two huge cigar-shaped objects that had the appearance of polished chrome reflecting the sunlight. They looked like mirrors reflecting the full brightness of the sun, and they seemed to be effortlessly floating side by side, headed toward the New Haven area. I just had to see this, so I pulled my car off to the side of the road a short distance past the railroad tracks and focused on these strange objects, which were like nothing I had ever seen before. They were huge and had no wings or tail section. There was no visible means of propulsion either in the form of propeller or jet. They were absolutely silent. What happened next was even more incredible, as two smaller disc-shaped craft emerged from the underside of these craft. One headed off toward the New Haven area, and the other went in the opposite direction, probably headed toward Durham or Middletown. I thought, *This is totally amazing*, and I watched until both craft were no longer visible in the clear blue sky. I then started my car and headed off to the beach. After getting only a short distance down the sparsely populated rural road, I noticed that one of the smaller disc-shaped craft was coming toward me. It actually came to a halt hovering only a few feet off the ground in a field to my left. I was totally amazed and frightened by the sight of this strange object floating silently above the ground. I did not remember seeing it leave, and the next thing I knew, I was continuing my drive to the beach.

I arrived at the beach and was hungry, so I decided to go to a local restaurant and get some lunch. That is when I noticed it was now almost two in the afternoon. I thought it was impossible, as the ride to the beach from the point where I had seen the unusual object should have taken no more than thirty to forty minutes—especially as there was no heavy traffic to slow me down. I still clearly recall this experience, as one does traumatic moments in life. For instance, I clearly remember where I was when I heard President Kennedy had been shot. These things are indelibly stamped on one's mind. This unusual sighting occurred in 1967, when it would not have been a good idea to talk about it. Even though I had both a need to get it off my chest and an excitement that was hard to contain, I more or less muzzled myself and told only my wife, who did not believe or support me; my parents; and Art, a friend since grade school, who listened intently as I related my sighting to him and accepted what I said as fact. My parents believed me, probably because my own mother had once seen a UFO and was fearful of it, to the point that she would never talk about it and refused to undergo hypnosis. She did not want to know any more about it. My dad was an engineer involved in aerospace projects, but he would never discuss the subject, so I never did find out just how much he might have known about the UFO phenomenon.

It was not until much later, when the researchers enlisted a hypnotist to see what, if anything, had happened when I had stopped my car beside the road to watch the craft, that I learned what had happened. While I was under hypnosis, the experience came alive again in my mind, and I realized a very intense red light had somehow drawn me out of my car and into the craft. While in that round room, there was light everywhere. But I could not see any physical lights, and there were no shadows. A gray-skinned being with a large head and huge, black, slanted eyes was standing near me. He was dressed in a one-piece fitted red suit with a belt. I could see a gold lightning-bolt patch on the left side of its chest. It told me to undress. The next thing I remembered was that four identical beings came into the room, and I was floated to a table, where I could not move. They communicated through the mind and assured me they would not hurt me, yet I was stuck on the table. At this point, it looked like I was in for a physical examination, whether I wanted one or not. One of these odd beings was at my feet, apparently interested in the composition of my toenails, as he began scraping the underside of my large toe with what appeared to be a chrome or shiny metal tool that reminded me of the pick commonly used by dentists. He also rotated my feet in different directions. Sometimes it was a circular motion, as if to check the range of travel on these particular joints.

Another of these beings held my head and rotated it in a similar fashion, and I also underwent what appeared to be an x-ray or a total body scan. This object emitted a pinkish-white light that came out of the ceiling and passed slowly from my feet to the top of my head. As frightening as I found these beings and their examination of me, there was something that freaked me out more than the examination itself: As one of the beings passed to the side of me, I witnessed his body fade as he turned into a form of light. I could still see his form, but it was almost like looking at a ghost. My mind had trouble understanding how could this be happening, for I was physically there. I was wide awake and fully aware of my surroundings. When they finished with me, they put my clothes back on me. But now I was back in my car, moving away from the farm country and pressing toward my original destination, the beach.

CHAPTER 11

Wherever You Go

• • •

Now I, BETTY, WILL RETURN to our continued life story. I will reveal in my own words what took place during our relationship and eventual marriage. It was fall; leaves were changing colors and falling to the ground. Evenings were starting to feel cool, and thoughts of winter came to mind. For transportation, I used an unreliable, beat-up green station wagon with a leak in the gas tank, which I had stopped up with some chewing gum. Seeing the situation, Bob insisted on leaving his Mercury Marquis for me to use, and he took a bus back to Connecticut. Time passed, and we were still living in Massachusetts. It was winter when I finally put the large house in Ashburnham up for sale. It made no sense to freeze up north when I had a perfectly warm house in Florida that did not need oil to stay warm.

Bob came to Massachusetts to get his car, went back home, hooked up his trailer, and came back to Ashburnham to take us to Florida. We packed our clothes, housewares, and bedding into Bob's small trailer. My mother and the two girls piled in the car's backseat, and we pulled out of the drive headed for Pompano Beach, Florida, to the small ranch-style home I had purchased a few months earlier. At this time, Becky and my two granddaughters were settled in an apartment located in the Old English Village area. Scott, his wife, and my new granddaughter were living in Gardner, Massachusetts, and Mark had returned to the navy to finish his tour. After 1,037 miles of continuous highway travel, we finally reached our new residence and unloaded the fully contained trailer, which Bob would be living in while seeking a job.

I enrolled the girls in high school. But Bonnie was having a problem accepting the circumstances, and because I was dealing with so many issues, I did not realize she needed some counseling to handle her brothers' deaths and some help to accept the direction life was going. She did not like the school, did not want to accept Bob in our lives, and wanted the family to return back to how it was. Before the boys' demise, she had been mad at Todd for teasing her; as with many children, when arguing with their siblings happens, she'd hastily said something to Todd that she now was having a difficult time dealing with or forgiving herself for. With everything that was happening, I could no longer handle her anger. She was being difficult, did not like the school, and wanted to go back north. It wasn't long after that I gave in and allowed her to fly back north to temporarily be with her sister Becky. After spending a few contented months in the warmth of the sunshine state, I was thinking of Bonnie and her unsettled future. I began to worry about her schooling and did not want her to quit as I had, because of unusual circumstances.

So once again, we decided to return to the north to the large house, and months later I sold the small home I had purchased and briefly used while in Pompano. First we stopped in Connecticut to drop off Bob's trailer, and then we drove on to Massachusetts, to the empty large house that had not sold as yet. My sister Shirley lived down the street from my small house in Florida, and my mother did not relish the idea of cold weather, so she decided to stay and live with my sister. Cindy, Bob, and I locked up the small house and headed back up Route 95 North. Bob returned to his old job in Connecticut and continued to call and come up to see me. It was then that he asked me to marry him. I received my divorce papers in 1978, and we were married on August 21. We had a small wedding in the beautiful Hubbard Park area of Meriden, Connecticut, with just a few friends present. Then we went out to have a lovely marital toast and meal, after which we took his trailer to Florida on our honeymoon. A week later, we were back to Massachusetts. By this time, Bonnie had settled down and accepted the fact that I was married to Bob, and she came back home. Later, when we moved to Meriden, we took Bonnie to a psychologist to help her understand and overcome her sorrow and anger over the loss of her brothers and father. Bonnie and Cindy continued high school and graduated in Cheshire, Connecticut.

I finally sold the large house in Massachusetts at a loss, as the economy at the time was very poor in the entire state. It was many years later that I learned about the woman living there; she must have seen the lights outside or had some unusual things happening inside, because I was told she wrote a letter out of fear and taped it on the refrigerator door, saying in big letters, "Betty Andreasson does not live here anymore. Please leave us alone." Evidently she was hoping the spiritual intruders would stop scaring her and her family. One might think it's funny, but it isn't when strange and unusual things happen. I'm sorry if there was a residue of phenomena left behind, for there's nothing I could do about it. As for us, after selling the large Ashburnham home, we bought a small two-story house in Meriden. Bob was working at his regular job and started taking flying lessons. He used the Piper Tomahawk and the Piper Warrior out of Connecticut's Goodspeed Airport. Anyone who knew Bob knew of his keen sense of humor, but it was not always appreciated by everyone, especially one of his flight instructors. One day, while flying with an instructor we will call Billy, Bob made a very bad approach to the airfield and had to do a go-around. This apparently caught the instructor off guard at the time, as he had not reacted quickly enough either. Bob applied full power to the airplane in order to keep it in the air and avoid going into the Connecticut River. The problem was that there is a steel-girder bridge at this end of the runway, which Bob barely cleared. This scared Billy so badly that Bob could see him visibly shaking when he asked Bob, "Aren't you afraid?"

Bob calmly replied, "No. We are past it now."

Several days later, when Bob returned for another lesson, he was told Billy had quit on him, and he would have a new instructor. After several weeks had passed, Bob inquired as to where his previous instructor was and found out he was now instructing seaplane flight. Bob went over to that area, found Billy, and told him that as soon as he got his license, he would be over to seek instruction on the seaplanes. Billy was obviously not happy with this prospect.

At that time, Bob was doing very well with his training and was up and away in the wild blue yonder by himself. He said he would try to fly over the house if he could. I think the next-door neighbor must have thought I was crazy, for I took a roll of white toilet paper and some pebbles to hold the tissue down and wrote on our lawn "Hi, Hon. I love you." Little did I know they were having a big air show that day at the Meriden Airport, and all day, different planes circled above our house looking at my message to Bob. There were so many planes I couldn't tell if he saw it or not, but when he got home, he said he had. Another time, Bob wanted me to take a ride with him in the plane, for he was just about to get his license. I kept telling him no and "not yet." Well, a few days later he talked me into it, and he flew from Connecticut's Goodspeed Airport to Meriden's airport, where he stopped to pick me up, and away we went. I was still very reluctant to go until he received his full license, but I gave in. Everything was going along fine, but I was still pretty nervous about being up there.

My psychic energy was really kicking in, and it caused the plane's radio and navigation to stop working. Meanwhile, we were flying over a thickly wooded area below. I thought we were heading for Canada. It turned out we were over the Quabbin Reservoir in Massachusetts. I was all shaken up, knowing I should not have gotten on that plane in the first place. Bob turned to the east until he saw the Connecticut River, and we followed it back to Meriden. Once the airplane set down on the ground in Meriden, everything started working again. I was so glad to get in my car and head for the house. Bob took off once again for the Goodspeed Airport, set the plane down, parked it, and returned the keys. It wasn't long before he was safe and sound at home as well. It appears I may have been the cause of the radio and navigation going out, because it was fine when we first started off, and it turned back on as soon as I got out of the plane; Bob had no trouble with the electronics flying the plane back. Oh well, just another unusual episode of things that happened to us.

It wasn't that long in the Meriden house before we once again started to have very unusual things start to happen. We had trouble with lights and the doorbell. One evening, someone was at the front door ringing the bell. I was in my nightgown, ready for bed, and had started up the stairs to our bedroom, but I stopped as Bob went to the door to see who was calling so late at night. When he opened the door, there was no one there. He went outside and stood on the landing, wondering what had happened and looking to see if some kids were playing a prank, but he could not see anyone, and the bell rang again with no one there. Another day, the girls had two friends from next door over while we went shopping. They were talking and playing some music in the living room when the lights from the lamps suddenly went wild, started blinking off and on, and would not stop. Their friends were so fearful they quickly left for home. Then, another time, we were shocked one morning when we came downstairs to find all the kitchen's crown molding lying on the floor. It had been pulled off the wall, but the finishing nails were still sticking in the plaster. At the same time, our large stainless-steel spaghetti pot, which had a thick, round rim of stainless steel at the top edge, was split. Also, some clear drinking glasses had squiggly white marks embedded in the glass. Bonnie, Cindy, and Bob had seen shadow people in the house at separate times, but I did not. It was during the evening that Cindy thought what she saw was Bob wearing jeans and sneakers, but she saw only half of the form.

In our bedroom, Bob and I were awakened from sleep to see our bedroom bathed in a red light, and suddenly it sounded like hundreds of birds were singing in our room. It couldn't have been the birds awaking outside, for it was only three o'clock in the morning. We sat up in bed, stunned and amazed, until the red light and sounds of birds finally stopped. We had an additional phone put in on the second floor for the girls. Late evening, it rang, and Bonnie answered. It was a young man who wanted to speak to Cindy, so Cindy took the phone and began to speak to the caller. She recognized the voice and was temporarily surprised, for it was a young man she had befriended when we lived in Ashburnham. He was sort of a loner and had hardly any friends. Cindy's very outgoing and likes everyone, and she was easy to talk to, so while riding home on the bus, she would sit and talk with him. However, no one in Massachusetts but family knew this brand-new phone number or where we had moved to, so she thought someone was trying to play a joke on her...particularly because the young man who'd called and was talking about the past had died years ago. Yet here he was talking to Cindy. She became afraid, because she absolutely knew from what he was referring to that she was talking to the very young man who had been killed in an accident. She quickly hung up and told me the next day about the weird phone call.

It was now Christmas, and Bob and I asked the girls what they would like for their gift. Wanting to surprise them, we decided to take them to Disney World. The tree was up and decorated, with some gifts there for other family members, so I asked Becky if they might like to spend their Christmas at our house, even though we would not be there at the time. They said yes and thought it might be fun to get away from the snow up north. The four of them traveled to Connecticut and brought their large Belgian shepherd, Brutus, with them. We left them a key and plenty of goodies to eat, so they could spend an enjoyable weekend at our house for the holidays. During that first evening, they all went upstairs to sleep. For some reason, Becky, who is somewhat psychic, felt something was strange and sort of spooky in the house, so they all stayed in Cindy's room together. Their dog's unusual protective reaction didn't help, for the hair on Brutus's back was raised, and he was growling and showing his teeth, as though protecting them from something unseen. Brutus had never become so aggressive without a reason. Evidently the dog was sensing something in the house that he did not trust. This, of course, spooked all four of them, and because of the strange feeling they experienced earlier, along with the dog's reaction, they immediately left the house and went back home. I felt upset that their time there had turned out so badly. At another time, Bob's daughter, Wendy, was staying overnight to be with the girls. She was sleeping in Cindy's room, and Bonnie was in the other bedroom. It was years later that Wendy told us she remembered standing in the room looking outside through an open window and didn't know why. At first she thought she was at home when it happened, but we think it might have happened that very evening she stayed overnight with the girls. You might question why we think that, and it's because this was the particular evening Bob and I, in our bedroom across the hall from the girls' rooms, began to hear a loud noise over the house. We both started to hear a whirring sound above the roof of our room. I was in the bathroom brushing my teeth, and Bob was by the bed taking off his socks and getting ready for bed. The whirring sound got very loud, and as I turned to look at Bob and saw him suddenly rise up from the floor, I was shocked.

He was in two places at the same time, for while he was on the floor taking off his socks, he remained there in a state of suspended animation, but his other active self was rushing toward me. It would be years later that we would find out what had happened. The presence of his double state of being, where he was in two places at the same time, is called a doppelganger effect. He suddenly rushed toward me, stopped at the doorway, and raised his arms and hands up to the sides of the door casing, and we briefly looked at each other in shock. He grabbed me to hold on, and as I hugged him, I could feel us both starting to rise upward through the ceiling, into the air. It felt like there was wind and mist all around us. There was light as we were lifted upward. I started to feel us being pulled apart, like we were going in separate directions. I kept yelling for Bob, but I couldn't seem to see or hear him in this misty fog. I was still rising upward and began to see the color blue around me, though it was quickly changing into soft purplish lavender. My body seemed as if I had no flesh color as I began to move into some purple atmosphere. My body didn't seem to have any interior color to it either, like it had disappeared from my form. It seemed like my body was a ghost's as I continued to travel upward into a golden light. My whole body started to absorb the light, and it became a glowing golden color. As I moved through this golden light, I could see other forms of golden people there as well, but they didn't seem to have any features either. I could see and hear them, and we were all moving into this large room that had a walkway and a very high domed top. From where I was standing, I could tell this was a huge round room. There was a bottom floor, where there were three tables with people on them who were covered with white blankets, and there were some smaller beings around each table.

These beings had large heads and grayish skin, and they seemed to be standing over each one of those people, who were not moving. Three large orbs of intensely bright light hung in midair, just above the three people and gray beings. By now all the golden people I was with were moving along this walkway with me. We all stopped and started to touch the palms of one another's hands. I don't know why, but it felt as if we all had a oneness within and between us—something like a promise we would have to keep. The walkway continued to slowly revolve, and I once again was looking down over the railing at the big-headed gray beings and tables below. The walkway continued to slowly revolve. I glanced over to the right and suddenly saw Bob way on the other side of this rotating walkway, with two tall, white-haired people in white robes. I started to wave to him, but the white-haired people quickly escorted him into another room. I don't think Bob knew it was me waving to him, for I was covered with light, but at least I knew he was all right. My attention turned back to the beings and the three people lying on the tables below, for I was wondering what they were doing.

I leaned over the railing once again to try to see and immediately recognized who it was. I gasped in sorrow and total disbelief. Meanwhile, the other beings of light came rushing over to me, like they knew I needed them. They were able to sense my confused feelings of terror caused by what I saw. They crowded around me, touching my shoulders, back, and head as if they were mothering me by lifting away a burden. It was as though they shared in my sudden feelings of sadness but were able to brush the memory away. Their attentive touch made me forget. I stood and followed them along as if we had something important to do. We drew closer to another open door with a glass entrance. As we passed through, the inside had a rounded partial wall, made like a rolled banister with slanted curves. The whole area was moving counterclockwise. Close to the top of the curves were square metal plates that had many small multicolored lights in them, blinking and twinkling off and on. A wide, flat, colored ribbonlike strap of light was attached to each square plate. The bands of light were draped over the banister and hung in midair to way below. One after another, the beings of light stood before them, turned, and pressed their backs on and against the slanted glass, with their heads slightly above the embedded square plates. I followed suit. The glass seat flipped and rolled backward as our bodies of light suddenly curled into a ball-like position and each of us rolled downward, absorbing the entire band of colored light. Each ball-of-light being now sat on the floor with a sparkling glow, and suddenly the balls of light turned back into glowing beings again. Once again, our original golden light was still clothing our whole beings, but our bodies were now stationed in a strange manner. Our feet and toes were sideways facing out yet flat on the floor while our bent legs were in a tight sideway squat. Our arms were stretched out, bent upward at the elbow, with the palms of our hands faceup; in every hand, there was now a small lighted object, though they all had different shapes and colors. There were spheres, pyramids, curlicues, bars, diamonds, stars with points, doughnuts, disks, and orbs. Even though I was also partaking of this peculiar experience as a being of light, I did not understand exactly what was going on or why we were doing it.

While each of us had an object, one particular being carried something else, a long black-and-white cylinder rod with long points on both ends. And it seemed as if we were playing a game, for we were flinging these odd objects around through the air, and each being had to make sure to catch one of them. While they floated in air, the rod keeper used the pointed ends to try to catch them. Within this area, off to the side, was this huge, long cylinder of whirling bright energy with circular bars of intense light. There was ring after ring after ring that reached around this central cylinder. This multiple-ringed energy was casting off a sort of golden-amber light that was coming from between the many standing circular rings of bright white light. We continued to toss the objects to one another, when suddenly the rod keeper grabbed one. The being who ended up without an object had to immediately go to the rings and stand there. After a while, the rod keeper managed to catch more objects, and each being without an object had to stop and go to the rings of light.

After the last object was secured by the rod keeper, we all had to patiently wait on the rings; the collector floated over to the side and quickly thrust the completed rod through a door. The white side of the rod was pulled through the door, along with the accumulated objects, while the black rod and objects were still on our side; immediately they disappeared as well. Suddenly there was an opening where the door had been. One by one, we left the rings and floated toward the opening. Each being of light passing through miraculously changed into a normal-looking human being, just like regular clothed people; however, at first, they were like ghosts, with very little color to their skin, hair, eyes, and clothes. It surprised and amazed me to realize each one of the light beings that had been floating around with me, releasing and catching the objects, was actually a person, and we were of many different races and countries. This proves it's a small world, and the UFO phenomenon has affected us all worldwide. Standing by, there were some tall, white-haired, pale men dressed in long white robes. They looked similar to the two tall people or beings I had seen earlier with Bob. It would be much later that I would learn they were called the Elders. These tall beings were now quietly escorting us to some doors, where it looked like a lavender color. As the door opened, I swooped through it, and it felt like I was being swirled round and around. Next I heard a loud whirring noise. The whirling around me made me feel weak and strange, as if I couldn't understand what was happening and where or who I was. I must have been transported back to the bathroom, for at this point, I remembered standing there amazed at Bob, who had rushed toward me and stood at the door with an astonished and bewildered look on his face and then just as quickly moved backward into his body by the bed. At first we remembered the whirling sound above our bedroom but continued to get ready for bed.

It was much later that we both would learn under hypnosis that we'd once again experienced another strange encounter, triggered by the whirling noise over our bedroom and Bob's odd double presence. Before I close and you hear from Bob about his experience with the tall Elders that same evening, I want to explain the very last thing that happened—at least that I'm now aware of—concerning the Meriden house, which we sold. I was at a supermarket in Meriden, and I noticed the lady behind me was the woman who had purchased the home from us. We started talking, and I was wondering how she and her family liked the house. She was happy with it but said one evening something unusual had occurred. You can believe I was all ears, but I sort of cringed, thinking uh-oh. She said the whole family had gone out one evening, and much later when they returned home, they unlocked the front door, and every light in the house and outside went on without anyone touching a switch. She also said the upstairs telephone was still working, even though we'd had both phones turned off when we moved, so they are probably still having free telephone service upstairs.

But now to get back to what Bob experienced during our 1978 encounter, in Bob's own words. He will relate what he saw, what happened, and what he was told.

In 1978, Betty and I were abducted together after hearing a loud whirring noise over our Meriden, Connecticut, home. Once on the craft, we were separated. Betty joined a group of others, who like her, had been somehow changed into beings of light or spirit/soul and were involved in some sort of learning process that to me appeared to be a game. Meanwhile, I was escorted to another room in this craft, where I was given information by two of the tall white Elders. First, they told me it was a privilege to be here and that usually people at my level of spiritual development did not get to this point. This led me to think it must be because of Betty's level of development that I was allowed to be here. At any rate, this is some of what I revealed under hypnosis.

Hypnotist:	How do you know it is a privilege to be here?
Bob:	Because the two big guys told me so.
Hypnotist:	Do they tell you together or separately?
Bob:	It's hard to tell...they are almost like twins; it's like what one thinks, the other thinks at the same time, so I am not really certain who is saying what. In fact,

> I don't even think they are talking. I think it is just thought, but I am not sure.
>
> Hypnotist: What form is Betty in? Is she a light form or a solid form?
>
> Bob: He said she was one of those people who looked like a ghost or light.

The hypnotist went on to question me about how it was possible for me to be here, while my body was apparently still home in the bedroom. I explained to the hypnotist that these beings had told me Betty and I were present there in our spirit/soul bodies, the real person or real you—your light body. He further explained that this part of us does not die. This answer was not what any of the investigators present expected to hear. Later, when the tape was played back, I was amazed to hear what I had said as well.

> Hypnotist: Where does that part go from here?
>
> Bob: We move on in stages, and our earthly existence is only one step in a long learning process. It is a process that the human mind is unable to comprehend. The spirit has existed in different bodies at different times.

As the session continued, the hypnotist was beginning to lose his composure because of the answers I had been giving to these questions; in the investigators' opinions, these seemed to be completely out of my ability to know. After all, I was a technician, a nuts-and-bolts physical type of guy. Yet I had all this knowledge of the spiritual realm that just did not fit me.

> Bob: This is all part of what the Elders had been imparting to me.
>
> Hypnotist: Are you saying evil is positive?

Bob: Evil on the earthly plane is the negative aspect. Evil on the larger plane is part of the overall plan that gives us all a chance to advance and rise above it. Everyone in the earthly plane has the ability to do evil. Those who do not, those who fight evil, those who learn and overcome evil, and those who have advanced have gained tremendously in the next realm. Everything in nature has a plus and a minus, a light and a dark, a negative and a positive, a good and a bad. It must be, for without some content of evil, there can be no choice. There can be no growth.

Hypnotist: We need evil for good?

Bob: We do not need *evil* for good. We need *choice*. The Creator gave us choice. We cannot use that choice unless we have more than one choice to make. Evil or good, it is so simple—so beautiful. But there must be evil to have a choice. So on this plane, evil must exist.

Of course, the Elders told me much more during this meeting, including where animals fit in and distressing times to come for planet Earth, as a result of developing faster technologically than spiritually. They revealed much more then, which I will not go into here. After Betty and I returned to our room, the initial memories were gone, except for the loud whirring sound over our bedroom. Later, we remembered a few bits and pieces slowly. We had lived in this Meriden cottage for a year or more and decided there just was not enough land to garden or relax outside in the sunshine. So in the fall of 1979, we sold the house and purchased a ranch-style home in Cheshire, Connecticut.

And now back to Betty and our new residence.

Earlier that day, I had enrolled the girls in the Cheshire High School, and they were supposed to come back to this house as soon as school was over. Meanwhile, Bob and I were at the attorneys' office processing the closing, signing ownership papers, and receiving the keys. After school, the girls returned to the new house and found the door wide open, with a telephone man working inside on our new phone. This was odd, because earlier the doors had been locked, so that even we could not get in until we received new keys. You might question why that bothers me, but the answer is simple: because of the UFO phenomenon that seemed to following us. Over the years, we've been followed, watched, and indiscriminately listened to. Our telephone was tapped, and we have had our mail opened by the postal inspectors. For instance, we've had many disturbing telephone activities take place. At one time, my mother was ill, and I tried to call out to check on her. I was unable to get through, for someone on the outside had left the line open again, where there was no dial tone at all. I was upset and screamed into the phone, "Get off the line! My mother's sick. I need to call my mother." Suddenly the line became free.

Another time, I picked up the phone to call, and right away a woman's voice said, "The director's office."

I said, "Director of what?" She immediately hung up. Many peculiar clues continue to point to a large degree of hidden surveillance going on around us. After a while, you start to sense and feel when things are not normal and are out of context. What's irritating is that we're not hiding anything, so there's no reason to use the cloak-and-dagger attitude toward us. As of March 2014, it appears we are still having phone surveillance. It's absolutely obvious that off and on we are being recorded, especially when speaking with two particular family members, who have also heard it. When my call has ended, just before I hang up, I've heard the last part of my conversation repeating itself. Since moving to our Cheshire residence, things have continued to happen. They were not encounters but still were linked to the UFO phenomenon. I was still undergoing hypnosis to recall all I could remember, but a large number of black unmarked helicopters were constantly flying over our immediate area, and this was not a usual flight path. I had started to receive information from the beings through telepathy, and when it was happening, the unmistakable *wharp, wharp, wharp* sound of a fast-approaching helicopter heading our way sometimes broke off the communication. Most likely, the fliers of these black copters were trying to find out where it was coming from. Of course, the house had to be bugged in order for them to know what was going on as well. At times I received information and strange writings from the beings five stations back, and even though I did not understand what it meant, I would quickly jot it down on anything close by, in order to capture the strange exchange as quickly as possible. I have released some of these things to the public in a series of three small booklets I've named *A Step beyond Tomorrow*. Bob took many pictures of these particular un-marked helicopters as well. In his own words, he will reveal other details of our constant harassment by these unrelenting copters and will also reveal how and when we were both drugged by an unknown source.

CHAPTER 12

Surveillance Begins

• • •

IN 1978, JUST PRIOR TO the release of the *Andreasson Affair*, we started to notice some unusual air traffic over our home. Not only were the flights themselves unusual, in our mind, but they seemed to be directly targeting us. Shortly after purchasing the Meriden home, Betty was at a local store on South Broad Street in Meriden buying wallpaper for our home. The store had a large parking lot devoid of any trees or other obstructions. A helicopter appeared over the parking lot, and there was a man sitting in the open doorway resting his feet on the landing rail. He had a camera in his hand, photographing the front of the store and its large plate-glass window, in which Betty was clearly visible. This photo never appeared in the newspaper or anywhere else that we could determine, so it appeared this was the beginning of aerial monitoring of us that would last for years to come. We could not help but notice that these flights continued over our home as well.

I started taking photos of them and sent them to Raymond Fowler, who told me the images were too small to really make any accurate identification of these aircraft. That's why Betty purchased a good telephoto lens as a birthday present for me, which I promptly put to good use in photographing these helicopters. With the larger and clearer images, it became very apparent that these were no ordinary helicopters, as the ID numbers required by federal law were nowhere to be seen on these aircraft. Additionally, the flights became so frequent and so low that a neighbor began to document the times and dates of these flights. At first Ray thought perhaps we were in some flight path that would explain the frequency of these flights. That was a good theory, but it did not hold up. When we moved to Cheshire in the fall of 1979, the helicopter flyovers moved with us, and neighbors reported that they had ceased over the Meriden home. It now became painfully apparent that some sort of government surveillance had started on us, possibly because we were now doing interviews on TV and radio and were featured in magazine and newspaper articles as well.

Once we were settled in the Cheshire home, the flights became even more frequent, and it appeared they were not concerned about being seen by others. The helicopters were almost always Huey UH-1s at first. Later, Sikorsky Blackhawks and Huey UH-1s would both show up over our home, sometimes daily and sometimes several times a week. Although I was quite certain they were there to keep an eye on us, we were not sure why, as I had flown over our home myself and noticed there was not much to see from the air other than the home itself, the roof, and the yard. However, I realized these helicopters often carried electronic gear that I did not have access to, like shotgun microphones and thermograph equipment that can literally see inside your home through the walls, or roof as the case may be. Although we suspected as much, the question was whether we could be sure they were looking at us.

These questions were soon answered, thanks to a friend who'd been in the military and who also had a great sense of humor as I did. This friend constructed an exact replica of a surface-to-air missile (SAM) that he'd worked with when in the service. A day or two after we received the dummy missile, we heard the familiar sound of a Huey approaching from the north; it was time to have some fun with these unwanted intruders. The harmless SAM was quickly set up on a cement patio on the south side of the home, where it would not be seen by the low-flying helicopter approaching from the north until he was quite close to the house. I only wish we'd had a video camera at that time, for as the unmarked chopper came close enough to our home that the "missile" came into view, the pilot made such a tight turn away from our home that I thought the blades might just break on this aircraft. As it turned out, we all had a good laugh, and

I believe the pilot returned to wherever he came from and probably had a quick shower and a change of underwear.

That said, I want to make it clear that we never had any ill will against those flying these aircraft, as they were only doing what they were ordered to do by someone higher up the chain of command; however, I still enjoyed toying with them whenever I could. These helicopters also gave us a few problems away from home as well. One day, I was up with my flight instructor while taking lessons for my pilot's license, and he gave me a compass heading to follow. While flying on this course, I noticed a black Huey off in the distance to my right. I immediately banked to the right to chase after this Huey, hoping we could follow it to wherever it was going to land. My flight instructor asked me what I thought I was doing, since he knew nothing of the problems we were having with the helicopters and surely did not know of our UFO experiences. I just said something like "my bad" and got back on course. On another occasion, I was flying alone on my first cross-country flight from Goodspeed Airport in Connecticut to the Worchester airport in Massachusetts, where as required, I would get my logbook signed and then return back to the airport in Connecticut I had started from. It was a beautiful, clear day, and on my return flight, when I was at three thousand feet above ground level, I noticed four Black Huey UH-1s way off in the distance, and it appeared that we were on intersecting flight paths. As we got closer and closer, I got more and more apprehensive and wondered if they knew it was me in this aircraft and whether anything would happen to my airplane. Would I have a student-pilot accident? They got closer and closer until they passed underneath me by what I estimated to be five hundred feet. I breathed a sigh of relief. I then thought, *Good God, am I really starting to get that paranoid?* Looking back now, with all our government had put us through, I guess I had a right to be a bit paranoid.

As these flights continued, I became obsessed with finding out whose aircraft these were. I soon learned the US Army was the largest purchaser of these aircraft, but I did not see the connection with the UFO phenomenon. I started writing everyone I could think of to try to find out whose aircraft these were. The Federal Aviation Administration's district office in the Boston area had jurisdiction in this area, so I started with them. I sent them a number of clear photos of these aircraft, only to be told they could not identify ownership without the aircraft ID numbers visible. Well, that was a great help, especially since I was writing them *because* these aircraft were unmarked. One person at this office told me on the phone that this sounded like a CIA operation. Another person from that office, Sam Martino, was interested enough that he drove down to Connecticut on a Saturday to investigate on his own, but unfortunately, we were not home. Sometime later, *Connecticut Magazine* did an article on us and contacted Sam, who said he only vaguely remembered this. I thought that was quite unusual since he'd taken the time to drive down on his own time, and when I called the district office a few days later to talk to him, I was told he was no longer at that office and they could not tell me where he was. The thing they did not count on was the fact that he'd left a note taped to my front door, which I had saved. Strangely enough, one of the IRS agents I named in the article also said she only vaguely remembered us. I also found this unusual, as I am certain the IRS does not often have audits as harassment for UFO whistle-blowers, which we were at the time. After being disappointed by my communication with the FAA, I tried the National Guard, air force, FBI, CIA, and the helicopter manufacturers—all to no avail.

I also contacted Bell Helicopter in Texas who manufactures the Huey helicopters. I enclosed a photo of one of the choppers that had circled over us earlier in the year with my letter and asked if this was one of theirs. I received a reply from the Bell Helicopter public-affairs person, Dick Tipton, stating that this particular craft was a Huey UH-1f BF that had been modified by the military, as the body configuration had been changed. He said this particular helicopter, which was designated as a UH 1P, was one of a number of the UH 1F BF helicopters modified by the air force for psychological warfare in the Vietnam conflict. The question this raised for me was why this type of helicopter was monitoring us. The closest I got to finding out who was flying these particular helicopters came one summer day in the early 1980s when I was putting new shingles on our roof. By this time, my camera had become like an American Express card, in that I would never leave home or even go out the front door without it. I took my camera everywhere I went, including up on the roof while putting on the new shingles. Out of the southwest, I heard the now also familiar sound of a Sikorsky Blackhawk, a relatively new helicopter at that time. Since it was flying low and nowhere near the required five-hundred-foot distance laterally away from structures, I snapped a few photos and then got a compass heading on it as it circled our home and headed back in the same direction from which it had come. I was going to act quickly on this one. I knew this chopper was headed in the direction of Sikorsky Aircraft Corporation, the manufacturer of this helicopter. I quickly contacted the tower at Sikorsky and asked if they had a large black helicopter in my area. I was told they did and that it was an army Blackhawk. Elated, I fired off a letter that day, demanding an apology for the low flyover.

Several days later, I got a letter from Sikorsky, apologizing for the low flight of a navy helicopter over my home. I wrote back and called the discrepancy to their attention. Several days after that, I received a letter explaining the helicopter was an army helicopter being flown by a navy acceptance crew. As far as I know, the navy does not determine whether helicopters are acceptable for the army, but in all fairness I do not know for certain if this is the case. The flyovers of these unmarked aircraft continued for years, often even following us on vacation. Betty's niece and nephew in Florida had remarked that they knew we were in the area when they began to see the black helicopters. On one occasion, we stopped with our camp trailer at a beautiful campground called Fort Christmas off Route 50, west of Cape Canaveral. The campground is wooded with many pine trees, and we had secured a parking spot for our camper just under a small clearing in these trees. We had barely parked and leveled our trailer when along came a small two-man observation helicopter, which stopped directly over us. The pilot was obviously photographing us, as he was low enough that I could see him clearly. I decided to reciprocate by taking his photo and managed to get to my camera in time to take a quick photo of this craft before it rapidly made its way out of my field of view and disappeared behind the tree line.

On yet another trip to Massachusetts, where we were planning on visiting Betty's relatives, we were driving along a sparsely populated area on Route 2 when two black Hueys rose from a nearby field and crossed over the front of our car at an altitude of between fifty to seventy-five feet. I believe this is also illegal by federal law. If the objective was to intimidate us, it did not quite work, as I gave the pilots the single-finger wave as they passed over us from left to right. Some of these flights were quite bold and very visible to the public, as in the following instance. I was in a sporting-goods store on East Main Street in Meriden, purchasing an AR-15 rifle, while Betty waited in the car. Along came one of these now-too-familiar choppers; surprisingly, it stopped and hovered, without making a lot of rotor noise, low over the store while I was in there. They may have been using thermography to view the inside of the store. Otherwise, I do not know what they could accomplish by just looking at the roof. This was confirmed by an onlooker who witnessed this unusual event and took the time to let Betty know, although he did not want to become involved because of his position with a local newspaper.

When I spoke about the helicopters at a conference in Phoenix, Arizona, a man approached me during a break. I could not help but notice that this man appeared to be military, because of his appearance. He looked to be in his midthirties. His hair was a close-cropped buzz cut, and he was clean shaven. He wore his shirt buttoned so the buttons directly lined up with his belt buckle, and his pants were perfectly creased. His black shoes were almost free of dust and were highly polished. All of this, coupled with his very erect posture, made me certain he was of a military background. He informed me that all the helicopter surveillance and flyovers were meant to intimidate us, *so they would not have to hurt us.* I thanked him for the information, and he walked off without another word. One thing I found out for certain is that whoever was ordering these particular aircraft did not want too much publicity. I had taken a photo of one of these low flights over our Cheshire home and sent it to a Kodak processing facility in the Boston area to have it made into a twenty-by-forty-inch poster. Once again, there were unusual circumstances. The poster-size photo arrived at my home in a mailing tube six weeks later, with a Washington, DC, postmark on it, as witnessed by a police officer named Larry Fawcett. Undaunted, I displayed this poster on a network TV show we did some weeks later, and suddenly there were no helicopters over our home. This lasted for about two weeks before the flights suddenly resumed. Another baffling circumstance of these craft was that they seemed to know where we were at all times. This was probably due to the tap on our home phone or possibly a bug planted within our home or other forms of eavesdropping.

We were lecturing to a small group of people at the home of a Connecticut psychologist, and Betty had just finished speaking of her UFO experiences. I had just started to discuss the helicopter problems we were having when out of nowhere came the unmistakable sound of the rotor blades of a low-flying Huey UH-1. This aircraft was low enough and loud enough that the windows in this home rattled; all who were present, approximately twenty people in all, witnessed this incident. You might chalk this up as coincidence, if not for the fact that twice more it happened as we were lecturing to groups of people in private homes, both in Meriden and New Britain, Connecticut, in the following weeks. One of the lowest flights over our Cheshire home occurred on Sunday, October 28, 1979, at a quarter to ten in the morning. Betty and I were headed out for a typical Sunday breakfast at a local restaurant and had only reached our car in the driveway when we were startled to see a large black helicopter coming down the street, almost directly in line with our driveway. We watched in disbelief as this helicopter flew directly over the center of the road at an altitude just slightly above the roofs of the houses on either side of the road. It soon passed over us, only slightly higher than the maple tree at the end of our driveway, and passed directly over our house. I wished I'd had a paintball gun at the time, as I could have marked it, although I doubt anyone would have complained or arrested me for doing so. At this altitude, it was easy to see and describe this large vehicle, which had twin jet engines that trailed a light smoke on both sides of the cabin; a red, rotating beacon on the bottom; and a flat black paint job, with very dark windows and absolutely no markings anywhere on it. Strangely enough, the chopper was not as loud as one would expect at this altitude. This was clearly in violation of federal regulations, which state that a helicopter must maintain a five-hundred-foot lateral distance from dwellings on the ground. Since this passed directly over our home at this extremely low altitude, it was beyond a doubt in violation of two specific FAA regulations: first, for passing directly over the house, and second, for having no ID or tail numbers.

The next day, I tried to find out where this aircraft had come from. I contacted the tower at Bradley International Airport, where National Guard helicopters were housed, as well as the helicopter manufacturers in Connecticut. I also contacted the military in our general area and the FAA. No one owned up to or had any information regarding this aircraft. It seemed, too, that no one had filed a flight plan for this particular run. Obviously, *someone* had to know who owned these aircraft, and *someone* had to give the order for these flights, but no one was talking. Can you imagine what this type of surveillance—which could have been avoided if they had just come and asked us whatever questions they may have had—cost the taxpayers?

OTHER FORMS OF SURVEILLANCE

Apparently whichever agency, or more than likely agencies, was harassing us was not satisfied with using the helicopters alone to try to keep us on edge, as we began to be followed by cars as well. This was one of the most enjoyable of the harassment tactics. As mentioned earlier, as a young man, I'd taken pride in the fast cars I put together and in my skills as a road racer. These skills would now come into play and provide us with some entertainment and just plain fun. One early morning, we started out from our Cheshire home for a shopping trip to Meriden. After a short time, it became obvious that we were being followed. The road we were on had a speed limit of forty-five miles per hour, so I sped up to around seventy-five for a short distance, then slowed down and quickly took a sharp left; I took a couple more turns and maneuvered us up behind the car that was following us, which was now stopped at an intersection. I stopped behind it and recorded the license plate. The driver of that vehicle had stopped in the middle of the road and put on the emergency flashers to make it appear that the car was stuck on the road, while in fact, she was looking all over to see where we'd gone. I knew this car was not stuck, and I knew what she was up to, so I went around the vehicle and again started out at a high rate of speed. I ducked behind an automotive-parts store a couple of miles down the road that was owned by a friend of mine. The store was on the corner of a major intersection. Only a few seconds passed before the car that was supposedly stuck could be seen coming up the road at a high rate of speed, and it came to a screeching stop at the intersection. My wife and I watched, quite amused, as the driver looked several times both left and right, trying to determine which way we had gone, never noticing us sitting off to one side of the building observing her.

On yet another occasion, the person assigned to watch us parked on the same street our house was on. As we headed out that morning, I picked him up immediately as someone who was going to try to follow us. I told Betty to watch as I went up the street to a church that had a sign at the bottom of the driveway that said "No Throughway." I turned up there knowing there was another way out of that yard, which our tail was not aware of. I drove slowly up the drive and watched the driver of the tail car pull over and wait next to the curb at the entrance of the church drive. I exited the drive from another direction, unseen by our tail, turned, and came face-to-face with the driver of the other car. Even from inside our car, we could see this fellow was quite embarrassed as he quickly accelerated by us and headed back in the opposite direction from where we were originally headed. Unfortunately, we were so caught up in laughing and enjoying the moment that we neglected to take down the license-plate number.

This type of surveillance was not limited to our local trips. While vacationing in Lake Worth, Florida, we visited a local Laundromat to wash our clothing. It was early morning on a bright, sunny day, and the place was empty other than the manager, Betty, and me. A car pulled into the yard rather quickly, and a man jumped out and started taking pictures through the large window at the front of the building. Betty, thinking the place was perhaps up for sale, asked the manager if this was the case. The manager replied that it was *not* up for sale, and she had no idea why anyone would be taking these photos. I managed to get outside before this person got completely onto the roadway, and I got the plate number, which I gave to police officer Larry Fawcett when we returned to Connecticut. No big surprise—again, the plate number came back as unissued, just like the others.

I believe the people or agents assigned to track us were probably entry-level employees, as they appeared to be relatively young and not very experienced. Another example was when we purchased a condo in West Palm Beach, Florida. The very first day we arrived, we were followed into the place by a young woman. The fact that we were being followed was obvious to me as I made a number of turns and took side streets instead of heading for the condo we had purchased. Finally, I sped up and took several streets that brought us to a position directly opposite the car that had been following us. Since this was Florida and the weather was hot, the windows in both cars were open, making it easy for us to hear this young woman speak apparently into an unseen microphone. As we pulled up next to her, we heard her say, "They're here. They're here." Her excitement at apparently finding and identifying us was unmistakable. This may sound like the ranting of paranoid people, but proof of this surveillance had already been verified in the past. One cold winter evening in Connecticut, Betty and I decided it would be great to get away from the cold and enjoy the warmth of our favorite winter state, Florida. Without saying a word to anyone, we arose at about two in the morning on a Sunday and went over to the home of a friend who was kind enough to let us store our camp trailer in his yard. We quietly hooked the trailer up to our truck and headed off to Florida. A few days later—on Wednesday, I believe—two men with FBI photo identification showed up at my place of employment and wanted to know where I was. The fact is no one knew exactly where I was headed, even though everyone I worked with knew of my dislike of cold and love of Florida.

At any rate, the FBI men, if they were really FBI, gleaned no information from their inquiry. Their visit was verified later, when *Connecticut Magazine* wrote its article on us and interviewed my coworkers, who verified the men's appearance at my job and their questioning regarding my whereabouts. Of course, when we returned and learned of this, Betty and I went to the federal building in New Haven where the FBI office was located. An agent came out to talk to us and said, "We can neither confirm nor deny that we were looking for you or were at your place of employment." Again, there was no big surprise here. While talking with this agent, I asked why they were tapping our telephone and explained that we had verified a tap by using an electronic tap detector to check our phone. He did not appear to be surprised that our phone was tapped, but he did say that, in our case, it was not the FBI but rather air-force intelligence monitoring our phone. This is in itself was strange, as we'd never mentioned we were involved with the UFO phenomenon and had given only our names, yet he assumed air-force intelligence was involved in tapping our phone.

Sometime later, I had an occasion to talk to someone from air-force intelligence regarding our phone tap, and he told me they would have needed a court order to do so. More than likely, he said, it would have been the FBI tapping our phone. So goes the endless circle of trying to get answers from government. There *is* one thing that leads me to believe the culprit, at least for the phone surveillance, possibly was air-force intelligence. This is because I was told that abductees Betty and Barney Hill did, in fact, find out their phone was being monitored from the nearby Pease Air Force Base. Another interesting facet of the phone tapping is that security people from the phone company seem to have been coached by someone, or some agency, to not find anything wrong with our phone. Here is what I base this opinion on: After suspecting for a period of time that our phone was tapped, I purchased an electronic tap detector and tried it out on the phones of friends and family. In all cases, I found no indication of a tap. However, when this device was installed on our home phone and Betty's work phone, it indicated a tap on the line. Now, to me, the next step seemed obvious—call the phone company and request that our line be inspected for the presence of a tap. A "security person" was dispatched to our home, and this is what transpired. He came into our house, and after introducing himself, he went to our phone and tried to unscrew the mouthpiece. He claimed it would not come off; therefore it was secure, and no one had been in there. He stated he would check the line and inform us of the findings. Here is where it gets interesting: As soon as he left, I grabbed the phone and easily unscrewed the mouthpiece, which this "security person" had said was secure and he could not open. The next interesting thing was that, later that day, I photographed the phone-line junction box on the telephone pole in front of our house, and it had been left with the cover in the open position, leaving the electrical connections inside it exposed to the weather. This is obviously an error, as no electrical devices or junction boxes should ever be left open, exposing the electrical components to the weather, especially rain and moisture. Lastly, we never got a report or anything else from the phone company regarding the so-called inspection of our phone line.

Possible Scare Tactics

In addition to using the helicopters to try to scare or intimidate us, they had a few more surprises waiting for us. Once Ray Fowler published the first book, the IRS was kind enough to keep track of our finances by giving us an audit every year for several years in a row. The first audit was pretty normal except for some of the questions asked, which included these: (1) What did you see? (2) What were the beings like? (3) What was the craft like? These are unusual questions for an audit. But we did not think much of it at first. Later audits became heated, as my CPA accused the IRS of harassment, an accusation that turned out to be true and resulted in very loud exchanges between us and the IRS agent. During some of the following audits, I was asked to provide documents that were more than seven years old, and I refused. The agent told me they could audit my ex-wife to get the information they'd requested. Since she and I did not get along well at that time, I told them to go for it. They also refused to take my canceled checks as proof of payment for property, water, and sewer taxes, and they were difficult about statements for my mortgage and saving accounts as well. I had to go to the bank and get signed statements from bank officials and from the town to prove all was paid and properly reported to the IRS. If this was not a clear case of harassment, I do not know what would be considered one.

After this, I found that when I overpaid my taxes a bit, they no longer had reason to call me in. Another interesting tactic they tried took place at the airport in Connecticut. Betty and I were flying with police officer Larry Fawcett from Bradley Airport to O'Hare Airport in Chicago, as we were scheduled to do some publicity for the book on both radio and television shows in the area. When I got to the desk at Bradley Airport, the ticketing agent told me Mr. Luca had boarded the plane already. Thinking it may have been another person with the same name, I explained to the person at the desk that I was Robert Luca, and I gave them my Cheshire address. The representative told me that was the name and address of the person who had boarded the plane. By this time, Larry had spotted me and came over. He confirmed my identity, and we all did get on the plane; however, I found no one in my seat. Perhaps this is a way of trying to make you nervous or paranoid, but it is not very effective, in my opinion. On yet another occasion we were camping in our camp trailer at a KOA campground in Rockledge, Florida. We had been there only a few hours when we got a message that Betty's son had called. This was unusual because no one knew we were there, as we'd decided on that campground more or less on the spur of the moment as we were driving on 95 South. Betty's two boys had no idea we were there, and neither did anyone else. Then there were a number of other harassing phone calls, one of which I managed to catch on tape. Since we had an unlisted, unpublished phone number, it would have been difficult for the average person to get it. One night I got a call that went something like this:

Caller: Is this Robert Luca?

Bob:　　Yes.

Caller: We are coming to your home to beat your a—.

Bob:　　You will need the right address. Do you have a pencil?

Caller: Yes.

Bob:　　Good…stick it up your —.

I hung up, but the recorder kept recording until the other party hung up as well. You could clearly hear the caller telling someone, in what I could only describe as a low, moose-like voice, "He told me to stick it up my a—." I then loaded my twelve-gauge shotgun just in case this was a serious call, but apparently it was not, as no one showed up at our home.

CHAPTER 13

What? Not Our Government?

• • •

THE WORST THING DONE TO US, and there is no doubt in my mind that this was the work of our own government or possibly the shadow government, was the following.

Betty and I had retired for the night, probably around half past eleven, and drifted off to sleep. Sometime later, I awoke and clearly heard two male voices in our kitchen. I looked to the side of the bedroom where our 110-pound Belgian shepherd, Brutus, usually slept on the floor at night. I was wondering why he did not bark. I saw him try to get up, and his front legs slipped out from under him. Down to the floor he went. Now aware that something was terribly wrong here, I reached for my revolver, which was in the nightstand next to the bed, so I could confront these men.

The next thing I knew, it was morning, and I awoke with a killer headache. Betty woke and complained of a bad headache as well. We ate breakfast, got ready for our respective jobs, and went off to work. All day long I had pain in my right arm (I am left-handed) for seemingly no reason. When I got home, Betty told me of the pain she'd endured all day in her left arm (she is right-handed). We both removed our shirts and were stunned to find we each had a black and blue circular area on our nondominant arm approximately one and a half inches in diameter that had what appeared to be a puncture mark in the center. I can surmise only that there must have been a sleep agent in the form of a gas put in the house, probably through one of the bedroom windows, to put us out long enough that the two men could enter the house and give us a shot that would keep us out for hours while they searched our home for whatever they were looking for…or perhaps they were there to question us while we were under the influence of whatever drug they administered to us.

An examination of the front door confirmed my suspicions, as there was evidence that someone had broken in. I had just a few days earlier painted the white trim around all the doors and windows. Since the front door did not have a bolt lock on it, it could have been opened easily by someone slipping a thin plastic or metal tool in to open it. In fact, locks like this could be opened with a credit card, something I had done myself in the past. Apparently this was the case, as it looked very much like someone had slipped a thin metal or plastic tool in to open the door, which had scraped off some of the fresh white paint. Unfortunately, we really did not know what could be done about this at the time, and we both felt completely helpless. We did consider calling the police, but would they even believe us, or would they think we were crazy? We decided the latter would more than likely be the case, so we did not make the call. During a visit to our family doctor, I asked him if any drug in our bodies could have been detected through a blood test. He was of the opinion that unless we'd had blood taken the same morning, it was highly unlikely that tests would have found anything.

Another interesting tactic was used while we were doing a radio show live from our home in Cheshire. Just before we had to call the station, I noticed a plain white van had pulled up and parked directly in front of our house on the opposite side of the street. This was followed by a black Cadillac, which parked right at the curb by our driveway and faced the wrong direction. Since the phone was on the wall in front of the glass in the front door, I could observe both vehicles from this viewpoint even while we were doing the hour-long radio interview. Interestingly, no one ever got out of either vehicle for the whole time we were on the radio. As the show drew to a close and the hosts were talking to Betty, I quickly went out to the front yard to see if I could determine who was in the car or at least see the license-plate number. I did not have much luck here, as it was a dark, moonless night, and the Cadillac apparently had dark tinted windows and no license plate on the front that I could see. I thought of going right up to the door and asking who this person was, but in light of past experiences, I thought better of it. The show was not even over, as Betty was still on the phone, when the van left; only seconds later, the Cadillac did too. The funny thing is that neither vehicle turned on its lights until they were down the road, which guaranteed I would not be able to see the license plates on either one.

Sometime after selling the Cheshire home, we purchased a thirty-foot-long fifth-wheel trailer. We lived in this year-round for some time, as I was more and more tired of working at my trade during the cold winter months in Connecticut. I was able to secure full-time employment in Florida during the winter months and return to my full-time job in Connecticut for the summer months. I really loved this, as during this period, we had the best of both worlds, so to speak.

One fall day when we were living in Higganum, Connecticut, we went off to do a lecture out of state, which meant we left the trailer unoccupied for a week or so. When we returned home, we were surprised to find our trailer wrapped with rope going completely around it top to bottom and securing the front door. Later I learned a thoughtful neighbor had done this after he returned home and found our trailer had been broken into. So again someone had broken in to our residence, which was no easy task, as the metal-frame doorjamb held two deadbolt-type locks very securely. The door had been destroyed, and the only things missing were some of Betty's drawings of the craft's interior. This ruled out a robbery, as our jewelry, computer equipment, and firearms went untouched. Apparently whoever had done this was familiar with the times people were at the campground, or he or she had spent some time casing the area, as no one saw or heard anything when this took place, even though there were trailers on both sides of us. We were in a rural area, so I had to call the local state trooper to investigate and verify the claim for my insurance company. I did explain to the trooper that we were heavily involved with the UFO phenomenon and that I felt it was probably some government agency that had done this, as opposed to a common thief. The trooper did not seem surprised to hear this and promised he would let us know whatever he found out. About a week later, I went to the trooper's office to ask if he had turned up anything. I was met by another trooper, who told me the trooper I had spoken to had been transferred out of our area shortly thereafter, and we never found who was responsible for the break-in. But because only the drawings were taken, we suspect government agencies, as these drawings would be of little interest to anyone else.

As time went on, the surveillance even progressed to the Department of Defense trying to hack into my computer. This turned out to be a big mistake on their part, as my security software caught them in the act. In a period of forty-eight hours, there were two attempts to gain access to my computer. The first one occurred on March 26, 2004, and was from a computer located at 7990 Science Applications Court in Vienna, Virginia; this was a DOD computer assigned to the Naval Space and Warfare Systems Department. The second attempt was two days later and originated from the same physical address; this attack came from a DOD computer assigned to the National Guard. I sent inquiries to both the army and navy asking why they were trying to get into my computer. I did receive a letter from the army Inspector General admitting that the computer numbers I had listed from my security software were, in fact, from the US Army National Guard and the navy's Space Warfare Systems Department, both of which were under the DOD's control.

As of this writing, I have never received an answer to my questions, and I have now filed Freedom of Information requests on both the army and navy for all relevant information pertaining to these attempts and any others that may have been successful. Now, in this particular instance, I was able to catch them; however, I believe they may have been successful at either an earlier attempt or perhaps even a later one using more sophisticated methods or hackers. I am pretty sure I know what they may have been looking for, and that information is not in my computer and never will be. I've included copies of the documents pertaining to the hacking of my computer on the following pages, along with my correspondence with the FBI, which finally admitted they did in fact have a file on us. If there is any further resolution to this situation before this writing is completed it will be included in this chapter. The thing that really irritates both my wife and me is that had they come and asked us for whatever they were looking for, we would have given it freely, meaning there was never any reason to put us through all they did. As it stands now, I personally would not give them the proper time of the day because of all they have unnecessarily put us through in the past. Just try to imagine what this operation cost taxpayers.

Again, on the following pages, readers will see the actual information displayed by my security software, as well as some of the Freedom of Information requests and letters I've written in an attempt to find out why the government was so interested in us or our computer, particularly as they claim UFOs pose no threat to national security.

Above the Law and Unaccountable

Many of you who are familiar with some or all of the Andreasson Affair books know that, because of our experiences, we have been trying to bring *truth* to the public, and it has been costly in a sense. Once we went public, the government began its program of trying to intimidate us to stop talking, using the following agencies.

The FBI—The FBI placed us under its surveillance, and we have witnesses who can verify this. The surveillance included our home being watched, and we were followed by cars whose license plates came back as unissued when run through police computers. FBI agents visited my place of employment when they lost track of us.

The IRS—We were subjected to yearly audits, starting the first year the *Andreasson Affair* was published. The audits were pure harassment and at times resulted in shouting matches between our CPA and the IRS auditor.

Air-Force Intelligence—I can't prove this one for certain, but when we questioned the FBI, they said they weren't tapping our phone and suggested it was air-force intelligence.

Department of Defense—My computer was hacked by two Department of Defense computers, which my security software identified. The first computer belonged to the US Navy Space and Naval Warfare Systems Division; forty-eight hours later, my computer was hacked again by the US Army National Guard. The government verified ownership of these computers, and the US Army Inspector General promised in writing that an investigation would be done. This never happened.

Unknown Intelligence Agency—Our home was the target of many flyovers by black military helicopters with no ID numbers, which is a violation of FAA regulations. These flights passed directly above our home, which is also a violation of FAA regulations, which state there must be a five-hundred-foot lateral distance between buildings and the helicopter. These helicopters also flew over us at a very low altitude (less than one hundred feet) while we were in our car. None of the government agencies I contacted could or would identify the owners of these aircraft, even when I sent them clear photos that included the date, time, compass heading, and approximate altitude of these flights. People I spoke to at the FAA General Aviation district office in the Boston jurisdiction said this sounded like a CIA operation. I could never verify that, but I *can* say that when I requested an interview with the CIA, they promptly turned me down.

Unknown Agency—Two men broke into our home in Cheshire and drugged us as we slept. I do not know which agency was responsible for this one, but I have my suspicions. Someone also broke into our home in Higganum, and although we had computer equipment, cameras, jewelry, and firearms in the home, the intruder took only two of Betty's drawings of the interior of the UFO craft she had been aboard. We reported the incident to the state police, but the intruders were never found.

There is more to this story than what I have written here, and even when queried under the Freedom of Information Act, none of these agencies admit to having information regarding any of these events, which is just another part of the cover-up. The FBI office in Richmond, Virginia, even refused to respond to my certified mail, as apparently I am on their PITA list. Also disturbing is the fact that none of the media outlets I have contacted, such as Fox News, are willing to do a story on this.

Apparently when it comes to the UFO phenomenon, these agencies *are above the law and not held accountable for their actions.* My wife and I have no criminal records. We are law-abiding citizens. However, in the eyes of these government agencies, we are criminals for trying to bring truth to the public, which has a right to know. Others have said, "The public has a right to know, and the government has a duty to tell.". It is a shame the government does not live up to this responsibility.

03/29/04

Office of The Naval Inspector General
1014 N. Street, SE. Suite 100
Washington Navy Yard, DC 20374-5006

Dear Sir,

I am writing your office to inquire about a recent attempt to hack in to my home computer by the DoD network information center, Space and Naval Warfare Systems Center, which is apparently located at 7990 science applications ct. M/S CV 50, Vienna VA. 22183-7000. Normally I would not be that interested in a random hack attempt on my computer, however as you can see by the attached documents there was a second attempt within approximately forty eight hours of the first one and it came from the same address only this time the computer workstation was different and it was listed as ARMY.MIL. I am sure you can understand why I am asking for your assistance in determining why these attempts took place at all.

Attached you will find copies of the information that was displayed from my security software regarding these attempts. I am curious as to why either of these offices would have any interest in the contents of my computer or even take the time and effort to attempt hacking in to it. I would appreciate your looking into this matter.

Sincerely,

Robert A. Luca

03/29/04

Office of the Inspector General
US Army Inspector General Agency
Department of The Army
1700 Pentagon
Washington DC 20320-1700

Dear Sir,

I am writing your office to inquire about a recent attempt to hack in to my home computer by the DoD Network Information Center, apparently located at 7990 science Applications Ct.. M/S CV 50, Vienna VA. 22183-7000. Normally I would not be that interested in a random hack attempt on my computer, however as you can see by the attached documents there was a prior attempt made from the same address approximately forty eight hours earlier. This attempt was initiated by the Space and Naval Warfare Center and the responsible computer was listed as NCC.NCTS.NAVY.MIL. I am sure you can see why I am asking for your assistance in determining why these attempts took place at all.

Attached you will find copies of the information that was displayed from my security software regarding these attempts. I am curious as to why either of these offices would have any interest in the contents of my computer or even take the time and effort to attempt hacking in to it. I would appreciate your looking into this matter.

The Navy has been sent a similar letter requesting assistance in this matter as well.

Sincerely,

Robert A. Luca

DEPARTMENT OF THE ARMY
OFFICE OF THE INSPECTOR GENERAL
1700 ARMY PENTAGON
WASHINGTON DC 20310-1700

May 3, 2004

Assistance Division

Mister Robert A. Luca

Dear Mister Luca,

We received your letter to the office of The Inspector General on April 12, 2004 requesting that an inquiry be conducted into several attempts to "hack" into your home computer.

We conducted a preliminary inquiry into your complaint and confirmed that the computer/servers you listed as supporting the incidents belonged to offices under the Department of Defense. Specifically, that one computer/server was controlled by the Department of the Navy and one by the Army National Guard. We referred this information to the Department of the Navy and Army National Guard Inspectors General for appropriate action and direct reply to you. We have assigned case number DIH 04-0533 to these matters.

Sincerely,

Jay Q. Smith
Lieutenant Colonel, U.S. Army
Inspector General

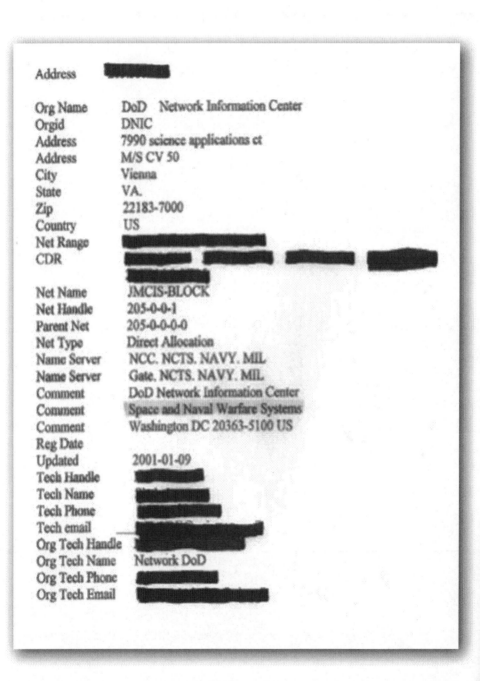

Address	████████
Org Name	DoD Network Information Center
Orgid	DNIC
Address	7990 science applications ct
Address	M/S CV 50
City	Vienna
State	VA.
Zip	22183-7000
Country	US
Net Range	████████████
CDR	████████ ████████ ████ ████████ ████████
Net Name	JMCIS-BLOCK
Net Handle	205-0-0-1
Parent Net	205-0-0-0-0
Net Type	Direct Allocation
Name Server	NCC. NCTS. NAVY. MIL
Name Server	Gate. NCTS. NAVY. MIL
Comment	DoD Network Information Center
Comment	Space and Naval Warfare Systems
Comment	Washington DC 20363-5100 US
Reg Date	
Updated	2001-01-09
Tech Handle	████████
Tech Name	████████
Tech Phone	████████
Tech email	████████
Org Tech Handle	████████
Org Tech Name	Network DoD
Org Tech Phone	████████
Org Tech Email	████████

Address   ▓▓▓▓▓▓▓▓

OrgName   DoD Network Information Center
Orgid   DNIC
Address   7990 Science Applications Ct
Address   M/S CV 50
City   Vienna
StateProv   VA
PostalCode   22183-7000
Country   US

NetRange   ▓▓▓▓▓▓▓▓▓▓▓▓▓▓▓▓
CIDR   ▓▓▓▓▓▓▓
NetName   RCAS
NetHandle   Net-▓▓▓▓▓▓▓

Parent
NetType   Direct Allocation
NameServer   ▓▓▓▓▓▓▓▓▓
NameServer   ▓▓▓▓▓▓▓▓▓
NameServer   ▓▓▓▓▓▓▓▓▓
Comment   Army National Guard Breau
Comment   NGB-RC-SDE
Comment   Newington VA 22020-8510 US
RegDate   1996-10-26
Updated   2002-10-07
OrgTechHandle   ▓▓▓▓▓▓▓▓▓
OrgTechName   Network DoD
OrgTechPhone   ▓▓▓▓▓▓▓▓▓
OrgTechEmail   ▓▓▓▓▓▓▓▓▓

Aug. 01, 2014

Senator Mark Warner
475 Russell Senate Office Building
Washington, DC 20510

Dear Senator Warner,

I am writing your office in the hope that you may help resolve an ongoing problem I am having with both the Army and the Navy under the offices of the Department of Defense. Some time ago an attempt to hack into my computer was made by both the Army National Guard and the Navy Space and Naval Warfare systems both located at the DOD network Information Center 7990 Science Applications CT. M/S CV 50 Vienna VA 22183-7000.

I have filed FOIA requests regarding these incidents and have in my opinion been totally ignored to the point that even though the Navy was sent my request via certified mail I never got my receipt back and in fact have never even had my request to the Navy acknowledged. I know it is illegal to hack personal or any other computers and I have a good idea of why these departments tried to hack into mine but that still does not excuse them. I believe I have a right to the information I have requested and furthermore I believe the responsible parties have an obligation to reply. I did get a response from the Army stating that I may be charged for search time if they honor my request and to be honest that angered me. They hacked into my computer, something I was not responsible for, and I have to pay for a records search when I sent them the exact date this took place? My anger was probably obvious in my reply and I apologize for that.

At any rate I have enclosed copies of all of the Documents containing relevant information and proof of the hack attempts. I am hopeful that with your help this situation may be resolved.

Sincerely,

Robert A. Luca

MARK R. WARNER
VIRGINIA

United States Senate
WASHINGTON, DC 20610-4606

COMMITTEES:

BANKING, HOUSING, AND
URBAN AFFAIRS

COMMERCE, SCIENCE, AND
TRANSPORTATION

BUDGET

RULES AND ADMINISTRATION

INTELLIGENCE

JOINT ECONOMIC COMMITTEE

October 17, 2014

Mr. Robert Luca

Dear Mr. Luca,

Enclosed you will find the response from the U.S. Department of the Navy Inspector General (NAVINSGEN) to my inquiry on your behalf. I hope that the information provided will be helpful and responsive to your specific concerns.

My staff and I stand ready to be of assistance to you in any other matter that is of concern to you. Thank you.

Sincerely,

Mark R Warner

MARK R. WARNER
United States Senator

MRW/kp
Enclosure

180 WEST MAIN STREET
ABINGDON, VA 24210
PHONE: (276) 628-8158
FAX: (276) 626-1306

101 WEST MAIN STREET
SUITE 4900
NORFOLK, VA 23510
PHONE: (757) 441-3079
FAX: (757) 441-6250

919 EAST MAIN STREET
SUITE 630
RICHMOND, VA 23219
PHONE: (804) 775-2314
FAX: (804) 775-2319

1255 SALEM AVENUE, SW
ROANOKE, VA 24011
PHONE: (540) 857-2676
FAX: (540) 857-2800

8000 TOWERS CRESCENT DRIVE
SUITE 200
VIENNA, VA 22182
PHONE: (703) 442-0670
FAX: (703) 442-0408

http://warner.senate.gov

PRINTED ON RECYCLED PAPER

DEPARTMENT OF THE NAVY
NAVAL INSPECTOR GENERAL
1254 9TH STREET SE
WASHINGTON NAVY YARD DC 20374-5006

IN REPLY REFER TO:
5041/201402916
Ser N615/1091
October 10, 2014

The Honorable Mark R. Warner
United States Senator
ATTN: Ms. Katie Pillis
919 East Main Street
Richmond, VA 23219

U.S. Senator Mark Warner

OCT 16 2014

Richmond

Dear Senator Warner:

This is a final response to your letter of August 14, 2014, to Ms. Elizabeth King, Assistant Secretary of Defense for Legislative Affairs, on behalf of your constituent, Mr. Robert A. Luca. Mr. Luca alleged he submitted a Freedom of Information Act (FOIA) request to the Naval Inspector General (NAVINSGEN) for all documents containing relevant information regarding attempts made to hack into his personal computer in the 2004 timeframe. He alleged that NAVINSGEN ignored and never acknowledged his FOIA request. The Secretary of the Navy forwarded your letter to NAVINSGEN to respond on his behalf.

We reviewed Mr. Luca's allegations and the supporting information. Our records indicate that Mr. Luca submitted a FOIA request to NAVINSGEN on April 3, 2014. Enclosed you will find a copy of Mr. Luca's request and NAVINSGEN's response dated June 25, 2014. As stated in our response, we searched our database for any records responsive to Mr. Luca's request but were unable to locate any such record. Additionally, NAVINSGEN forwarded a copy of Mr. Luca's request to the Commander, Space and Naval Warfare Systems Command, FOIA office for their consideration and appropriate action.

We hope this information will be of assistance to you in responding to Mr. Luca.

Sincerely,

ANDREA E. BROTHERTON
Deputy

Enclosure:
1. FOIA Request
2. NAVINSGEN Response

November 28, 2014

United States Attorney General
Executive Office for United States Attorneys
United States Department of Justice
950 Pennsylvania Ave, NW, Room 2242
Washington DCX 20530–0001

Dear Attorney General,

I am filing a complaint with your Office regarding <u>two illegal hacks </u>into my personal computer. One by the United States Navy Space and Naval Warfare Systems Division and forty eight hours later a second one by the US Army National Guard Bureau both of these illegal intrusions were captured by my security software (see copies enclosed). Both of these Hacks originated from The DOD Network Information Center located at 7990 Science Applications Ct. M/S CV 50 Vienna VA. 22183–7000. As you can see by the enclosed Documents when I requested information on why these intrusions took place I was promised by the US Army Inspector General that an investigation would be done. To this Date this has not happened. I have on more than one occasion filed FOIA requests on both the navy and the US Army responsible offices and still have had no explanation forthcoming, in fact I have been ignored. The last filing on these incidents was approximately three months ago and was done by my state senator Mark Warner, on my behalf, again with the same results, that being no answers. The claim has been that the Documents, or files can not be found. I find this hard to believe since the information I have provided includes the exact date of each incident as well as the responsible parties and even the ID number of the computers involved as well as the physical street address.

I have enclosed all related Documents for your viewing in trusting that your office may obtain the information I have requested from these DOD departments. The information requested has included why these hacks or intrusions took place, What information in my computer was being sought, what information was taken and what files are these offices in possession of regarding myself? Since I have virtually no criminal record of any type and am a law abiding citizen I can't help but wonder why I have received this type treatment from these offices or what they consider to be of such interest or value that may be in my computer in my computer.

I sincerely believe that your office can assist me in finding the answers to the questions that I have posed in my prior requests to these offices. Quite frankly I believe these offices had no intention of ever answering my requests and that is the real reason for the run around I have experienced with them for so long. I have no doubt that appealing this will produce no results which is why I have contacted your office directly.

Sincerely,

Robert A. Luca

These are a few of the many correspondences I have had with government offices regarding the hacking of my home computer. It's clear from these letters that there is no desire on the government's part to confirm these hacks, even though the Inspector General's letter included in this section above shows that he acknowledged the hacks. I find it amazing that they can so conveniently misplace documents that are clearly labeled with case numbers, names, and dates.

The documents on the following pages again represent only some of the correspondence I had with the FBI regarding their having us under surveillance and their refusal to investigate the hacking of my computer by the Department of Defense.

Jan. 25, 2015

FBI
170 Marcel, Drive
Winchester, VA 22602

RE: Request NO 13

Dear Sir/Madam,

I am writing to request information regarding the status of my Freedom of

Information Request which was received by your Office on Oct 07 2015.

Attached please find copy of the certified mail receipt verifying that your Office

Did receive my request on Oct. 07 2015.

Sincerely,

Robert A. Luca

FBI Richmond
1970 E. Parham Road
Richmond VA 23228

Feb. 28 2015

Dear Sir / Madam,

I am writing you as directed by the US Attorneys office regarding what I am
sure is a federal crime which is the hacking of my home computer by the
DOD US Space and Naval Warfare Systems Dept. and forty eight hours later
another hack attempt by another DOD computer belonging to the US Army
National Guard Bureau. Both of these intrusions in to my computer were
identified by my security software and ownership of the offending
computers was verified by the Army Inspector General. I was promised, in
writing, that an investigation into this matter would be done. This has not
happened and when I filed FIOA requests regarding this incident I was told
the related documents could not be found. I find this hard to believe since in
my requests I have clearly included the dates, physical street address of the
offending computers, computer ID and case numbers. In short I have been
given a runaround. The fact that these computers belong to the Military in no
way changes the fact that this hacking into my computer is a crime. If the
situation were reversed and I attempted to hack into the offending computers
in my case I am certain there would be swift and harsh punishment. I have
enclosed the Documents that are related to this incident which has dragged
on for too long now. Should you have any questions or need further
information you may contact me at the above address or phone
        My email is   I am sorry to have to bring this
to your office but the parties responsible have not lived up to their promise
of an investigation and as I mentioned this has gone on too long.

Sincerely,

Robert A. Luca

FBI Richmond
1970 E. Parham Road
Richmond VA 23228

June 22 2015

Dear Sir / Madam,

Enclosed you will find a copy of a letter that was sent to your office six
months ago regarding the hacking of my computer by the US Navy Space
and Naval Warfare Systems Dept, and forty eight hours later another hack
by the US Army National Guard Bureau. Both of these computers obviously
committing illegal acts are under the control of the Department of Defense.
Regardless of that fact the hacking of my computer is in violation of Federal
law as is the violation of my personal privacy rights.
I realize the offices of the FBI are in fact busy, however according to recent
news articles not so busy that time can not be taken to investigate the
hacking of the Huston Astros sports team by the St Louis cardinals team.
Quite frankly, I, along with many others that I have spoken with don't think
the sports team hacking is anywhere near as serious as hacking done by the
United States Department of Defense computers from the US Navy Space
and Naval Warfare Systems Dept, and the Army National Guard Bureau.
Once again these acts are illegal under Federal law and according to
information I received from the US Attorney Generals office fall under the
jurisdiction of the FBI to investigate.

The president of the US has stated repeatedly that he promotes and expects
transparency in our government. I sincerely would like to see an example of
that transparency in this case.

Sincerely,

Robert A. Luca

Certified Mail #7013 3020 0002 2464

U.S. Department of Justice

Federal Bureau of Investigation
Washington, D.C. 20535

March 7, 2016

MR. ROBERT A LUCA

FOIPA Request No.:   -000
Subject: LUCA, ROBERT

Dear Mr. Luca:

This is in response to your Freedom of Information Privacy Acts (FOIPA) request.

Records which may have been responsive to your request were destroyed on February 08, 2010. Since this material could not be reviewed, it is not known if it was responsive to your request. Record retention and disposal is carried out under supervision of the National Archives and Records Administration (NARA), Title 44, United States Code, Section 3301 and Title 36, Code of Federal Regulations, Chapter 12, Sub-chapter B, Part 1228. The FBI Records Retention Plan and Disposition Schedules have been approved by the United States District Court for the District of Columbia and are monitored by NARA.

By standard FBI practice and pursuant to FOIA exemption (b)(7)(E) [5 U.S.C. § 552] and Privacy Act exemption (j)(2) [5 U.S.C. §552a] , this response neither confirms nor denies the existence of your subject's name on any watch lists.

For your information, Congress excluded three discrete categories of law enforcement and national security records from the requirements of the FOIA. See 5 U.S. C. § 552(c) (2006 & Supp. IV (2010). This response is limited to those records that are subject to the requirements of the FOIA. This is a standard notification that is given to all our requesters and should not be taken as an indication that excluded records do, or do not, exist.

For questions regarding our determinations, visit the www.fbi.gov/foia website under "Contact Us." The FOIPA Request number listed above has been assigned to your request. Please use this number in all correspondence concerning your request. Your patience is appreciated.

You may file an appeal by writing to the Director, Office of Information Policy (OIP), U.S. Department of Justice, 1425 New York Ave., NW, Suite 11050, Washington, D.C. 20530-0001, or you may submit an appeal through OIP's eFOIA portal at http://www.justice.gov/oip/efoia-portal.html. Your appeal to OIP must be postmarked or transmitted within sixty (60) days from the date of this letter in order to be considered timely. The envelope and the letter should be clearly marked "Freedom of Information Appeal." Please cite the FOIPA Request Number in any correspondence to us for proper identification of your request.

Oct. 05, 2015

FBI
170 Marcel, Drive
Winchester, VA 22602

Dear Sir/Madam,

RE: Request NO 1336773-000

I am writing to request all information that your Department may be in possession of concerning myself. To the best of my knowledge my wife and I were under surveillance for the whole of the 1980's and a portion of the 1990's as well. The reason I am certain of this is that while living at   around the period of 1984 – 1986 my wife and I left home for a FL vacation at around 2:00 – 3:00 am on a Sunday morning. During the following week two FBI agents with photo ID came to my place of employment which was   and questioned my co workers and supervisors as to my whereabouts. Also during the 1980's our home phone was tapped and this was verified by Lawrence Fawcett a Coventry CT Police lieutenant. During this time period we were often followed by vehicles whose license plates, on occasion, I was able to record. Several times these plate numbers came back as "un-issued" which again made me suspect FBI ownership of these vehicles. When I visited the FBI Office in New Haven CT during this time period I was told they "could not confirm or deny they had been at my place of employment" even though my former co workers have stated they were there as a matter of public record. As far as the telephone being tapped the agent I spoke to in the New Haven office claimed it was not the FBI tapping our phone but more than likely it was Air Force Intelligence. When I questioned Air Force Intelligence they replied it was not them and more than likely it was the FBI. Also during this time period we were repeatedly over flown by Black unmarked helicopters both at our home and while on vacation. The Helicopters were usually Sikorsky Blackhawk or Huey UH 1 models and displayed no ID numbers which was verified by viewing them through binoculars as well as photographing them. I have hundreds of photo's of these very low flying Helicopters, which at times flew less than 100 feet AGL, directly over our home or car, which is in total violation of Federal regulations. I also have numerous witnesses including police officers, newspaper reporters, local politicians and professional photographers as well as neighbors, to verify these over flights. Also during this time period I had Contacted The FAA GADO in Boston, FBI, CIA,

The Pentagon, all branches of the Military and Helicopter Manufactures in CT as well. I included with my letters Date, time, Photos, compass heading, and approximate altitude yet no one could tell me the owners of these Helicopters as there were no ID numbers and apparently no flight plans filed, however it is a given that these aircraft are owned by some branch of the US Government or Military as far as I am concerned. I have enclosed four photos for your viewing.

I also had contacted Bell Helicopter in Texas that manufacture the Huey Helicopters and was told at least one of the photos I sent of a Helicopter that circled us several times was a particular model that was modified by the Air Force for psychological warfare in Vietnam, please see Document enclosed.

I am also interested in the 2014 time period as I had contacted the FBI office in Richmond VA regarding the hacking of my home computer by the US Navy Space Weapons Systems Division and a second attack forty eight hours later by the US Army National Guard Bureau. These hacks took place back in 2004 and when I wrote the Inspectors General of the Army and Navy I was promised, in writing, that an investigation into this would take place. To date this has not happened. When I filed FOIA on both of these offices the claim was that they could find no documentation on this even though I gave them very specific information including the case number assigned (see documents enclosed). Even though this much time has passed the information copied from my security software can not be denied. The Richmond FBI office never gave me the courtesy of a reply and when I sent them another letter six months after the first one, sent certified mail with a return receipt, it was never signed for and was returned to me unopened. I am aware the FBI has investigated the hacking done by sports teams and I consider the hacking by these two DOD computers to be a much more serious offense, especially, considering that if you check my background you will see I retired from the Palm Beach County Sheriffs Dept. in 2004 and have No criminal record and neither does my wife. When I lived in Florida and worked for the Sheriffs Department my home address was

There is much more than what I have put in this letter but I realize how valuable your time is so I have tried to keep it to a minimum.

If any further information is needed please feel free to contact me at the phone number provided   or at the above address.

Sincerely,

Robert A. Luca

U.S. Department of Justice

Federal Bureau of Investigation
Washington, D.C. 20535

March 7, 2016

MR. ROBERT A LUCA

FOIPA Request No.:   -000
Subject: LUCA, ROBERT

Dear Mr. Luca:

This is in response to your Freedom of Information Privacy Acts (FOIPA) request.

Records which may have been responsive to your request were destroyed on February 08, 2010. Since this material could not be reviewed, it is not known if it was responsive to your request." Record retention and disposal is carried out under supervision of the National Archives and Records Administration (NARA), Title 44, United States Code, Section 3301 and Title 36, Code of Federal Regulations, Chapter 12, Sub-chapter B, Part 1228. The FBI Records Retention Plan and Disposition Schedules have been approved by the United States District Court for the District of Columbia and are monitored by NARA.

By standard FBI practice and pursuant to FOIA exemption (b)(7)(E) [5 U.S.C. § 552] and Privacy Act exemption (j)(2) [5 U.S.C. §552a] , this response neither confirms nor denies the existence of your subject's name on any watch lists.

For your information, Congress excluded three discrete categories of law enforcement and national security records from the requirements of the FOIA. See 5 U.S. C. § 552(c) (2006 & Supp. IV (2010). This response is limited to those records that are subject to the requirements of the FOIA. This is a standard notification that is given to all our requesters and should not be taken as an indication that excluded records do, or do not, exist.

For questions regarding our determinations, visit the www.fbi.gov/foia website under "Contact Us." The FOIPA Request number listed above has been assigned to your request. Please use this number in all correspondence concerning your request. Your patience is appreciated.

You may file an appeal by writing to the Director, Office of Information Policy (OIP), U.S. Department of Justice, 1425 New York Ave., NW, Suite 11050, Washington, D.C. 20530-0001, or you may submit an appeal through OIP's eFOIA portal at http://www.justice.gov/oip/efoia-portal.html. Your appeal to OIP must be postmarked or transmitted within sixty (60) days from the date of this letter in order to be considered timely. The envelope and the letter should be clearly marked "Freedom of Information Appeal." Please cite the FOIPA Request Number in any correspondence to us for proper identification of your request.

U.S. Department of Justice

Federal Bureau of Investigation
Washington, D.C. 20535

April 11, 2016

MR. ROBERT A LUCA

Request No.:
Subject: A request for a criminal
investigation regarding the hacking of a
home computer

Dear Mr. Luca:

This is in response to your Freedom of Information Act (FOIA) request.

Your request for a criminal investigation regarding the hacking of your home computer under the control of DOD is not searchable in our indices. For your information, the FBI Central Records System is not arranged in a manner that allows for the retrieval of information in the form for which you have requested. Items are indexed according to individual investigatory interests and not for a criminal investigation regarding the hacking of your home computer under the control of DOD.

The FOIA does not require federal agencies to answer inquiries, create records, conduct research, or draw conclusions concerning queried data. Rather the FOIA requires agencies to provide access to reasonably described, nonexempt records.

For questions on how to reasonably describe your request, please email us at foipaquestions@ic.fbi.gov. You may also visit www.fbi.gov and select "Stats and Services," "FOIA/Records Requests," and "Requesting FBI Records" for additional guidance.

You may file an appeal by writing to the Director, Office of Information Policy (OIP), United States Department of Justice, Suite 11050, 1425 New York Avenue, NW, Washington, D.C. 20530-0001, or you may submit an appeal through OIP's FOIAonline portal by creating an account on the following web site: https://foiaonline.regulations.gov/foia/action/public/home. Your appeal must be postmarked or electronically transmitted within sixty (60) days from the date of this letter in order to be considered timely. If you submit your appeal by mail, both the letter and the envelope should be clearly marked "Freedom of Information Act Appeal." Please cite the FOIPA Request Number assigned to your request so that it may be easily identified.

Enclosed for your information is a copy of the FBI Fact Sheet.

Sincerely,

David M. Hardy
Section Chief,
Record/Information
 Dissemination Section
Records Management Division

Enclosure

CHAPTER 14

Defensive? Not Us

• • •

When the first Andreasson Affair book came out, Betty and I had already been forewarned about the government's policy of spreading disinformation, debunking, ridiculing, and doing anything they could to discredit those who tried to tell their stories of UFO sightings or abductions. Who could forget some of the ridiculous explanations—such as swamp gas or Venus, when the planet was not even visible in the night sky—that were put out to make witnesses look foolish? Even those considered credible at the time like astronomer Dr. J. Alan Hynek, former scientific advisor of three air force UFO-related projects. Sign Grudge, and Bluebook. Dr. Hynek worked on Project Bluebook, which lasted from 1952 to 1969, and admitted he had found that some of the more credible cases were never listed in Bluebook files.

Dr. Hynek approached Betty while she and I were attending a conference at MIT. Betty was alone at the time, and he told her quietly, "Betty, stick to philosophy, and leave the military out of this." Apparently he was referring to my constant questioning of various military and other government offices. I must have been striking a nerve someplace in the military community for Dr. Hynek to relay this warning to Betty, which I thought was very considerate and kind of him. I believe now, as many others do, that Bluebook was nothing more than a public-relations program to make the public think the air force had everything under control though, in fact, they did not. The truth is they were powerless to do anything other than observe when UFOs flew over our nation's capital on July 19, 20, 26, and 27 back in 1952. And apparently that had not changed by 1969, when the air force used a bogus study known as the Condon Report to publicly extricate themselves from the UFO problem altogether. This was another display for the public that was not entirely true, as documents found after 1969 indicate that the air force were still very much interested in this phenomenon. As for Dr. Hynek, he had an obvious change of thought as time passed. In his 1977 book titled *The Hynek UFO Report*, Hynek admitted he had enjoyed his previous role as a debunker, which was what the air force expected of him.

As you will see, the government, or possibly the shadow government, began a program of intimidation on us even before the Andreasson Affair books were published. Betty and I had decided we were not going to lie down or bend to any pressure they would apply. As you have seen in this book, government agencies used a number of methods to try to intimidate us but never took a really direct approach, though we took an aggressive stance with them almost from the start. They started with the black helicopters flying over our home or any other place we happened to be.

The second thing we were aware of was the tap on our telephone, which police officer Larry Fawcett verified. After Larry and I finished a phone conversation, I hung up, and Larry was just about to hang up as well when he heard a man's voice ask, "Did you get them both on tape?" We further verified this with an electronic tap detector I purchased after this occurred. The tap detector did, in fact, indicate the presence of taps on our home phone and on Betty's work phone.

I decided to investigate both of these situations, starting with the helicopters. I started taking photos of the flights, being careful to document the date, time, compass heading, and approximate altitude of these flights. Once I'd collected enough of these incidents, I started trying to track down these helicopters' owners. I contacted the Federal Aviation Administration's General Aviation District Office in the Boston area. The fact that these military helicopters were flying so low, and so often, over a residential area meant they should have been traceable. But when the FAA responded, they said they could not identify these helicopters, as there were no identifying numbers on them. The fact that they were all black and had no ID numbers was why I had contacted the FAA in the first place. One FAA employee, Sam Martino, was interested enough to drive from his home in Massachusetts down to our home in Cheshire, Connecticut, to talk to us. Unfortunately, he came unannounced on a Saturday, and we were not home, but he did leave a note on our front door. A few years later, when questioned about this by *Connecticut Magazine*, Mr. Martino responded that he had only a vague memory of this. I thought this response was strange, considering he'd taken his own time on a weekend to drive down to Connecticut. Yet another FAA person I had contacted said our experiences sounded like a CIA operation. A CIA operation? They are not supposed to do any domestic spying, as far as I know. But finally new evidence surfaced. I had already contacted the FAA, CIA, FBI, air force, US Army National Guard, helicopter manufacturers, and Aircraft and Pilots Association, and no one was able, or willing, to identify the owners of these helicopters. Finally, I contacted Bell Helicopter in Texas, who manufactures the Huey helicopter, and sent a photo of one of the helicopters that had flown over us. I received a letter from a Mr. Dick Tipton, who at the time was the public information officer for Bell Helicopter. He notified me that the helicopter in the photo was one of theirs; however, Mr. Tipton said this helicopter had been modified by the air force for use in psychological warfare in Vietnam. I still have that letter to this day. Now, the question is, what in the world does this type of helicopter have to do with Betty and I? Is it just keeping track of our whereabouts, or is it supposed to be trying to intimidate us?

Over the years that followed, I contacted air-force headquarters at the Pentagon to try to get some sensible answers from them regarding the statements they had publicly issued regarding the UFO phenomenon. I soon found that no such answers would be forthcoming, and eventually an FBI representative told me no one there would talk to me. Of course, there was always the possibility that someone might slip up and answer one of my questions honestly, so I recorded my phone conversations with them in the hopes this might happen. I also contacted Wright-Patterson Air Force Base and got the same nonanswers from them as well. Unwilling to give up so easily, I contacted the CIA at Langley and explained that Betty and I were planning on writing a UFO-related book and would like to set up an interview with them. The CIA quickly turned us down, offering no explanation of why our request was denied.

On yet another occasion, Betty and I were doing a three-part series on the channel-eight news in Connecticut. I mentioned that the FBI was in fact involved in the UFO phenomenon. They quickly denied this accusation, saying they had enough to do in dealing with crime here, which made it look like I was lying about their involvement. I was not. Somewhat angered by this, I challenged the FBI to appear on a radio or a TV show with us and discuss not what Betty and I had experienced, but rather talk about the FBI documents I was in possession of, which organizations such as Citizens Against UFO Secrecy and I myself had obtained legally. As expected, they declined.

Moving on from there, Betty and I decided on a trip to Florida that it would be nice to spend a day at Cape Kennedy, taking in some of the marvels our space program had developed. We also thought it might be a good idea to interview the NASA administrator while we were there. We approached the guard station and explained that we were doing research for a book and would like to interview the administrator while we were there. The guard made a phone call, and in just a few minutes, we were told to proceed to the administrator's office to interview him. To say we were elated to be granted an interview on such short notice would be an understatement, as we hoped to put forth some hard questions regarding NASA's knowledge of and involvement with the UFO phenomenon. The long walk from where we were to the office seemed to take forever, as we could not wait to get started. Well, our hopes were soon dashed. When we reached the office, a visibly shaken secretary told us the administrator was not in his office, even though we'd been told only minutes earlier that he was. We hadn't said what the interview was about, only that we were doing research for a book we were writing. Neither of us had mentioned UFOs, but apparently someone had recognized us or at least had an idea of who we were, and it became apparent that NASA wanted no part of us or the questions we would ask regarding UFOs. It now appeared that these government agencies did not like being on the receiving end of this situation, which they had tried to keep us on.

Well, if they were not happy with us then, they would soon see that they had reason to be even more upset with us. In September 1982, the *Hartford Current* published a newspaper article on us; Mister Larry Warren read this article, which only made things worse for those in government who were working so hard to keep facts regarding UFOs from the public. You see, Larry Warren was one of the airmen present when the now famous landing at Bentwaters Air Force Base in the United Kingdom took place. Larry called me at my job and explained that he had been in the military and was witness to a UFO incident while on active duty in the service. To be honest, I did not know if I believed him at that point. As it turned out, Larry had just had dental work done, and his speech was kind of strange. Since we had been pranked before by jokers, I really did not know what to make of this person on the other end of the phone line. I decided if there was a chance he was legitimate, it certainly would be worth talking to him, so we invited him to our home. This was a wise choice. Larry arrived at our home and turned out to be a very friendly, serious, honest, and likable person, which we determined after spending many hours interviewing him and recording his testimony. There was no doubt in my mind that this young man was relating to us an actual event that had taken place in his life, exactly as he remembered it. We spent hours listening to and recording Larry's explanation of what he saw, as well as viewing the diagrams he drew for us. Now there was a problem for Betty and me, as I realized we did not have the experience or necessary resources to treat this extremely important case with the necessary expertise. We decided to put Larry in touch with Larry Fawcett, a police lieutenant and UFO investigator who was involved in our case. Larry Fawcett and Barry Greenwood, a Massachusetts UFO investigator, were both heavily involved in investigating the phenomenon and, at the time, were penning a book titled *Clear Intent* on the government's cover-up of the UFO experience. Since Larry Fawcett was one of the founders of Citizens against UFO Secrecy (CAUS), the pair had access to attorneys and researchers, which we did not. It was obvious to us that they could do more good for Larry than we could.

As time went on, I wrote the British Ministry of Defense and questioned them about the Bentwaters UFO incident. The reply was as expected. In their letter, a copy of which I have posted on my Facebook page, they stated that the whole story was a hoax. I also filed a Freedom of Information Act request on the US Air Force, and they responded that, because this was a nonevent, the air force had done no investigation. In my opinion, this is just another load of BS from the air force. I posted this response on my Facebook page as well. Today, of course, we know the Ministry of Defense and the air force were the ones who were lying, not Larry Warren. Larry's contacting us and the resulting story that came out due to CAUS's research and hard work, coupled with Larry Warren's bravery in bringing this important information forth, was just one more reason for the powers that be to be even more upset with us, as well as with Larry. It appeared that after Larry contacted us, the surveillance became even more intense.

ANDREASSON AFFAIR...A HOAX?

I am sure many of you whom have read the account of the Andreasson Affair being a hoax may wonder if this is true. Well, someone *was* perpetrating a hoax...but it wasn't us; that misinformation came from those who put forth this story without doing any investigation at all into the information's source. This is shabby journalism at best.

The real story here is that Robert Luca Jr. was not a close family member at all, as these articles stated. Unfortunately, in his adulthood, Robert became involved with alcohol and drugs, possibly due to the amount of prescription medication he was on earlier in his life. This led him to create serious problems with me when my father passed away. Robert Jr. accused me of changing the will and made numerous calls to the attorney who'd made the will and even threatened to sue the attorney. The fact is that in my father's original will, he left nothing to his grandchildren. When he revised his will, I suggested that it would be nice for him to leave something to each of them. He agreed and left the sum of $5,000 to each of them. Robert was not satisfied with this and created the previously mentioned problems. This, along with a number of other situations Jr. had created with family members, led me to disown my son and inform him that, when I passed, I would leave him absolutely nothing. Robert Jr. obviously was not happy about this, and the fictional account he posted on his website was his way of getting back at me. Any rational person who read what Robert Jr. had to say could see instantly that this whole account simply did not make sense. As for Betty, he knew very little about her life or the lives of her children. On the rare occasions when he did visit, it was with me, and once in a while, he would stay long enough to have a meal with us. Unfortunately, due to his addictions, he became more and more unstable and would not admit he had a problem. Robert was taken more than once for psychological evaluation because of his actions. Skeptics should consult the Meriden, Connecticut, *Record-Journal* newspaper for the story on Robert J. Luca. I've included a copy of the front page of this newspaper below. This story gives a good indication of Robert's mental and psychological state back as far as 2002. Sadly, Robert Jr. passed away at age forty-three. This, in my opinion, was a result of his lifestyle. There is of course much more to this, but it would not be proper to bring anything more up, as Robert is no longer with us, and I don't think it would be right to do so.

Record-Journal

HOME • NEWS • OPINIONS • CELEBRATIONS • SPORTS • CLASSIFIEDS • OBITUARIES
ARCHIVES • FEATURES • BUSINESS DIRECTORY • SUBSCRIBE

TODAY'S W

18
more

The Record Journal
E-Paper

New Search   Return to results   Printer Friendly

- Login to the
  E-Paper

About your archives purchase:
Your purchase of articles expires on .
You have viewed articles and have articles remaining.

- Subscribe to
  the E-Paper

- Purchase a
  single copy

- See how it
  works

Record-Journal (Meriden, CT)

INDEX OF
TODAY'S
EDITION

SUBMIT A
CLASSIFIED AD

ARCHIVES

SUBMIT A
LETTER TO
THE EDITOR

SUBMIT AN
ANNOUNCEMENT

PHOTO GALLERY &
REPRINTS

MARKETPLACE

ABOUT US

CONTACT US

LOGIN

Resident talked out of taking his life

Evan Goodenow, Record-Journal staff
Published: March 12, 2002

MERIDEN - With his .44 magnum by his side, Robert Luca telephoned police Monday morning and told Sgt. Michael Zakrzewski that he wanted police to remove his mother from his 14 Genest St. residence so she wouldn't be there when he committed suicide.

Police notified the SWAT team and evacuated neighbors, but after about 30 minutes, Zakrzewski talked Luca out of suicide. "It's very satisfying. That's why I do it," said Zakrzewski, a member of the police department's crisis negotiation team, which works in tandem with the SWAT team.

At 10:30 a.m., Luca, 36, telephoned police. Dispatcher Diane Larson tried to calm him while summoning Zakrzewski. Police evacuated a handful of neighbors from around the one-family house in the quiet neighborhood off Murray and Dyer streets. "We had no idea who was in the house or the danger there was to surrounding residents, so they activated SWAT," police spokesman Sgt. Lenny Caponigro said.

Negotiators try to get the subject they're dealing with to talk for as long as possible. "Time is your ally," Zakrzewski said, adding that Larson did a good job keeping Luca calm. Police said Luca's mother was asleep at the time of the incident and was never in any danger. Luca surrendered at about 11:15 a.m. and was taken to MidState Medical Center for psychiatric evaluation. He was not charged, but the magnum and a .22 caliber semi-automatic pistol were seized.

"It was a nice effort by the sergeant to talk him into surrendering without further incident. As we know, these scenes can sometimes turn ugly and dangerous," Police Chief William C. Abbatematteo said.

Our Publications:

The Berlin
Citizen

The Plainville
Citizen

The Southington
Citizen

CHAPTER 15

What? Liquid Mercury!

• • •

FOR THOSE WHO ARE INTERESTED in the science of UFOs, I have revealed and added what I have seen during my encounters within the Andreasson Affair series. All I can give are the details I was able to see while in the interior and exterior presence of the craft. One time I remembered seeing a circular arrangement of triangular boxes and a large round tube. Another time I was told that mercury was one of the substances they were using within their craft. Of course I passed this information on to investigators, Raymond Fowler, and Paul Potter many years ago and then forgot about it. I did sketch a quick drawing of the honeycombed box in an upper room and an elongated tubelike extension below, including the lower circular tube around the three-stemmed crystal orbs and crystal wheels that were centrally located beneath the craft; I've included that drawing in this book.

This is what happened to jog my memory concerning the beings' mention of mercury: I had forgotten all about the mercury until recently, when Bonnie visited me the day before Thanksgiving 2014. She said she and her brother were curious and were trying to recall where the location of the outside entrance to the cellar was when we lived in the South Ashburnham home. During the course of the conversation, I described to her the layout of the house before we changed some rooms and later sold it. Outside of this house, about twenty-five feet to the right, there must have been a large barn or building at one time connected to the property, because there was a five-foot-high wall of concrete foundation there. Half of this foundation had been capped and made into a wooden garage, while the remaining half of the cement wall, at the end of our property, was like a concrete *U* shape, with the opening toward the front. The children would play in there quite often. And forty-seven years later, my daughter happened to mention to me that when she was little, she'd found a pool or puddle of shiny mercury on top of the foundation wall. Being somewhat curious, my children never realized the imminent danger involved with handling and playing with the pretty, shiny substance, which happens to be a poisonous metal. She said she'd slid the mercury back and forth in the palms of her hands. Some had dropped to the cement floor, where it had formed little silver bubbles.

Shocked, I said, "What? Mercury is poisonous! Why were you kids playing with it? Why didn't you tell me?" Of course they hadn't realized its danger. Where in the world had it come from? You can believe I was very upset and full of questions. Even though it had happened many years ago, I was very alarmed to learn my children had handled mercury like liquid Play-Doh. She continued to tell me the mercury had been on top of the cement foundation and that the other kids had seen and handled it as well. My mind was racing. Thank God the children had been all right. But the question remained: Where could that mercury have come from? It is not something that grows on a cement foundation. Today, in my mind, I tried to think back to what the being had said about the craft's use of mercury. Back in 1967, a UFO had quietly landed on the slight hill behind our house. The new information concerning mercury on the cement wall, which Bonnie had innocently mentioned to me, helped to jog my memory, for it was during my abduction that they'd briefly revealed that they used mercury in their ship. I went through so much during the abduction that it was hard to remember everything they were showing me.

Fortunately, I had drawn and labeled pictures of the machine's mechanism, which helped me to remember that they used mercury and a gel. The picture I drew of the lower half of the craft was published in 1979, within the pages of *The Andreasson Affair*. Drawing the craft helped me to remember. But once I was taken aboard their craft, I had no idea what was about to happen to me. Fear rose up within me, especially when I was put through two frightfully painful physical examinations with needles, where I could not move or cry out for help. I was alone in a strange and scary place with unusual-looking beings standing over me. Much earlier they had told me they wanted only to check my body for light. After the examinations, I was escorted by two silver-suited beings to the most unbelievable places that seemed out of this world. I couldn't understand everything the beings were transmitting to me through my mind. It was after undergoing regressive hypnosis that I began to draw and write down what I had seen and what I'd been told.

But for now, I want to return to the mercury my children had found in the yard on top of the cement wall. It made me wonder if their craft might have hovered over the small trees located behind the foundation so it would not be seen. It would have been very dark in that area. As for the strange deposit of mercury, I'm thinking the possibility exists that the ship either may have discharged or leaked some mercury on the cement foundation, where my children happened to discover it sometime later. But before the kids found the mercury, the power in our house went out on the evening of January 25, and a UFO set down on the small hill in the backyard of my home. There had been a January thaw, and mist had settled around the yard and house. Now, after learning the children had found mercury on the cement foundation, I wondered if the ship could have left a residue of mercury on the hill as well. We never understood why grass would no longer grow there, but I think now that a discharge of mercury might have accidentally let go beneath the craft at the time of my encounter. If the craft had leaked mercury below, I wonder if a mixture of soil and heavy moisture could have changed its substance into a methyl mercury poison. Unfortunately, the area has now been dug up.

The UFO's powerful energy cut off the electricity, plunging the whole neighborhood into darkness for a time. The researchers investigated the strange outage to find out what could have happened to turn off the electricity. The power company's records revealed there was a power outage at the time, but they had no idea what had caused it. Considering Bonnie had informed me so recently about finding mercury in the yard, I wondered if any of my other children knew about it. She said she was going to her sister's home the next day for Thanksgiving and would question her. During dinner, Bonnie asked both her brother and sister if they remembered the mercury over by the foundation wall. Both my son and daughter answered yes. They definitely remembered seeing and handling the mercury while playing out there. Their father, Jim, was also present at the table and was as shocked as I was to learn that they had been handling mercury. They had no idea it was a poisonous liquid metal.

Now, as far as the mercury is concerned, scientists such as David Childress who are connected with the mercury-vortex technology may help to explain the way heated liquid mercury could have been used to lift a craft, making it possible for the craft to float along in Earth's atmosphere. This exciting research will certainly open eyes and minds to this new and phenomenal information that is finally finding its way into today's news. It is claimed that a lot of these ideas are taken from ancient Vimana Shastra manuscripts, and the mercury-vortex system may have been used in India's flying ships centuries ago, as mentioned in their ancient books.

The Sandia and Livermore Laboratories developed MFD technologies, where the plasma-based mercury resulted in superconductive plasma. I'm not going to even try to explain what it's all about, because I'm not a scientist, but I do know that the beings also used crystals on the particular craft I was on. Since the beings mentioned to me that they have used mercury in their crafts, and some actual mercury happened to show up at our residence, it appears that this is much more than just a coincidence. The fact that scientists today are pursuing the use of mercury for its possible antigravity effects is encouraging, as it could be a tremendous boost to our future space programs.

Now, I would like to mention Paul Potter, whom I worked with off and on for almost five years concerning the craft I've experienced. Paul has done a phenomenal job of putting information together of how he believes the craft I've seen and been on could function. He has written an excellent, informative book called *Gravitational Manipulation of Domed Craft* about UFO propulsion dynamics. Paul has a great mind and speaks about the crystal-glass spheres and the helical field-tube technology of propulsion. His work includes subjects such as the plasma, electronic state of matter, and polarized fields. Paul is an artist in his own right and has painstakingly computerized each rendition of the craft's working ability to lift, move, and fly. He thoroughly reveals his understanding of the "AA Craft" and has included these working scientific pictures throughout his book. I am proud to have worked with this man, who has detailed the craft I saw and was on. Evidently, his knowledge and understanding appear to be on the same line as the Vimana technologies I mentioned earlier. If readers are at all interested in information concerning the craft I saw and experienced, I highly recommend this man's work. He also reveals within the last half of his book some scientific information on Bob Lazar's work, when Bob was employed at Area 51. Thank you, Paul, for all the research and hard work you have accomplished regarding the propulsion system as described in *The Andreasson Affair*. And now Bob will continue to add more information concerning the UFO phenomenon and the propulsion system, which I described as accurately as I could after the beings allowed me to view it while inside and outside the craft.

Bob's Thoughts on Propulsion Systems

As a person who has always been interested in science and technology, I was quite surprised and a little skeptical when Betty first told me mercury was part of the craft's propulsion system. I thought surely she must have been mistaken in her description. Betty is such a sincere and honest person, however, that I had to consider that her description probably was accurate. You can imagine my surprise when, years later, I learned of the ancient Sanskrit writing *Samarangana Sutradhara*, which translates to *Controller of the Battlefield*. It is written here that the body of the Vimana must be strong and durable, made like a great flying bird of light material. It goes on to state that, inside the craft, one must put the mercury engine with its iron heating apparatus underneath. It also goes on to state that by means of the power latent in the mercury, a man sitting inside may travel a great distance in the sky. This writing reveals that this Vimana can travel in any direction and is capable of flight both out of our atmosphere and underwater.

So what is up today with mercury and the possibility of using it as an antigravity source? For one thing, there are presently experiments going on regarding a theoretical device that employs mercury rotating in a superconductive ring to create a graviton magnetic field to overcome Earth's gravity. I personally believe our government has gone way beyond the theoretical stage and actually produced more than one working model. Let's look at the rumored TR-3B aircraft for an example. This craft is rumored to use highly pressurized mercury accelerated by nuclear energy, which produces plasma that, in effect, creates a field of either antigravity or weight reduction around the ship. There are said to be conventional thrusters located at the tips of the craft that enable it to perform all manner of high-speed maneuvers about all three axes. As an additional bonus, the plasma generated around the craft reduces the radar signature to the point that the craft becomes almost invisible to radar. As far-fetched as this all sounds, we need to remember that these developments have been withheld from the general public for decades.

Of course we are aware of this thanks to people such as astronaut Gordon Cooper and others who have come forward. In his excellent book *Leap of Faith*, Gordon states that while he was in the military, they were using digital technology a good thirty years before it became available to the public. There is no good reason to believe that the TR-3B, which officially does not exist, and other new technologies are not presently in use today by the military. I am certain we can all believe the statements made by Ben Rich, former head of Lockheed Martin Skunk Works, where some of our most sophisticated weapons and futuristic technologies come from, when he said there are two types of UFOs: the ones *we* build and the ones *they* build. This is a very strong statement coming from a man in a position to have knowledge of these things. As difficult as it is for us, the general public, not to have firsthand knowledge of these technologies, we must remember that if our government told us about these developments, they would be telling our enemies as well, and that would not be good for any of us. If we look at Betty's case, which was known for many years, our government may have thought there was possibly more information stored away in our computers. This may account for the illegal hacks on our home computer by two Department of Defense computers within forty-eight hours.

Recently I filed a complaint with the US Attorney General regarding these illegal intrusions into our computer. As of this writing, there has been no reply. I also contacted the FBI, as hacking comes under their jurisdiction, and asked them to investigate the hacking of my computer by the Department of Defense. Apparently they want no part of this situation, as they ignored my first request, which I sent to the Richmond FBI office on February 28, 2015, as certified mail with a return receipt. After receiving no response from them for six months, I sent a second letter on June 22, 2015, also sent as certified mail with a return receipt. This time the response was much different. The FBI refused to sign for the letter or even pick it up from the post office, which resulted in the unopened certified mail's return to me. I could not help but wonder how the FBI had time to investigate the hacking of the Houston Astros' computer by the Saint Louis Cardinals, which is by no means an earth-shattering event, when they apparently did not consider the hacking of a US citizen's computer a serious crime, even though this citizen had no criminal record and had not committed any crime. Perhaps it's just the good old boys protecting one another again. After all, what would the FBI be able to do once they determined that two agencies, the US Navy Space Weapons Systems Division and the US Army, were responsible for these hacks? They knew I had the proof from my security software and a letter from the Inspector General admitting the computers detected by my security software were DOD computers. Yet they refuse to act on it to this day.

CHAPTER 16

Life and Family Go On

• • •

SOME MONTHS AFTER MY TWO daughters graduated from high school, they decided to join the air force together. It felt strange without the girls being home, but I was so thankful that they were both in the same barracks in Texas and were not separated. After they finished basic training, they said their drill instructor told them they were going to have a party and celebrate. I mailed a large box with loads of cookies, cupcakes, and brownies I'd made for them and sent them along with balloons and colored rolls of crepe paper to hang up for their party. In the next letter I received, I found out it wasn't that kind of party. They told me later that the party was a GI party, where they had to clean the latrines using a toothbrush, which I'm sure their female officer must have had a moment of laughter over—especially because their clueless mother had sent so much party paraphernalia to the girls. Even so, she was very kind and let all the girls enjoy the sweets anyway, though they were told they could not use the other stuff.

With Bob working and the girls away, I had too much time on my hands, so I decided to get a job. I was hired and went to work at the Johnson Publishing Company in Cheshire, updating the city directory. There were six of us women constantly using the phones to access information for the directory. The boss could not understand why all of a sudden there were so many telephone people coming and going from his office. One of them even said they had to put a froggy on the line (Whatever that meant!). The city-directory salesman had to travel around with his job. He knew the company's main number by heart and frequently contacted the office several times a day to speak to the boss. One day, he came into where we ladies were working with the phones and appeared to be shocked as he told us what had just happened to him. He said that when he'd called the office, he'd been connected to the Pentagon. Of course the office number was nowhere near the Pentagon's number. Everyone turned and looked at me, because they knew about my UFO experiences. I asked him if he would be willing to write down what had happened and sign it for me, which he did.

Because of my 1967 encounter, a television station contacted us and asked if they could broadcast a four-part news series about what had happened. We had done a few radio shows already, and we were asked to do a lecture at the Cheshire Public Library, which was filled to capacity, though there were not enough seats and many had to stand. Regardless of the attention and weird happenings, we tried to live a normal life by planting flowers and a vegetable garden, playing with our dog, going to the drive-in, and having many cookouts with family and friends. But still strange things kept happening, no matter where we lived. For example, one summer we went to the Southington Drive-In to see the movie *Short Circuit.* We had parked our car very close to the projection booth when suddenly there was a loud bang on the back of the car. I urged Bob to get out to see what had happened, as it actually had shaken our car. He didn't want to move. So instead, a man who was parked next to us with his windows wide open had also heard the loud bang and was curious enough to get out of his car to check both his and our car. He said he thought a tire had exploded, but everything seemed to be all right. Later that night we would find out that was not the case.

After the movie ended, we started home to our camp trailer, which at that time was located at a Higganum, Connecticut, campground. We had to pass Lyman Orchards Farm in Durham. We learned through hypnosis after the fact that, along the way, we found out our car had been picked up and brought into an odd place, where an old rusty van and another car were parked with doors left wide open, as if they'd been abandoned or searched. Bob and I were unconscious at this time. It was as though my spirit sensed something was wrong and came partially out of my body to view what was happening. It was not good. Several small beings, evidently the bad ones, were by our car, and two were on top of the roof. One was toward the back. I saw it remove a metallic light from off the trunk of our car. Evidently they'd used this invisible magnetic object, hidden from natural sight, so that when it hit the car, it created the loud noise we'd heard at the drive-in. They must have also used it as a beacon to follow us. The beings appeared to be aggressive when a loud clap of thunder from a streak of powerful lightning occurred, and a tall, white-haired Elder appeared, along with other gray beings in blue suits.

He pointed and waved his hand, and the next thing I knew we were just about home. I said to Bob, "I don't remember passing Lyman's farm, do you?" Bob looked at the clock to check the time. We should have been home much earlier. It appeared we were missing about forty-five minutes of time, between the drive-in and our usual route home.

Another odd thing happened to us at the same drive-in, when a woman came up to the front of our car, took two flash photos of us sitting there, and quickly walked away as if nothing had happened. I guess someone wanted our photos for whatever reason. Throughout our life, we've had some very unusual things take place that just don't seem normal, or for that matter, possible. Bob's mom had died in 1980. Her only child, Bob, inherited her house. She also had left her beloved red Toyota, but somehow, before her passing, the main wire harness had caught on fire while she drove and burned all the wires. The Toyota had not been fixed and sat in her backyard after her death, until Bob had a chance to tow it to our house in Cheshire. The car was parked outside in front of our garage. We were out shopping during the day, and as soon as we arrived home, Bonnie said she heard a loud horn honking outside, but no one was there. As the three of us were standing in the kitchen, we also heard a loud horn honk and stop. Bonnie said, "That's the same horn I heard off and on all day today."

We rushed outside and stood by Mom's car, and the horn honked again. Stunned, Bob lifted the car's hood, and being an expert Toyota technician, he said, "This is impossible." The whole wire harness was burned and disconnected. There was no way the horn could work.

The strange thing was, Bob had dreamed about his mother the night before, where she called him on the telephone and said, "It took me three days to get here. But it's beautiful." Because of the dream, Bob was worried about his mother and prayed for a sign that she was all right. He realized she was letting him know by performing the miraculous feat of honking her disabled car's horn to let him know it was her, and she was fine. His mom was a wonderful lady, thoughtful and kind.

Some other unusual things also happened at his mother's house. Bob's mom rented the lower apartment to a close friend, who experienced a few unusual things while living there. When she awoke in the morning, her large, heavy rocking chair had moved from its original place and was sitting in the middle of the living-room floor. Another time heavy rock-maple kitchen chairs from her round table were pulled away from the table and sitting in the middle of the floor. She was astonished and could not figure out why it was happening, for only she and her cat lived there. Her cat would stand on the bed and look up, meow, and swat the air, as if seeing something invisible to the human eye. After Mom Luca's friend had moved, I helped her paint, and rewallpaper the rooms of the lower apartment. When it was finished, Bob used his camera to take pictures of the rooms. When we picked up the prints, there was a picture of what can be described only as a male ghost in three of the prints. There was no one physically there at the time he took the photograph shots, but the man appeared in at least three photographs. One was taken in the front bedroom, and two were from the kitchen. We still have the photographs of the ghost and have no idea who he is. After Mom Luca passed away, we sold the ranch house in Cheshire and moved into the lower apartment. We lived there for a short period of time. The bathroom had the older, heavy twist-type metal faucets on the sink, and while we lived there, the heavy faucets at times would turn on full force by themselves. Another time, Bob put the downstairs apartment up for rent, and a young couple with their little boy came to see if it was something they might like to rent. After showing them the rooms, we stood out on the porch, giving them more information on the area, while the boy was happily running from room to room.

Suddenly it became really quiet, and the parents called their son to them. The father asked him what he was doing in there, and the boy replied, "I was talking to the nice lady." When we questioned the little boy about what the nice lady looked like, he described Bob's mother perfectly. It's a known factor that people who have had UFO experiences usually have some paranormal activity happening in their lives as well.

While we were living in the Cheshire home, we wanted to make some changes. I worked inside, painting and decorating, while Bob put cedar shakes on the outside of the house and later started to shingle the roof. It was summer. As he climbed up his folded thirty-foot aluminum extension ladder, which he'd placed against the garage roof, he realized too late he could not get down the same way, for it had stirred and angered a large nest of swarming bees ready and able to take care of the trespasser. At one point Bob was ready to jump off the roof. But a second thought of a possible broken leg changed his mind. Instead, he quickly moved to the opposite end of the house to get away from them and yelled for help. Cindy and I came out and went to get the ladder for him. This is going to sound stupid, but there were only six feet between the garage and an incoming electrical wire, and the border on that side had thick, very tall bushes that closed the area in even closer. This meant we couldn't lay the ladder down to get it off the garage wall. For us to be able to remove and carry it safely, we had to grab the lower end. Cindy was standing underneath the ladder, and I was on the opposite side trying to balance it, which was next to impossible to do. We managed to pull the heavy vertical ladder away from the roof, but it felt like a ton of bricks swaying back and forth. Cindy and I held on to each side while giving conflicting directions like, "Whoa, whoa, whoa, this way, Mom," and, "No, no, no, that way, Cindy. More to the right."

We continued to dance in a haphazardly back-and-forth motion, struggling to get it under control, to keep it from falling. We were making progress, but once again, the vertical ladder began swaying in the air, with a mind of its own. We jumped out of the way just in time, as the ladder suddenly fell forward and crashed into the driveway. Bob was still standing on the roof with his hands on his hips, laughing while instructing us to carry the ladder the flat way. While laughing, he said, "You two looked like a couple of Keystone Cops carrying that ladder vertically." At that point, we felt like leaving him on the roof to teach him a lesson of humility. This "life in the Luca family" happened way before the girls joined the air force. Thank God Cindy was at home to help.

Because so many other odd and unusual things were going on at times, I kept praying for protection for the family. We tried to live a normal life and stayed in touch with family and friends, and Bob still made his famous spaghetti sauce that everyone loved. When the girls joined the air force, I was so proud of them. Bonnie and Cindy were adjusting to the service life, but I missed them terribly at times and hoped they were all right. As it happened, Bonnie was on leave and had called from Virginia, where she was stationed, as she was coming home for a visit. I couldn't wait to see her. It was around three o'clock in the morning when she arrived; I rushed to the door, gave her a big hug and kiss, and helped her into her room with the luggage. Bob was in bed half-asleep, and my daughter and I were still tired. After talking for a few minutes and seeing if there was anything she needed, I returned to my room and got back into bed. It wasn't very long after that I heard my daughter yell for me. I said, "What? What's the matter?"

She didn't answer, so I thought she must have fallen asleep and was dreaming, as the lights were out, and it sounded as if she was mumbling. The next morning she told me what had occurred. She had shut off the bedroom light, so the interior of the room was still softly lit from the window. She'd changed into her pajamas and climbed into bed. Located at the bottom of the bed, off to the left side against the wall, was the large mirrored bureau. She had been in bed for a few minutes when suddenly she saw me standing at the bottom of the bed, wearing my purple bathrobe, looking at her. The form she thought was me turned toward the bureau and mirror, stood there, and silently started to slowly move back and forth in a swaying motion. Startled and wondering what was going on, she asked, "Mom, what are you doing?"

The form said, "I'm going into your mirror."

It was then she realized it was not me, and she screamed, "Mom!" When I heard her call, I answered with a very loud "What?" from my bedroom. This really frightened her, as it made her realize immediately that the lookalike form in her bedroom could not be me but was a vision wearing a robe that looked exactly like mine. She quickly covered her head under the blanket and attempted to tell me about the stranger in her room. That's when I thought she was saying her prayers or mumbling in her sleep. In the morning, I was very surprised to hear what had taken place that night. All three of my daughters have had some unusual things happen to them. My eldest daughter, Becky, has experienced the psychic world and UFO phenomenon, while my two younger daughters quietly shun the phenomenon, for they personally feel it would draw its activity closer to them, and at this time they do not want to open such a door. My two sons have also had experiences, but they refuse to talk about them.

CHAPTER 17

Who Is the One?

• • •

THOSE WHO HAVE HEARD ABOUT or have taken the time to follow the strange and complicated lives of those subjected to the UFO phenomenon may wonder, *What does it all mean?* I believe it is bigger than we can possibly imagine and truly understand. It is so profound it is next to impossible to absorb or wrap one's mind around its truth. Let us see, and let us hear, to hopefully open the understanding of the One's totality. Some people may be a little fearful of the UFO phenomenon. I know I was at times when I couldn't believe what was happening to me—especially each time I was brought before the One. The intense white light was so awesomely bright and beautiful that I felt afraid. It was as if I were being absorbed into its peculiar yet beautiful intensity of oneness. It was overwhelming. I was

experiencing it, but half the time, my mind couldn't comprehend what was going on or what I was being told.

I do remember the powerful words the voice of the One spoke to me in 1967. They were, "Betty, you have seen, and you have heard. Do you understand? I have chosen you to show the world." Many years have passed since I received such an awesome and thought-provoking statement of responsibility, and I have earnestly struggled to understand what direction the Creator in my life will take to somehow show the world. No matter how long it takes, I have faith in his words and patiently wait upon his will to lead me to that absolute truth. At times I feel the Spirit guiding me. During the writing of this book, I felt the need to somehow, for the sake of all, once again attempt to understand the One, for there have been many people wondering who he truly is.

And suddenly, I stopped writing about Bob's and my life experiences with UFO encounters to draw a fictitious picture of a face as a reference and centered starting point to spiritually connect to his presence. As for the One's face, there was no physical image to see. Each time I stood before him, he had no visible form, only an extremely bright, shining light filled with love and his voice. But drawing a physical picture helped to clear my mind, to see beyond my eyes, to understand the invisible One, who dwells in and *is* total light. It was as if the beings had shown me something extremely important, for as you can see, the finished picture I have drawn takes in the entire One, consisting of all there is. I realize we are not supposed to draw a physical rendition of the One (or the One most people consider to be God), as it is impossible to do so and impossible to capture, but drawing was a way to help me understand and hopefully help the world to see and understand who the One is and who we are as well. As I continued to draw, it felt as if the One wanted me to try to understand and possibly see everything about him, including what he looks like, who he is, and what he does. We have a small view of what actually exists before, within, and around us. But through spirit, as I continued to draw the penciled form to help me pull together a possible likeness of his Oneness, I realized the Creator, who forever is, created everything. And every form of creation in time continues to exist, evolve, or end. Nothing can exist without him or his Word. All works of creating with a beginning or an end depend on the good or evil principles involved in its full existence.

Concerning the human creation, he made it to have a physical form, made of earth, then breathed his breath of spirit within it, and the form and spirit became a living, breathing soul or being. Our creation was made from his spirit word, and we were blessed with a power and an ability to choose and create, for we have been made in his image; however, because of choice, our physical knowing often overrides the true spiritual insight before us and causes people to make unrighteous judgments at times. As for the One's righteous judgment of the good and evil experienced in each soul's past life, there will exist either a continued new destination, which will possibly be a good place to be, or a very hard or difficult destination. And as I thought, if humankind's likeness was made in his image, I continued to draw the picture of him as a person to better understand what it meant and how our likeness is to him. Our bodies, souls, and spirits seek the truth of the unseen, but the human soul often refuses to believe what exists. It is too busy living in the physical realm to believe we belong to and are part of the One, the great Creator. As I've attempted to show in the drawing, the Creator, whose powerful energy of word from the beginning created, and the creation was with him and yet *was* him. Because he creates, he can be as small as an atom or particle or as large as trillions of stars and space, which he created in the first place, to have more room to create. He oversees all. He is all there is, all that is not, all there has been, and all there will ever be. He is spirit and is much greater and more magnificent than we could possibly imagine, for he is life. And yet he is death. He has made and formed everything that exists, will exist, or ever has existed, and he continues to recreate more of him in so many different ways, over and over again.

Now every race on Earth has a specific religious or divine name for the higher powers or gods. Depending on a country's origin or spiritual motivation, different forms of religion or worship have developed in the world, for he is the Almighty. Different faiths could not be, unless they were spiritually conceived and manifested through the Creator, who has created everything, good *and* evil. And even though there are times we don't understand why he allows what is to be, he knows the end from the beginning; in order to fulfill a final work, it will become, change, or end to fit his creation. We as human beings, who have been given a mind and an ability to create, have the right to remove any obstacle that may threaten the existence of the human race, but the main theme is we are all a part of the One's creative body. That makes us a part of one another, and everything that exists is because of him. The Creator has provided everything good for his human creation.

As for humankind, while dwelling on this earth, we have been given a natural and a spiritual body. Our natural bodies are companions to the physical earth and earthly things, while our spirit bodies are companions to the soul's life within the blood, the mind, and the heavenly realm. The beings told me, "Jesus was the hypostasis," which meant he was "united, human and divine." Oh, that we all might reach that oneness through him. Our will to choose creates a path in life to reach its final goal. Everything the Creator allows to be will eventually come to its completion. The Creator loves every one of us, for he is the Creator of us and in us.

During the hypnosis investigation of my time as a child within the world of light before the One, I vaguely understood that everything is one. At that time, the hypnotist asked, "What do you mean?"

I replied, "Everything fits together. Everything is one. It's beautiful." For it exists through its creation, either by Him or by His creations, which are in or of his creation. Therefore, there is truly only one Creator. As for the many established beliefs, they are here for a reason and purpose, or they could not exist. The one I believe in and am aware of allowed me to see within the mind and heart of the one Creator, a picture of his will.

There are three original eternal powers, which always were, are, and forever will be. These three powers were not created, but are the eternal powers of will, love, and life within the heart of the One. And it seemed as though the Spirit was consciously attempting to reveal and clarify something to me concerning his eternal power. As I continued to draw and study the picture, I noticed these three moving powers, which always are and were the active part of the One's will. To me, the flow of these three eternal powers dwells forever as one within the heart's love center of the one Creator. And because I am a Christian, I choose to understand this oneness of his will, love, and life through my faith. I understood that the first eternal power in the heart of the One is law, the Father. The Holy Spirit mother's eternal power is absolute truth. And the third group of eternal powers, which is held by the Son, includes mercy, forgiveness, and eternal life. These three divine powers agree and express the One's eternal love of order, truth, unity of family, and all life. Extending from the three eternal powers within his heart, there are levels of angels and beings that also are the creations and expressions of the One. The Creator's mind and will made everything through his three powers that are one. He created every universe, every galaxy, every star, every planet, every natural form of vegetation, and every kind of creature, big and small.

Then, for his special last earthly creation, the One created what was to be his pride and joy: his children, the human race. With joy in his heart, he formed a natural male and female body from the dust of the ground and breathed his spirit within them, so they each became a living soul. The Creator was pleased with his children of light, but during the course of the day, darkness came upon them, and they fell short of the glory of the Creator.

Let us start from the very beginning after the One created the children; he planted fruit trees within his garden for their very own food. As the story goes, all the fruit from those trees was good for them to eat, with the exception of the forbidden Tree of Knowledge of Good and Evil. This particular tree of knowledge belonged to the One, because the Creator who had made everything, including good and evil, understood the difference between the positive and negative influences involved and knew when, why, and how the knowledge was righteously used. Near his entrance to the garden was the Tree of Life, which stood protected by his angel, who held a two-edged, flaming sword of fiery power, moving every which way. This meant none could go in until the work of the One was completely finished. As soon as the first two human children were created, they stood within the garden of fruit trees. Right away, because of love, the job of the first and second eternal powers that protect, spoke to the children about the forbidden fruit tree that possessed good and evil knowledge. It was then that both eternal powers of law and truth warned the newly created children about the One's tree of judgment, saying, "Do not eat of this tree, lest you will die."

But as time passed, the human race denied the eternal truth, disobeyed the eternal law, and consumed the deadly fruit of good and evil that caused division. Dwelling within the tree of forbidden fruit was the split-tongued Serpent, who tempted, received, and knew the first-born female. As she consumed the fruit, the Serpent supplanted his seed within her mind and womb. After the knowing, the female gave her brother the fruit to know, and she received his seed as well. Two boys, each made from different seed, were born. Later, out of jealousy, the Serpent's son killed his half brother, Abel. Once again the created male knew the created female, and another son was born. Thousands and hundreds of thousands of years passed, as the cursed tree's poison of judgment and death continued to claim generations of humankind. The love in the heart of the Creator's truth and law was broken, as the human souls teetered between good and evil, waiting for death, while dwelling in darkness from disobedience. Ages passed, and humankind was under the law with no provision to lift them out of the darkness, to recover his soul with light. Their sorrowful cries reached the heart of the One, where the eternal power of life dwelled. The blood and power within the son of life was moved with mercy and wanted to help.

The One knew in his heart that his Son's life was the only one able to pay the sacrificial debt. The eternal power of life, mercy, and forgiveness veiled the Son's being and was the only way to freedom. When the Son lifted the veil and covered the two-way tree with his being, the eternal power of love, mercy, and forgiveness released the true meaning of oneness: one for all, and all for one. Such love makes all things possible. Hate destroys. We were all created from love. The great Creator is, was, and will forever be the One. I would hope the reader will understand I am not trying to push religion; it is up to each person what he or she chooses to believe, and I judge you not. I am hopeful others will not judge me either, for we all have a greater judge who judges righteously. But I am compelled to tell exactly what has happened to us, even if it sounds religious, crazy, or impossible. As I see it, in the continuum, there appear to be countless levels of created dimensions, which appear to be populated with a variety of beings with specific degrees of unusual abilities, intelligence, and work. The deciphered Sumerian information reported and delivered by Dr. Zachariah Sichen alone has to open the minds and eyes of readers.

And the Old and New Testaments of the Holy Bible have been available for many years to the world and have to awaken people to the truth of who we are. And if what the One revealed through the picture I have spiritually received and drawn in the hope of understanding the *all* in *one* is correct, may it be a blessing to you.

Concerning my UFO contact, the beings told me there were seventy races visiting our planet, and one was detrimental and should not be trusted. During one of my encounters, the beings told me they were caretakers of nature and all natural forms and have been with humankind since our very beginning. They claimed they love humankind, but they included the worrisome fact that we were walking in the wrong footsteps. Unfortunately, many footsteps taking place in today's world seem to be all about greed, big money, wrong thinking, and separation from the One who gave us life. The messengers also said, "We have the ability to watch the living spirit in all things." One wonders how the human soul's spirit might appear to them. Could our spirit souls be a form of light or shades of darkness? If so, might the color of a spirit reveal to them the works of the living soul that is present? Now back to the messengers who have faithfully collected various plant, animal, and human seed for thousands of restorative years. Of course they must use this ability to watch over the continued growth and existence of the main body of physical life on Earth. Like our being, the systems of renewal, which are constantly moving and growing, exist along with the elimination process going on as well, for all life contributes to take in and give out. I believe most substance is changed or transformed into other forms or dimensions to become more of the framework and embodiment of the Creator's work; however, another message from the beings said, "Humankind will eventually become sterile." Unfortunately, we possess that very problem today. This means the inability to produce human offspring is happening now.

To realize the beings' alarming message, we must first look at our environment. Sadly, the air, water, land, and oceans have been somewhat polluted and poisoned by the careless release of toxic gases and other waste products. To understand the causes of sterility, I'll grant you this has not happened only because of our physical and spiritual neglect. Our brains, mouths, and muscles must work to change the situation. Our lives are held in jeopardy by allowing this pollution and not holding huge industries and companies making billions of dollars accountable. Their dumping of illegal waste has created a worldwide bad situation, and they've gotten away with it. Lack of cleanup in certain areas will make the world a silent, disease-ridden cesspool. Not only our lives, but the earth's goodness, suffer with pollutants. We are not only breathing it in, but are indirectly eating poisonous chemicals that have been sprayed on some of our foods, and in my opinion, the companies pushing genetically modified organisms (GMOs) in foods or seeds haven't done us any favors. They claim this is for our benefit, while in fact they are poisoning us and making huge profits from doing so. Today the leading disease is cancer. I wonder why...

The One is always totally aware of what is happening and looks to his children to figure out how to clean up the mess. So far, during my encounters, I've been physically taken to see the One four different times. The first time was in 1950, when I was thirteen years old. It all began when I was taken aboard a bright orb-shaped moon ship, where small white-suited beings with large heads and big black eyes transported me to an underground misty room. After they finished with me there, I was taken into another room and placed upon a tubelike wheel. Something was put in my mouth to hold my tongue down. I automatically sank into the tube, as the wheel turned swiftly around and around and finally came to a stop. There was a window overhead that allowed me to see what was happening and where I was going. Although I was on the wheel, the craft I was in had taken flight as well. The ship entered some water below, and it became very dark. To my relief, the craft lifted out of the deep, briefly hovered in place, then entered a very large and lengthy, icy tunnel. As the craft moved past the tunnel's ice-covered walls, there appeared to be a group of peculiar irregularly sized blocks of ice stored up ahead. The craft passed them and continued its route forward. As it slowly moved along, I could see another cluster of these odd-looking blocks of ice before us. The craft drew closer, and I realized these blocks seemed different. Some were big and tall and cut into a rectangular shape. The craft drew closer yet, and I made it a point to check these large, smoothly cut blocks of ice and was stunned. Within the solid blocks of ice were frozen human bodies of people young and old.

Much later, toward the end of my 1950 experience, I was transported from a crystal forest within a different glass-like orb that had taken me toward the great door to the world of light. The wondrous shining door appeared like many glistening doors within a great and glorious door that stretched upward beside the slanted, crystalline walls, which seemed to continue as far as I could see. It was then the small being I was with told me to lift my feet, and the funny glass shoes I had been wearing much earlier automatically fell to the floor. I could not understand what had happened, for I came out of myself and was now in two places at the same time. The small being brought me before the beautiful crystallized doorway and said, "Now you shall enter the great door to the world of light and behold the glory of the One." As I stood before the beautiful doorway, I was lifted up and placed in the world of light. I stood bathed within the light of his awesome realm of wholeness and could barely move. It seemed alive with hidden energy of unseen wonder, power, and mystery. I was young and unable to fathom the depth of his beautiful oneness, surrounding me within his light. Suddenly, to my surprise, I was drawn back from the world of light to the other side of the great door.

The hypnotist and research team, hoping to get some answers, had drawn me back into the room, for they wanted to know what was happening. Once again I was sitting in a chair, being questioned by the hypnotist. He continued to ask, "What did you see? What did you hear when you were before the One? What did he tell you?" For some reason, I was unable to answer his or the researchers' questions about what had happened. At the time, all I remembered was bright light everywhere, with the sudden appearance of a much brighter form of overwhelming light, which was the One. Even though it was peaceful, I felt a little afraid not knowing what I was there for, until I was told I had something I must do. As time passed, I could no longer remember what it was.

Seventeen years later, the beings took me before the One again. It was 1967. I was thirty years old and married, and I had seven children. My husband was hospitalized from an auto accident, and my parents were staying with me to help out at the time. It was evening when the electrical power went out, and a red flashing light shone through the back pantry window. Thinking it was either the fire or police department, my father rushed past me to check. After calming the children, I went into the kitchen, where five strange-looking beings entered my home, right through the closed wooden door. Because of their astonishing ability, I believed they had to be angels. It was during this encounter I was taken to places I had never seen before. As I stood before the glowing light, I heard the One say, "Betty, you have seen, and you have heard. Do you understand? I have chosen you to show the world."

The third time the beings brought me before the One was in 1989. Twenty-two years had passed. I was now fifty-two years old. It was late at night when I was drawn outdoors. Bob was fast asleep, and as I stepped outside, it felt like the area was unusually still and deserted, for we were staying in our large fifth-wheel trailer in a wooded campground. In the distance, I could see a blue ball of light, which appeared to be moving toward me among the large trees. Suddenly I couldn't move. I felt paralyzed, and before I knew it, I was inside the blue ball of light, traveling away from the campground toward another small waiting craft. Three beings took me aboard their ship, and we traveled to a beautiful crystalline forest. The craft stopped, and one of the beings escorted me outside. We moved into a misty area, where I was once again ordered to put on some odd glass-like shoes. The being and I moved out of the mist into the beautiful crystal forest.

I had no idea why we were in this forest or what we were doing there. Suddenly, huge translucent sheets of light appeared, falling everywhere and briefly trapping us within the forest. The small being said, "The One has moved to open the great door." It was unbelievably bright. I was told to run as the sheets continued to fall. It was difficult to move while wearing the thick shoes, and suddenly I was in trouble, for I had slipped. The shoes fell off my feet, and I fell into a crystal lake, which had turned into water. I was soon rescued by six beings of light, and the small being quickly led me to another clear orb, which immediately transported me to a different place, where I once again, was brought aboard another ship with watchers. We moved out into deep space, where a huge, elongated mother ship was stationed. The being took me aboard and brought me before a group of white-robed Elders performing an unusual ceremony while chanting. A beautiful purple orb of swirling light miraculously appeared, and the beings placed it in my hands. The entire activity of this outer-space encounter took place in a cylindrical mother ship stationed in deep space.

On my way home, the beings brought me once again to see the One, along with an Elder and a watcher. We stood before the great open door, where I could hear wonderful sounds of beautiful music and singing. The feelings of warmth and joy radiating from the living orb I held were wonderful. The music seemed to dance within the lights as if they were one. I felt a sweeping feeling of peace and love everywhere, and something strange happened to the three of us. Our bodily forms changed into beings of light as we entered the open door. The Elder immediately turned to a shining white light, while the gray being turned to a body of blue light, and I became a glowing form of yellow light. The precious oneness, unity, and feelings of peace and love rippled through my body. It was indescribably wonderful, but it seemed as if we were not there very long before it was time to go. I wanted to stay, but I knew I had to go back for others, so they would see and understand the oneness of our Creator. As we stood outside the door, a large amount of different-size, colored orbs of light were floating in the air above us, creating their special sounds of beautiful music. They slowly moved back into the light of the great door.

The fourth and last time I remember being brought to see the One was on July 21, 1994, five years after my last known encounter. I was fifty-seven years old. Bob and I were living in our fifth-wheel trailer just before we moved to Virginia. It was early in the morning when we awoke from sleep and I happened to see a three-fingered handprint on one of the mirrors to our closet door. I was shocked and could barely believe what I was looking at, for there before me was an actual piece of physical evidence, an image of the three-fingered hand I had seen in the past on Quazgar and other beings during my 1967 encounter in my home. Even though it was only a smudged print of one being's hand, I was so excited and happy we were able to capture it on sticky paper. There, at last, was proof, so skeptics could no longer think I was crazy for reporting everything I had been experiencing over so many years—although I have to gratefully say the human race is wonderful, for there has never been anyone I know of who has openly criticized me or made me feel embarrassed for reporting the facts of my strange and unusual life dealing with the UFO phenomenon. Thankfully, the strange print was the catalyst that helped open my mind to what had happened during the night of my last encounter.

It was then that Bob put me under hypnosis to find out exactly what had taken place that evening. Once again, the memories of when and how I was taken before the One were recovered. Much later during this encounter, one Elder made it a point to inform and remind me of the forgotten job the One had given me to do when I was thirteen. Back then, the sheer wonder of where I was and what had taken place as a child was overwhelming. At thirteen, I definitely had not understood what was happening, because the beings hadn't spoken to me. But years later, through the Spirit, without even realizing it, I managed to finish the work, which turned out to be a pictorial book of Revelation.

Finally, in 1994, I found out what had happened after my return home from the One. At the time of this last known encounter I was sort of nervous concerning the fact that I had been called for and was being escorted by an Elder, who claimed the One wanted to see me. It had been almost six years since my last experience. The Elder refused to tell me why, no matter how often I asked. The being traveling with us also entered the clear, glass-like orb we had boarded. We lifted off toward our destination, which was filled with amazing wonders. To my surprise, after traveling through two frightening fields of moving waves of energy, we arrived in a rather cool area, which was covered with mist and bright white light. We stopped. The Elder took me out of the craft but left me alone to approach the One by myself. I lowered my head to humbly stand before his powerful and most glorious presence. While abiding within the One's light, I learned and received what the One was to give me, which I had first thought appeared to be a personal gift and message. What he placed within my mind would be required to understand and be used for something I would have to do in the future, to show the world. I know, and believe, some spiritual dreams and visions I've received in the past have a spiritual connection somehow to what was given during the last time I was before the One, which may somehow reveal something that will help humankind to see and believe, for we are not only flesh and blood, but have living souls that continue to live on.

I do not know specifically what I am to tell the world. I am still waiting on the One to reveal the big secret to me. At first I thought it was concerning my encounters, so people would not be afraid and would realize if I lived through it, they could too. The purpose of this book is to allow the interested reader to know what has happened to us since the information recorded in the fifth book was printed. Bob's and my life may differ from other people's lives because of the continued UFO encounters we've gone through, but we've tried to live as normally as possible. As for the newest and most recent UFO experience, an Elder took me again to see the One. During this new encounter, the One delivered something personal and imprinted it on my mind. Once again, our meeting proved to me that in the future I will definitely have something I must do for the One and the world.

Raymond E. Fowler has written five books concerning the UFO experiences. Ray's spirit was profoundly capable of handling the high strangeness of the awesome phenomenon, for he has been groomed spiritually and indirectly by the One. There could not be a better or more intelligent author for this material, as Ray is careful to research and cover every aspect of this otherworldly information. Bob and I, on the other hand, are unable to compare or give an account of other similar experiences, for we are not professional authors. We also aren't knowledgeable of other people's experiences or related cases of encounters, so the information you receive from Bob and me is what it is. Not many explanations are forthcoming, only raw data. This is what happened to us. You have to decide for yourself if it is of value to you or not.

CHAPTER 18

Paranormal Visitations

• • •

As PROMISED AT THE BEGINNING of this book, we decided to report some
of the other paranormal activities we've experienced, as well as all the
strange and unusual UFO encounters we've had. Paranormal activity
seems to follow those involved in the UFO phenomenon. This has been
the case for Betty and me, practically since day one. Betty had experienced
this activity long before we met, and it continues to this day with both of
us, no matter where we happen to live, and has even accompanied us on
vacation and affected our animals as well.

Once Betty and I started dating in Florida, I could not help but notice
that there were some unusual things occurring. One night while we were
on the beach, we saw white and black orbs swiftly moving back and forth
on, or more than likely over, the water, perhaps a quarter to a half mile or
so offshore. Obviously the first thing you would think of is boats being out
there; however, these would have had to be jet-powered boats at the speed
they were traveling. The orbs moved much too quickly to be conventional
boats of any kind, and there was no up or down motion as they traveled
along, as you would expect to see from any object moving on the water.
Therefore, I reasoned that these objects must have been slightly above
the water. I just put that aside in my mind as something interesting and
unexplainable. There were also a rather unusual number of streetlights
that would turn off as we passed under them, numbers far too high to be
a coincidence, and I started having some problems with starting my well-
kept car. As a technician, I found all of these things interesting, although

I could not explain them. Little did I know this was just the beginning of paranormal experiences that would be with us for years to come.

My vacation time was almost up, and I was ready to head back to Connecticut and my job as a service manager for a Toyota dealership. Betty also needed to head home, so I offered to give her a ride back to her home in Massachusetts. She was hesitant at first, thinking she did not know me or my friend that well, but she did know my friend's sister-in-law, with whom she had worked at the restaurant. I guess I seemed harmless enough, so we all set out for the trip back north together. I resumed my job and would make the trip up on the weekends to be with Betty. One of the first unusual incidents at her house happened while we were sitting at the kitchen table and a chair I was sitting in started to vibrate quite strongly. I moved from the head of the table to one of the chairs on the side of the table. Again, the chair started to vibrate or shake, even with my full weight on it. Betty, sitting a short distance from me, put her hand on the chair and could easily feel the chair move with me in it, yet no other chairs were affected by this strange vibration. Being a logical, technical person, I thought perhaps something in the basement, such as the furnace or water pipes, might be the culprit. I went to the basement only to find that the furnace was not on, and there was no sign of any disturbance coming from water pipes or anything else that I could determine. What was further mystifying to me is the fact that only the chairs I sat in would do this. I never let on at the time, but this did kind of creep me out a bit, as I had always considered myself a logical person, and I especially did not like being involved personally in situations like this, where I could find no reasonable explanation for what was happening.

Time passed, and we continued dating. We were married in August 1978, and we moved into a house in Meriden, Connecticut. No sooner had we moved into the house than something made its presence known. Betty and I were downstairs in the living room, and Betty was in her nightgown ready to go upstairs to bed when the doorbell rang. I went to the front door and opened it to see who might be coming here at this late hour, as it was nearly midnight. I opened the door only to find no one was there. I looked to both sides of the house and still saw no one. The bell rang again while I was the only one out there, and I thought possibly I had leaned against or hit the button myself, and to this day, I am not sure exactly what happened. What followed left no doubt in my mind that there was some unusual energy at work here.

It was not long before the girls, Betty, and I began to hear footsteps in the house. Sometimes they were upstairs, and on occasion, when we were upstairs, we would hear the footsteps downstairs. The footsteps were followed shortly after by a shadow person. Once, one of the girls came downstairs and thought she saw me in the kitchen; however, I was upstairs in the bedroom at the time. I came into the kitchen from the living room another day and saw a man going into our basement. There was no outside exit from the basement, so whoever it was would be trapped. Thinking, *Now I got this guy*, I went into the basement, looked all over, and couldn't find anyone there. I gave up at this point, knowing there was nothing else I could do. On yet another occasion, Bonnie saw a man in the basement entrance through the glass pane in the door, and I investigated only to find no one was there. Even our parrot was not immune to whatever was moving about in the house. Many times when we let him out, he would perch on the highest shelf in the living room and be content to look around from this vantage point. After we were in the house a short time, however, this would change, as he would stare in one direction and squawk and reach out with his clawed foot, as if trying to grab some invisible object.

In addition to these shadow people and many unexplainable noises, we also had numerous problems with electrical devices and appliances. The lights in the living room would blink off and on when they felt like it, and we never found any loose wires, bad switches, or connections. The electric range in the kitchen was not immune to these problems; sometimes one or more of the burners would not work, then the next time you turned them on, they would be fine. On one occasion, the light in the hall leading to the basement had gone out, so I put a new bulb in it, thinking that was the problem. I flipped the switch off and on several times, with no result; however, later that evening, the light came on again without any human intervention. As I wondered what the heck would happen next, we had another very unusual happening in the house. During the night, there must have been an extraordinary amount of energy released in the kitchen, even though we never heard a sound during the night. When we came down to breakfast in the morning, we could not believe what we were seeing. The first thing we noticed was that the crown molding on all four kitchen walls was lying on the floor of the kitchen, while the finishing nails that had the day before held the molding to the wall were still in place. A large stainless-steel cooking pot was cracked right through the rolled-top edge, which is the strongest part of the pot. As we looked around for any other damage, my wife noticed that a couple of our clear drinking glasses had strange squiggly lines in them, almost as if they had been etched. We had no idea what could have caused all of this, especially since none of us had heard any noise the night before, and we had no idea whom, if anyone, we could call for help. So this event went unsolved.

Later, a professional photographer from Massachusetts contacted us and made arrangements to come to Connecticut. While in town, he photographed the pot, and as luck would have it, while he was there, we were visited by one of the black helicopters, which he also photographed. We lived in this home for about one year and then moved to a home in Cheshire, Connecticut, thinking that would at least be the end of those unusual experiences. Well, as it turns out, we were totally wrong. The strange occurrences moved right along with us to Cheshire. One evening after returning home from the nearby outdoor theater, we had no sooner gotten in the house and closed the door when Betty and I heard the most beautiful music I have ever heard in my entire life. It was as if there was a choir of angels right in the house singing to us, and though it lasted for several minutes, we could not determine where it was coming from. There were no radios, record players, tapes, TVs, or anything else on in the house. As the evening was on the cool side, all the windows were closed. This music was so beautiful that it seemed to reach right into my soul, and to this day, I wish I could hear it once again. We had never before heard anything like it and have not heard anything like it since.

On yet another occasion, when police officer Larry Fawcett and his wife visited us, we were sitting at the dinner table having lunch. Larry was sitting in a position that allowed him to have a good view of the tall chrome case with glass shelves that was behind the table on the opposite side from his chair. Larry jumped up from his seat and went over to the shelves, somewhat mystified by what he was witnessing. On one of the glass shelves was a small glass dinner bell that you could see through, and Larry could clearly see and hear the bell ringing. The interesting thing was that there were other bottles of liquid on the same shelf, yet none of them showed any sign of movement or vibration. There was no movement from the floor, or the shelf itself, yet the clapper inside the bell continued to move with a soft tinkling sound. To say Larry was totally amazed and uncertain as to how this could be happening would be an understatement.

MIB

Betty and I had decided to take a trip down to visit her sister in Pompano Beach, Florida, in the fall. This was a trip that usually took a solid day of driving from Connecticut, as I did not like to stop overnight unless it was absolutely necessary. I am one of those people who likes to get where I am going without a lot of side trips or stops. This trip, however, was different from most of the other times we had made the trek down Route 95. It seemed there were endless delays due both to accidents and road construction. By the time we got to Lake Worth, Florida, I was just plain exhausted and thought it would be unsafe for me to drive any farther that evening.

I pulled off of Route 95 and headed up Lake Worth Road, where there was a campground I had stayed at in the past with my camp trailer. My thinking was that this was a safe place where we could get a good night's sleep, then get up in the morning, shower, eat a good breakfast, and be on our way totally refreshed. It was around ten o'clock at night when we drove up to the campground's entrance. I pulled the car over by the side of the familiar office and went in to secure a lot to park in. While inside, I was surprised to hear the person behind the counter talking to another camper about a sighting of a UFO over the campground area, just the night before. Although I found this interesting, I did not get involved in this conversation, as all I wanted was to settle in and get to sleep. I drove the short distance to the lot we'd been assigned and parked the car, noting that the compass was pointing directly north. This was not unusual, as all the lots were in a grid formation (i.e., they were in a north-south position, while the roads they were off of were in an east-west configuration). I shut off the car, and we put the backseats down, which was a nice feature of our hatchback vehicle. This made it relatively comfortable to sleep in the car.

Then the unexpected disturbed our desire to lie down for some rest, when a multicolored ball of light approximately the size of an orange appeared on the driver's side of the car. The ball came through the driver's door and was inside the car. It hovered there in midair, at the middle front of the steering wheel. The ball looked very much like a small disco ball and emanated a variety of colors as it slowly and silently floated through our car, from left to right, passing right in front of Betty and me. I knew we were both tired, but I also knew this was no hallucination, as we both observed the same thing at exactly the same time. The object, whatever it was, finally made its way to the passenger side of the car and disappeared. I thought we were going to get some sleep finally, as we both stretched out as comfortably as we could in the space we had. Sleep came upon us almost immediately. It was not long, however, before I awoke due to a noise, probably after midnight, to see a Cadillac sedan that had pulled up behind us and parked at a ninety-degree angle to our car, a short distance from the entrance to our lot. I thought they must be trying to beat the campground out of its fee and would probably be gone by early morning. I was certainly wrong about this one. Sometime later, perhaps around two or three in the morning, I needed to use the restroom, which was probably twenty or thirty yards from where we had parked. I got out of the car as quietly as I could, so as not to wake Betty, who was now sleeping quite soundly, and I locked the car door behind me as I headed off to the restrooms. The campground was fairly well lit, and I considered it a safe place even at this early hour. After using the facilities, I headed back to the car, and that is when things got rather strange. As I approached the left rear side of this black or very dark Cadillac, I noticed it displayed the familiar yellow New York license plates. When I passed the driver's side of the car, things got really bizarre. I was about seven or eight feet from the rear of the car when all four doors opened at exactly the same time. Four weird-looking men who appeared to be Asian got out of the car, and they were all dressed exactly the same, with black suits and shoes, white shirts, slim black ties, and rimmed black hats. They circled the car once, like children playing musical chairs might do, until each one was now next to a door on the opposite side of the car from where he had started out. They all looked at me as they stood next to the car and again just before getting back into the car as well. Strangely, I did not feel the least bit threatened by these odd people, as they were all very slender and looked like a good wind would be enough to knock them over. After pausing next to their respective doors for a second or two, they all got back into the car and shut the four doors at exactly the same time. The action was so precise that the sound was that of one door closing.

Thinking there was something wrong with these guys, I let myself back into our car and settled down to sleep. In the morning, it was apparent that something unusual had happened during the night. The first thing I noticed was that our compass was now pointing almost due east, which should not be happening, as the car was still parked in the same lot facing due north. As strange as this sounds, that compass never worked correctly again, even when I tried to recalibrate it. If I set it properly on magnetic north, it would not be correct on other directions. Needless to say, I finally just scrapped it, which I later regretted, as there might have been the possibility of having it examined in a scientific laboratory. When I turned the radio on, I was again shocked to see our digital clock that had been in perfect sync with the radio station the day before was now twenty minutes fast. I wondered how a digital clock could actually gain twenty minutes in one evening. In later conversations with electrical engineers, I was told this should be impossible, and the only thing they could think of was possibly a rather large magnetic pulse close to the car might have caused it, which as far as I was aware did not happen. The only thing I could think to do at the time was to walk around the car with a handheld compass, which I did, and I photographed the results. The results themselves were a bit unusual, for as I walked around the car holding the compass about a foot from the vehicle, the compass needle was attracted to the car's metal body, which I thought to be normal. However, when I got to the spot where the multicolored ball had entered the car, the compass needle swung rapidly away, pointing in exactly the opposite direction. I tried this over and over again, holding the compass farther and farther from the car with each trip around it. The needle continued to swing away from the car at that particular point, until the compass was more than four or five feet from the car. I have asked many people from various scientific disciplines about this, but no one has been certain as to what might have caused this unusual condition, although the suggestion of a magnetic pulse kept coming up pretty regularly, no matter whom I asked.

Unusual Events

In early 1980, Betty and I were on a publicity tour for the newly published Andreasson Affair book. We had been traveling through the northeast appearing on radio and TV shows to promote the book, and now it was time to head west. We had just finished the Chicago portion of the tour and were boarding an Amtrak train headed for Los Angeles. The publishers had booked us a sleeper car, which was quite comfortable, and we were enjoying the trip when the unusual once again struck. During the evening, we were sitting in our car when all the lights went out. As the train went along a long curve, we could see all of the other cars had lights in them; however, our car was the only one without power. We were given no reason for this one-car power outage, and to this day, I do not know if an explanation was ever found.

FLORIDA 1990

While vacationing during the winter, we visited with relatives in the Lake Worth, Florida, area. Betty and I went with two other couples to a church in the area, and after the service, we all headed for the International House of Pancakes to enjoy a snack and a cup of coffee together. We all ordered, and Betty had put sugar in her coffee and began stirring it. She withdrew the spoon and briefly held it in her hand, when much to the total amazement of all present, the spoon resting between her fingers quickly broke into two pieces. She held the handle in her hand while the spoon's bowl fell into the coffee. Again this was highly unusual, but we all witnessed it as it happened. I jokingly said that must be some pretty strong coffee. The restaurant let Betty keep the two-piece spoon. When we returned home, we sent the spoon to Raymond Fowler, who then sent it to a metallurgist for examination, but nothing much out of the ordinary was found that could explain the bowl falling off the handle. As things happened that were getting just too strange, I began to record some of them; below is a letter I sent to Ray Fowler concerning one such experience.

Hi Ray,

I've had a couple of unusual things happen in the past two days and thought for future reference you might be interested in them. I have copied them to a disk. First I awoke at approximately 4:45 a.m. on Friday morning and heard a deep male voice say the word eudane (sounds like—you dane) this was very clear and distinct, and I was wide awake. I could not find this word in any dictionary, and have no idea what it means, if anything. About ten minutes later I got up to use the bathroom, it was still dark at this hour, and when I returned to the bedroom, I was surprised to see what looked like hundreds of tiny sparkling lights filling every square inch of the room. There were no lights on at the time, and the room was dimly lit by what little light filters in around the shades on the two windows. I have never experienced anything like this since we have lived here. I got into bed and finally closed my eyes, and I must have fallen back to sleep. This morning Sunday Sept. twenty-seven, 1988, I awoke at 3:00 a.m. and felt some discomfort in my right ankle; I was sleeping on my left side at the time. When I looked down at my ankle, I saw the covers physically lift up several inches from me, and a dark form almost the size and shape of a football with a white band around the center of it, rose up from the bed and disappeared into the ceiling. One notes here, at the time the covers lifted, I did not move my foot, and am quite sure of that. Also at the same time I felt something similar to a light electrical shock traverse my right arm, from elbow to wrist, and had the impression that the hair on this arm was standing straight up. I have no idea what any of this means, but thought you would be interested in hearing of it. If you have any knowledge of the word "eudane," or it's meaning, please let me know? Bob

CHAPTER 19

More Paranormal

• • •

MAY 2005

WE PURCHASED OUR PRESENT RESIDENCE around mid-May. We had decided to do all the painting, wallpapering, and floor refinishing before we moved the furnishings in. On the first night in the house, after retiring for the evening, I heard three loud knocks coming from the basement. The door from the basement to the upstairs was locked, so I just ignored it and went back to sleep, thinking maybe something had followed us to the new location.

The second night got more interesting. We had settled down for a much-needed night's sleep after a day of cleaning and painting different areas of our new home. Since we'd just moved in, we were temporarily using a mattress on the floor of our sleeping quarters, which was in the room that later became our office. At about half past eleven that night, an extremely bright light came into the house through the window of the back-door entrance. What made this even more unusual was the intensity of the bright white light, which appeared to move swiftly within and throughout the entire twenty-seven-foot length of the hallway and was headed straight toward us. The smoke alarm on the hallway wall suddenly went off, and the light quickly disappeared. This all happened in a matter of seconds. We got up, Bob shut off the alarm, and we looked all around, but we could find no source either in the house or outside for this odd and unusual light to have occurred. There was no lightning storm, and a quick look out the back door revealed nothing but a quiet evening with nothing unusual in sight. The source of light would have had to cross over our open, raised deck; move toward our outside garage-door entrance; and make a ninety-degree turn to be able to enter the back door to the house.

One evening in January 2006, I had come down with a bad cold or flu and was resting in bed. It was approximately seven o'clock in the evening, and Betty was in the kitchen making a large pot of chicken soup. The house was dark except for the light above the stove. All of a sudden, while Betty was sitting there, she noticed a light appear under the basement door, which is opposite the kitchen. She quickly got up and came into the bedroom to tell me. She returned to check the light coming from the basement, and when she opened the door, she was surprised to find all of the lights were on in the basement. It should be noted that there are three different light switches that must be physically turned on for this to happen. This would not be the last time we would experience this phenomenon, as from time to time, the lights in one basement room or the other would go on when no one was down there. Also, as mentioned previously, the motion-sensor alarm would go off without anyone being found in the basement at these times.

I finally decided to leave a digital recorder in the basement overnight to see if anything could be heard. Much to our surprise, when the recording was played back, there were a multitude of sounds to be heard, ranging from loud popping noises to music, and at times, we could hear but not understand muffled voices. Bonnie, who has been kind enough to stay at our home and watch our dog when we have had to travel, can verify this as well. She has said she's heard music and what sounds like a party going on in our basement at night. Of course she did not venture down there to take a look, and I don't blame her, as this can be pretty frightening to someone who has not experienced it before.

Unusual Events: May 16, 2010

One night around ten o'clock, Betty and I were watching TV in the bedroom when I noticed the hall outside our bedroom was bathed in a red light that lasted for only a few seconds. An hour and a half later, after I'd turned in for the night, I felt as if someone grabbed my right arm just above the elbow. Thinking it was only my imagination, I moved my arm. Several minutes later, I returned it to the same position and again felt very strongly that someone had grabbed me. I turned over from my back to my left side and went to sleep. Several hours later, I awoke feeling as if someone had sat on my legs. Thinking it might have been a dream, I moved my legs and distinctly felt heavy weight on my legs, as if someone invisible sat there.

Finally, I drifted off to sleep, waking again at 6:12 a.m. to find the whole bedroom bathed in a red glow. I was now wide awake but thought this could be my eyes playing tricks on me. I opened and closed my eyes several times, only to find the room remained bathed in this unusual red glow. Three minutes later, the room returned to its normal color.

Related Red Color

1967: During her 1967 encounter, Betty saw a pulsating red-orange light coming through the kitchen window at the rear of the house.

1977: Betty and I had just finished visiting my mom in Connecticut. As we walked toward our car in the backyard, my mom said she saw us engulfed in a red light. There were no police, fire, or other emergency vehicles in the area that might have caused the bright red lights to surround and cover us.

1978: Betty and I awoke from a sound sleep in our Meriden home to find the entire bedroom illuminated by a soft red light with no apparent source. At the same time, we heard a multitude of birds singing as though within our bedroom, even though it was around three in the morning and still completely dark outside.

1986: We were staying at a campground in Higganum, Connecticut, in our thirty-foot travel trailer, which we'd parked at the lower end of the campground under two very large mature maple trees. I headed off to my job for the day, and Betty decided to relax and do some reading in the Bible. As it turned out, she was again visited by one of the small gray beings, who told her there were many ears listening, apparently by some kind of electronic means. The being took some sparkly stuff from what appeared to be a small backpack and spread it within the interior air of the room. Evidently this was used to prevent whatever electronics were being used from picking up anything.

My thought is that this electronic eavesdropping was our tax dollars at work. The being left behind some unusual physical evidence of this visit— as soon as I returned home from work and entered the trailer, I could smell burned plastic insulation. It did not take me long to find the source of this familiar odor: melted insulation on some of the wiring in the trailer. We were on the campground's water supply, so I had taped the trailer's switch for the electric water pump in the off position so no one would turn it on by mistake. I found the switch still taped in the off position, yet the wires from the pump had been heated enough to melt the insulation, and the pump had burned out. As if that was not enough, the leaves on the two large trees behind the trailer had now turned brown, *but only on the top*. The bottoms of the leaves were still a bright green, which was just beyond my ability to understand.

Fortunately we did know two electrical engineers in the area and asked if they would drop by to take a look. Even these educated people could put forth only the theory of an electromagnetic pulse (EMP) as being responsible for the condition of the two trees. It seemed that most technical people we told about this event agreed with the EMP theory, and this phenomenon went all the way back to 1945, when I'd had my first sighting as a child in my grandmother's backyard.

There were a couple of odd things that happened to Betty while in the same campground lot, which was kind of deserted at this time. We had our trailer parked in the lower corner, with only a couple of trailers farther up the hill. One day, while I was at work, Betty decided to go to the store, and she put Brutus in the backseat. She tried and tried to start the car's engine, but it wouldn't turn over. This was odd, because as a technician, I always kept our vehicles in good shape. After a while, Betty gave up, got out of the car to let Brute out, and started to walk to the trailer. She was holding the trailer key when it suddenly, physically popped out of her hand and landed somewhere in the grass. She could not see it, so she placed her jacket on the ground to mark exactly where it had fallen and went to the trailer to tie Brute back up. She quickly returned to her jacket and lifted it from the ground; there was the key, gleaming in the sun. She couldn't understand how she had missed it. Brutus was now barking at something in the woods, and as Betty continued to move back to the trailer, she said her attention was drawn to the bushes along the left side of the trailer and woods, where something large and unseen was pressing the thick branches and leaves backward, like something very large was silently moving along against the foliage. She rushed to the trailer to open the door, and not knowing what it could possibly be, she quickly took Brutus inside.

While living in this same trailer at the campground, Betty dropped me off at work one day, as she was going to use the car to do some shopping. She called me at work all shaken up and somewhat frustrated; she was stuck by the pumps at the gas station and was worried about the key to the car. She said that when she stopped for gas, she took the key from the ignition, got out of the car, and accidentally hit the door lock. She put the key into the door to unlock it, and the key twisted in the lock. She somehow pulled it out, but the metal key was now bent sideways at an awkward angle that would no longer fit in the door. While holding the key in her hand, she was so shaken that she began stroking it, almost trying to smooth it out. She said it suddenly felt soft like butter as she continued to rub it between her fingers, and it miraculously became straight again. She called me upset, because she was afraid if she put the key in the ignition and turned it on, the key might break off. I told her to try it anyway and to go home to get the spare key if it worked. She drove to the trailer, found the other key, and later picked me up at work, still amazed she had been able to somehow straighten the bent and crooked key with her fingers.

Unknown Year: We were once again visiting relatives in Florida when I awoke to find the guest bedroom bathed in this familiar red light. Shortly after seeing the light, I saw one of the small gray beings next to the bed. This mysterious red light has appeared numerous times since.

2010: I awoke at 4:21 a.m. to the sound of our motion-sensor alarm in the basement going off. A quick check of the premises revealed that no one was there as usual. This alarm had gone off several times in the past month, leading me to believe it might have been an insect or something small triggering it. This is why this particular incident is so interesting. I had moved the sensor to the top of the basement stairs and placed the front of the sensor right up against the corner of the stairwell, so there was virtually no room between the face of the sensor and the wall, yet it went off.

I called to speak to Becky, who is very psychic, to see if she might have a clue to what was going on, after something odd happened to our clocks.

Hey Beck,

What do you sense (if anything) about 3:33 a.m. today? July o7, 2010, When I heard heavy footsteps in the hall that woke me up at 3:33 a.m., and as usual no one was there. When I got up this morning I found our clocks (all battery operated, and linked to the atomic clock) had different times? My office clock was accurate reading 9:15 a.m. The kitchen clock read 8:19 a.m. and the clock in the exercise room read 6:20 a.m. All of these clocks have alkaline batteries and have been replaced in the last ninety days. Normally I only have to replace these batteries once a year. So all I can say is ??????????
Bob

I checked the batteries in both clocks with my multimeter. The battery on the exercise-room clock tested at 1.4 volts—not low enough to make that clock fail. The kitchen clock battery tested at 1.2 volts, which was probably low enough to cause failure. What puzzles me on this one is how it got drained, in such a short period of time, approximately three months after having been replaced. I replaced the batteries in both clocks and wrote the date on the backs of the clocks, for future reference.

July 25, 2010: I woke this morning at exactly 4:55 a.m. I was on my left side facing the side of the room Betty's mirrored dresser is on. I immediately noticed that the mirror was lit up like a computer screen with a white background and a large image of a woman's face on it. I looked at this for about ten to fifteen seconds, which was long enough for me to be certain I had never seen this face before. After this time, the face simply faded away and was replaced by the face of a typical gray. That also faded after several seconds, and the mirror again darkened to how it usually looked in the dark bedroom. I am absolutely certain I was awake at this time, as I'd had to pick up the small digital clock and bring it closer to my face to read it without my eyeglasses on. I have no idea what this means, if anything, or why it happened.

September 3, 2010: Betty and I were in bed watching *America's Funniest Videos* when the motion sensor in the basement set off the alarm. I immediately got up and went to investigate. Once again there was no one there, all the windows were closed, and the door was securely locked. I had already moved the alarm to make it so spiders or insects couldn't set it off, though I doubt any insect would have body heat sufficient to trigger this alarm. I was still at a loss to explain this. The motion detector was infrared and should not be affected by any type of RF, as far as I know.

September 19, 2011: Betty and I woke at 1:52 a.m. to a very loud crashing sound that was so extreme I could actually feel the whole house shake. My first thoughts were that we were experiencing an earthquake, and I thought we should get out of the house. Once the sound and vibration died down about three to five seconds later, everything was silent, and I went back to sleep. When I got out of bed at half past seven that morning, I checked the house and outside for any visible damage, and there was none. I then checked the news to see if anyone else had reported hearing loud noises during the evening and found nothing. Once again I was left with no logical answer to this experience, but I have talked to several other people who have experienced exactly the same thing, and they never found an explanation either.

December 1, 2012: I awoke this morning at about a quarter past one and observed in the hallway just outside of our bedroom what appeared to be two red lights up close to the ceiling. Each light was about the size of a golf ball. I watched these lights change shape from round to more or less a football shape and flicker. They were getting brighter and dimmer, like a pulsing for maybe ten or fifteen seconds, then there was what I can only describe as an explosion of white light many times brighter than the midday sun. When this light was present, I could see everything in the hall or bedroom with exceptional clarity, even though I did not have my glasses on. The white light pulsed three times, lasting only a few seconds each time. I was propped up on my left elbow while this was taking place, and once it stopped, I thought, *What the heck was that?* By this time, I knew there was nothing I could do about it, and I went back to sleep.

December 3, 2012: I awoke at 5:55 a.m., and when I opened my eyes, I was surprised to see the hallway outside of our bedroom filled from floor to ceiling with gray see-through orbs. These orbs were different from ones I'd seen in the past, as they were mostly the approximate size of basketballs, with a few being slightly larger. They were a grayish color and transparent enough that I could see orbs behind orbs and even see the wall behind all of them. This lasted probably between thirty to forty-five seconds, and then they just slowly faded, leaving me once again to wonder why I was seeing these things. I had had a recent physical and eye exam and had been found to be in very good health, and my eyes were in unusually good condition for my age, according to the eye doctors, so I am ruling out any physical causes for the phenomenon.

I know some readers will think, *Oh wow, this must be a mental condition*, and I am sure many would like to believe this is the case, as they don't want to accept the idea that these things actually happen to people or that there is more to life than the physical world we live in. The truth is that this type of activity has happened to many folks who have had experiences with UFOs, and as we now know, there seems to be plenty of evidence of an unseen spirit world that can at times manifest itself in our physical existence. I think this has been more than sufficiently documented by the many *Ghost Hunter*-style shows that are now so popular.

As for Betty, she has had some unusual things besides her encounters to deal with. I had a motion-detecting camera set up on my bureau facing the door to the hallway to catch any nighttime activity that might transpire. One night, Betty got up to use the bathroom. When she returned to bed, there were three white orbs of light, each the size of an orange, that showed up on the camera; they were zipping around, darting upward over her head at our bedroom doorway as she entered the room.

On two separate occasions, while in our bedroom, Betty saw me walk down the hallway into the office, only to find out I was actually in the kitchen and had not moved from there. Several times, only at night, she has seen the hallway turn from its normal light to an intense, deep red light, but the color does not enter our bedroom. She also has heard loud bangs in the basement at times. We've been informed by two psychics that, in their opinion, we have two open portals downstairs; if this is the case, it is possibly where so much paranormal activity in this house stems from. The psychics told us one is under the basement stairs, and the other one is on the direct opposite side of the house, below the doorway that leads into the other half of the cellar. Our 120-pound German shepherd is bothered by something in the house that he will not pass. He often stops at our bedroom door, turns around, and walks into our room backward. He has done this in the kitchen and the living room at times as well, just as if he's going around something. When Betty sees this happening, she waves her hand in the air in front of our dog to push whatever it is out of his way, and he passes with no problem.

During times we've had to travel to different states to tell others about our experiences with UFOs, we've had some odd and unusual things take place. One such time was in the early nineties. Bob, Becky, and I were supposed to do a lecture in California at the Tim Beckley UFO Meeting and Conference, so we were driving west on Route 40 through Tennessee when our car's water pump broke and punctured the radiator. Within minutes, police came and called a tow truck to take us to a repair shop. It was getting quite late when the car was finally fixed, and we headed out again. We reached Alabama, and the weather seemed like there was a storm coming, so we stopped to eat and decided to get a room at a motel and start back on our journey in the morning, more refreshed. As we entered the motel room, there was a large window off to the left, a table with two chairs next to it, and two double beds. Bob and I slept in the first bed, closest to the entrance, and Becky used the adjoining bed. As we fell asleep, Becky suddenly awoke and started screaming for me. The room was very dark. I jumped out of bed and leaned down to feel her forehead, thinking she'd had a bad dream or a fever, and she grabbed both my arms and held me there, saying, "It's right in back of you, Mom. Look out; the thing is right behind you."

"What, Becky?" I asked. There was a look of absolute horror in her eyes. "What is it?"

Without realizing it, when I had leaped to my daughter's side, I'd jumped in front of a tall, black, hooded form that had a huge head like a cobra's and glowing red eyes. It rose from the floor to the ceiling. At that point, there was stark terror on Becky's face. I refused to turn to face the form, but could tell from the look on her face something horribly real was there. Immediately I began to call out loud the name of the Lord

Jesus, asking for his protection and for him to take away the unseen threat that evidently was residing in that room. With a loud voice of authority, I commanded in the name of Jesus Christ for the evil presence to be gone. Becky said the snakelike body suddenly fell from the ceiling to the floor. Meanwhile, Bob was also awake and sitting up in our bed, surprised to see the strange, slithering black form quickly move across the floor toward the table. Its body swiftly glided upward over the chair, across the table, past the curtains, and out through the solid glass window.

We don't know what it was, but we were thankful to the Lord for His protection. Both Becky and Bob saw it. I did not, but I believed what they had seen was possibly some kind of evil spirit. We looked out the window at the dark sky. Earlier the news and weather report had predicted possible storms or tornados in the area. Bob was concerned about the car's earlier problem, the weather, and the desert area we would have to travel through to get to our destination, so to be on the safe side, we decided we'd better go back home, as by this point we had lost enough time that we would be unable to make the conference in California. After returning Becky to her home in Virginia, we continued our drive to Connecticut.

I would like to add here something unusual that happened, where once again, strong faith played a role in both Becky's and my life. In 1977, after my two sons had died in an auto accident, I was still living in Ashburnham. The children were in school, so I decided to go to Gardner to see my daughter, who recently had moved into a new apartment. When I got there, Becky was in the living room speaking to a young man I had never met before. I heard her telling him she was not interested and wanted him to leave her alone. The young man refused to accept her rejection and became aggressive. He suddenly grabbed Becky and forcefully pulled her with him toward an adjoining room. Becky was resisting and trying to break away from his grasp, but he was too strong. I could not understand why this was happening, but I realized an out-of-control temper like his was dangerous. If he managed to get her alone in that room and closed the door, anything could happen. I immediately wrapped my arms around her waist and pulled with all my strength, for we were now in between the two sides of the doorway. He lost his grip and fell backward into the room on the floor. A surprised, angry look was on his face as he moved to get up and come toward us. I quickly prayed to the Lord for help. Immediately, I raised my arm and pointed my index finger toward him. I said, "In the name of Jesus Christ, stop."

Suddenly his body was pinned against the living-room wall. He could not move. His arms and legs were spread apart. He tried to move but could not get off the wall. He struggled ever so slowly to move sideways. Once again I pointed at him, saying, "In the name of Jesus Christ, be still." It was happening so fast, as if something was holding him against the wall. I knew it had to be the Lord watching over us.

He realized he was unable to break away from the wall and said, "Becky, tell your mother to stop. Tell her to stop it." Again he tried to move around the outer part of the wall but remained pinned to its surface.

A third time I raised my arm and pointed at him, saying, "In the name of Jesus Christ, be still." Becky and I quickly left the apartment, ran to my car, and drove to my home in Ashburnham. I locked the doors just as he pulled into my driveway. He jumped from his car, rushed to my front door, and started banging against it as if to break it down. I said to him, "You better leave, because I am calling the police, and you will go to jail. Now get out of here." He stopped kicking the door and went back to his car. He had taken Becky's pocketbook from her apartment, and as he sat there, he opened it up, emptied all her belongings out onto the driveway, and tossed her empty pocketbook to the ground. I'm sure he thought the police were on the way, because he suddenly whipped his car around and quickly left the area. I thanked God for watching over us, and after this, I believed even more strongly that faith can move mountains.

After a few days, I took Becky back to her apartment. I knew she would be safe, since we had family members living in the same complex. My sister Carol learned what had happened and said they would watch out for Becky and my grandchildren. A week passed with no problem, but the stalker showed up again. Becky's visiting cousin ran to tell her father the man was back and had forced his way into Becky's residence. My brother-in-law ran to my daughter's aid. As soon as the young man saw the anger on Becky's uncle's face, he knew he was in big trouble and quickly climbed out an open window to the rooftop, with Becky's Uncle Dell close behind. The young man continued to run from my fearless brother-in-law, jumping from rooftop to rooftop, until the trespasser finally leaped twenty feet or more to the ground below. Dell warned the young man that if he ever came back again, Dell would make sure he would not live to see another day. The stalker finally got the message.

Bob Continues

When we were living in Higganum in our fifth-wheel trailer, Betty decided to get a job. During those months at work, a wonderful friend taught her how to build and solder electronic circuit boards. Shortly thereafter, Betty had to quit for a publicity tour. One of the first shows we were on was *Sally*, with Sally Jessy Raphael. Much to Betty's surprise and joy, her friend and three of the other ladies from work showed up in the audience to support her. After the publicity whirlwind settled down and Betty had time on her hands again, she decided to take on a temporary job.

She was hired for two months at a shop that did some military work. She was building wire harnesses and so forth. One of the other workers was also named Betty, and the two women got along well. Betty confided in her new friend about some of the UFO experiences that had happened. Time passed, and the very day Betty's job was ending, something unusual started to happen. Betty and I were in our cars on the way to our respective jobs and were conversing though our CB radios, when both our CBs started making beeping tones, and we were cut off. She was passing the very trap-rock area where I had seen a UFO, but at this time, I was going in the opposite direction to Middletown.

Once Betty got to work, she and her friend were all alone. They worked by themselves at a table and chatted. Her coworker was cutting some wires, and my wife was dipping the ends of the wires into the melted lead in front of her to tin them. The square sunken basin holding the liquid lead was about three inches above the tabletop.

While the pot's four-sided, five-inch-high, perforated metal cover was attached to the basin with hinges, said lid was open and tilted safely backward, away from the tub of liquid lead sitting in front of my wife. Much to the women's surprise, the heavy metal cover started to bounce back and forth, up and down a number of times, with no one touching it. It eventually came to a stop. They sat there with their mouths wide open, wondering what the heck was happening.

Both women were surprised, and the coworker, remembering about my wife's encounters, put two and two together, turned, and said, "Do you think you should tie me down to my chair?" They laughed. She was so good-natured about it, which made my wife feel better. But in my wife's mind, she thought, *No more. Not now, please. This is my last day here. Please leave me alone. Don't do this. Not now.* They continued working, though they were a little frazzled over what had just happened. Suddenly, the coworker Betty turned in her seat and said, "What?" There was no reply. So my wife asked what was wrong. The coworker said, "Didn't you hear it? I just heard our boss call my name."

Of course my wife knew right away who it was doing the calling and why they were calling, "Betty." And once again she pleaded under her breath for the invisible force to stop bothering them. As it turned out, there was no boss present, only Betty and her coworker. My wife was never so happy to get home as she was that evening, and she let me know what had happened during her last day at work.

While living in Higganum, I started to have some heavy-duty back problems. The weather was cool in the winter, which tended to aggravate my condition, so we decided to move to Virginia. This meant Betty would have more time to see her three daughters and family settled there. We purchased a mobile home in Hayes, and because Betty and I each got a job, our dog was in the mobile home alone through the day. Because my job was not very far from home, I came home during my lunch hour to let Brute out and bring him with me to McDonald's for a couple of quick hamburgers. One day, upon arriving home to pick him up, I was surprised to see someone had tried to break into our new residence. When I arrived, the door was wide open, and there was Brutus sitting in the middle of the entrance. A thorough check of the mobile home revealed that nothing had been disturbed. It was obvious no one had made it past our dog. There were a few other things that happened in and around the mobile home while we lived there.

One late evening, about two or two thirty in the morning, we could hear two men close by in our yard, talking very loudly. It was obvious they had been drinking, and after about fifteen minutes or more went by, I decided enough was enough. It was time to put a stop to what was going on, so we could go to sleep. I took my separate laser gun sight, stepped up to the window and aimed it at the chest of one of the men. As soon as they noticed the red dot on the chest, they took off as fast as they could down the street. At last it was quiet so we could get back to sleep.

There were three other strange things that happened to us while living in this home. One evening I got up to go to the bathroom, and the bedroom was filled with tiny colored, sparkling lights. I had no idea what they were. Another evening, while in bed, we could see several long rounded poles of white light that kept appearing at the edge of the ceiling next to the sliding closet doors at the back of the bedroom. They kept appearing on the ceiling next to the closet doors. I don't know if it was UFO-related or not. One last thing that happened there in Hayes involved our laundry. Some sort of stain happened to appear on separate occasions. Our white sheets were stained with a pinkish red color in different areas, as were our pillowcases, towels, and facecloths. Also, my white briefs had these pinkish red stains on them in the morning, and when we took our showers, the facecloths and white towels would become stained with this strange color as we dried ourselves. We didn't know if it was coming out of our skin or what. We could not figure out what was causing it. Becky also had the same thing happen to her clothing at her home. Betty uses bleach when she washes white clothes, and that usually gets them white and clean. She thought it must have been the laundry detergent she'd used with bleach that caused it, but this had happened once before to us when we lived in Connecticut as well. We later found out that this happens to people involved in the UFO phenomenon and is being studied by Dr. David Jacobs, associate professor of history at Temple University. To the best of my knowledge, the first recorded case of one of these stains on an abductee's clothing occurred on the dress of Betty Hill. As far as I am aware to this date, the composition of this staining material has remained elusive, even under scientific testing.

The last paranormal thing that has happened to us has to do with our present residence. Bob was on the computer checking some land we had bought several years earlier, for we were thinking of having some trees cut down. He was using a program called Google Earth to check the land by satellite. He then decided to check our residence on Google Earth as well. This technology involves a camera that takes pictures by satellite of the whole earth as it turns. When he checked our property, we were totally surprised to see something huge hovering in midair over a portion of the back part of our garage roof, while the rest of the object was extended over a third part of our deck, about fifteen to twenty feet in midair. In its center was something that looked like a shining silver-white light, with a surrounding border of gray and black. The object was rounded with an elongated wing shape. After we showed the photo to two psychics, they both said it was a portal. This was strange, as we had been told much earlier that we had portals in our cellar, where we seemed to have had quite a few very odd things happening off and on.

Bob was tired of having to check the many noises in the cellar and in the house. He decided to try to close the portals. He used a bouquet of burning sage in all the rooms and in the cellar and then prayed over both portals, asking the Lord to close them. It seemed to work, but then this large outside portal suddenly appeared. This outside picture of the odd large portal was taken in 2014. A picture of it is included in this book. Bob would like to add here that, as a logical-minded technician, he thought this object was nothing more than a reflection of something very shiny. The problem that presents itself here is that at the time there was nothing on the deck or in that area of the house that could have caused that large of a reflection. There is a grill on our deck, but the angle and size of the object do not seem to match. Also it appears to be above both the deck and garage roof.

CHAPTER 20

The Strange and Exotic

• • •

As we've mentioned, Bob and I sold our home, bought a fifth-wheel trailer, and moved to a wooded campground in Higganum so we could go to Florida in the winter and enjoy our summers in Connecticut. The trailer was very large and comfortable. Its entrance brought us directly into the kitchen area facing the large refrigerator; beside it were the stove, some counters, and the kitchen sink. Across from this area was the kitchen table with large seats that could easily seat four people comfortably, and it could be converted into a bed. Of course there were cabinets on both sides of the room. Beyond the kitchen was the living room with an easy chair, a television area, and a large soft sofa at the back end, with a second door off to the side. Going upstairs near the entrance doorway, to the right, there was a sliding door to the second level, where we had a bathtub and shower with sliding doors on the left, and to the right were the toilet and sink. In the third level, there were large closets with mirrors and lower drawers, and the fourth level was where our queen-size bed was located. This layout information is all to provide context for an encounter with the One.

But first I want to share the unusual things the beings did to catch my attention and take me into their time element. One late evening in the summer of 1989, we had retired to bed in the trailer. After a busy day of work, Bob quickly drifted off to a deep sleep, as I lay awake listening to the quiet night. The window was open, but the air was stuffy and too warm. I felt drawn to go outside, thinking it would be much cooler. I quietly got up and opened the door. As I stepped outside, everything was eerily still. It seemed deserted, for there were only a couple of trailers in the whole campground at the time, and only one couple besides us was living there. I could see a haze of mist down toward the field, and as I turned toward the woods, I happened to notice there was a bluish light there. I stood there amazed and interested, wondering what it could possibly be. It looked sort of like a blue ball of light glowing among the tall trees, and it seemed to be moving toward me. Standing there alone, and not knowing what the thing was, I decided to go inside, but as I tried to turn to get back into the trailer, I couldn't move. The blue ball of light came closer and hovered in mid-air—whoa. At this point in time, I don't know what happened, but I was suddenly back in my home in Virginia, typing and reliving in my mind the old experience. I abruptly stopped typing, because of something that happened. It was uncanny and right on target. Bob was in the bedroom still fast asleep when I awoke very early this morning, got up alone, and went to the office to punch away at the computer keyboard. The house was dead quiet, and my mind was locked into the last memory of being para-lyzed from the odd blue light, while standing outside of the trailer. At that very moment, the lights in the office went out, and the room went black. Goosebumps covered my body. I held my breath and sat very still, think-ing, *Uh-oh. Here we go again.* I gathered my courage and slowly glanced around the darkened room, half expecting one of the beings only to see a hand wrapped around the light switch. To my surprise, it was Bob's hand, while the rest of him remained hidden in the hallway.

He saw I was shaken and claimed he'd left his hand there on pur-pose, for me to finally see it was him. He couldn't help but laugh at the expression on my face when I told him, "You scared me. I still have goose bumps." In a way it was funny, but the timing was incredible, for he didn't know I was almost reliving the blue-light event. I just wanted to share Bob's sense of humor and what happens in our household, which in a way is good for me, as I am a very serious person and need to lighten up once in a while, especially after all I have had to go through. After a shower, I dressed, had breakfast, and started to type about my encounter once again.

Now back to the experience with the actual blue ball of light in the Higganum campground. A stream of blue light shot out from the ball moving toward me. I was suddenly inside it, moving away from the trailer and over the road and trees. I was covered in blue light, wondering what was happening to me, while standing inside a different room that appeared to be another craft. The strange blue orb covering me suddenly felt like liquid draining off my body. The blue substance congealed in midair and formed a small ball of blue light that drifted upward and settled by the side of my head. There was a small being standing by, talking to my mind and telling me to kneel, while two other beings came in carrying some sort of clear, domelike headgear. They secured one of the apparatuses over my head, and the little being placed the other one on his head. The little being and I were then escorted into another room that felt like we were slowly moving through a lightweight form of gray jelly. After a while, the small being and I were taken out of this room into another, where the other two beings removed our headgear. The craft had stopped, and the small being and I moved outside, followed by the blue light that hovered next to me. It felt cool, and right away I knew I had been here before. It was very misty as the small being brought me over to an area, where the same glass-like shoes I had worn once before were stored. After securing the odd shoes to our feet, we moved past the misty atmosphere, and once again I was able to see the glorious crystal forest. As we moved along the crystal pathway, I remembered seeing this area before. Way off to the right was a craft parked in the tunnel entrance. There beside this entrance were the enormous crystal walls that reached heavenward. The being and the small blue light trailing beside me continued moving over the crystal pathway. The crystal forest of trees, bushes, flowers, and grass was magnificent. My mind was thinking about the crystal butterfly that had come to life briefly the last time I was here, and I wondered if I might see and touch it again. Then the area was bathed in a flash of extreme light, as a loud sound of rumbling occurred.

The small being told me to run, as the One within the world of light was opening the great door. I could not understand why, but thought

I had better do as he said, and I ran. It was difficult to do while wearing the shoes. All at once, it felt like the path below me was moving. The area became extremely bright as translucent sheets of light flashed down from above and settled within the crystal forest, making it next to impossible to move. I struggled to run between the barrages of falling lights. Somehow I got off the original pathway. The being told me to keep on running and not stop. I was afraid. I kept moving, but the small being was not catching up to me. While trying to run, I turned to check on him, and bumped into one of the peculiar sheets of light. I fell backward, and the odd shoes lifted off my feet into the air and landed in different directions. I fell through the crystal floor in shock and began to sink downward. I had gotten off the path and was on a smooth body of solidified crystal that was now quickly turning into a watery pond from my touch. I struggled to swim. The more I splashed and touched the crystal and my hands and body made contact, the more I turned the area into deep water. I kept trying to move and kick my feet and legs to stay above the water and get to some solid ground.

Finally the small being caught up to me, as I struggled to pull myself out of the water near the edge of the shore. He told me he'd been unable to move past one of the strips of light and had had to stop, for there was light all over the place. The light had definitely grown even brighter, and the being kept saying to me, "The One has moved to open the great door. The great door is open." There was such bright light everywhere, and the odd slices of mirrored light began to diminish and disappear. I rested on the ground with the small being and with the blue ball of light above me, not knowing what to do. We could see six beings of light moving through the forest toward us. They had no visible facial features, such as eyes, a nose, or a mouth like a human. Their entire physical form was a body of golden light. They were moving along, beside a floating machine. This looked like a clear, double-hollow barrel. I felt very cold while sitting on the path. Two of the light beings were carrying some odd fanlike tools and immediately began to sweep and smooth out chunks of crystal where the water and ground had been disturbed.

I was told to get inside the barrel, which I did. I watched as they used the odd fanlike tools to straighten out the disheveled crystal. I was amazed at how they were able to put the crystal back to what it was before I had fallen into the water and disturbed the ground. As they quickly worked to fix the crystal, I noticed little sparkly things floating around. Even while I sat inside this barrel, there were tiny sparkles floating all around. I began to dry off and feel much warmer. Tiny crystals were falling off my clothes, and I thought, *I better be careful not to touch them*, thinking they would probably turn back to water. To my surprise I touched them anyway, and they quickly broke down to tiny sparkles. The small being and one of the light beings were now carrying the glass-like shoes I had lost and immediately placed them on my feet. As I stood up next to the small being, the ball of blue light returned and floated over to me. We continued to watch as the six beings silently finished the cleanup; returned to the side of the revolving barrel; and, without a word or nod, moved along the path into the deeper part of the forest. I could still feel the ground shaking as the little being and I, for some reason, were heading back on the same path we had come from earlier. A clear, large orb within the tunnel rose above the crystal trees and came toward us. The little being stepped back as my glass shoes fell from my feet to the pathway, and the blue light and I were lifted up into the waiting orb. It immediately moved into the tunnel below.

I was now alone but not afraid, for I remembered I had been in a similar orb as a child, when I was taken to see the One and had been fine. I could see the tall mountains of crystal just before we entered the glass-like tunnel. As we floated along, suspended in space, the blue light filled the orb, which made me feel safe and comfortable. I started to see a shining light up ahead and noticed as we drew closer that there were many glass orbs below. At the end of the tunnel to the left, I could see a multitude of different-size clear orbs resting on the floor. The floating orb suddenly came to a stop, and the blue light and I moved out of it. Up ahead, there were two beings standing in front of a shiny metallic sphere, waiting for me. The beings greeted me through my mind. I was silently standing by their craft looking at the many orbs, and I asked them what the clear orbs were for. The being revealed that they were record keepers of intelligence and could become as small as an atom and as large as possible, like the sun and planets, which are also forms of a living, intelligent being. Each of them has an intelligence of its own.

After explaining what the orbs were used for, the beings insisted I had to go with them to see someone. They escorted me into their craft, which sat on the edge of space; once inside, I was surprised to stand before a large window that could not be seen from the outside. The craft had lifted off the crystallized area and headed out into the heavens. As we moved away from the light, it began to grow dark. The higher we ascended, the more my fingers seemed to hurt. Beyond the darkness, the sky seemed lit with a million stars. We were traveling deeper and deeper into space. As I gazed into the darkness, I realized we were moving farther from home. My mind wondered, *Where are we, and why is this happening to me?* I was bewildered, yet I was unable to pull my mind or eyes away from the window and the wonders that might exist within the beyond.

CHAPTER 21

Masters of OH

• • •

SOME DISTANCE AHEAD, THERE APPEARED to be an enormous cylinder-shaped craft coming into view. We were definitely headed toward the strange-looking vehicle. I could see it had a metallic cigar-shaped body. Three slowly revolving wheels stuck out from the main frame, yet the craft remained stationary. There were portals on the inner edges of the wheels where light and steam or mist poured outward, causing a misty cloud that seemed to hug or cover some of the outer surface of the craft. The front and back wheels were revolving one way, while the central wheel was revolving the opposite way. The big ship was hanging in midair, as the beings' craft drew closer and circled around toward one end that was lit up with white and red lights. The huge entrance to the elongated ship automatically opened with a dual separated twisting system that allowed the beings' small spherical craft to enter the wide opening that looked like it was made of metal and glass. Within this open space, there were graduated landing levels that had indented spaces for craft to park within. There were two large doors and some stairs that went into the main part of the craft. The beings parked the orb, and we got out. As we were standing there, an Elder came out to greet us. He escorted us into the inner part of this enormously large ship.

Keep in mind that this was the third time I would be brought before the One. At this time, we came out of the small craft and stood there waiting. A tall, white-haired being came down the stairs toward us and motioned for us to follow him back up the stairs. As we did, we passed through the large door into a long, very brightly lit hallway. He then communicated to the two beings I was with to wait there, and he wanted me to follow him. As we moved along, I was surprised, because I was able to walk on my own and was not being floated along. As we moved down this long hallway, there appeared to be other rooms and doorways on both sides. We walked up some more steps, and it seemed like this was a very long hallway. Then we stopped at another set of steps and went up another level, and he told me to wait there. As he left, I could see some light coming out of another room and decided to see what was in there. When I looked, I could see there were three skinny old men dressed in black sitting with their heads bowed. And there were two of the gray beings there. One of the old men noticed me standing there and pointed toward my way. All three men lifted their heads to look at me. I rushed back to where I was supposed to be waiting, and the gray being stuck his head out and looked at me. I got the feeling I wasn't supposed to be there.

The Elder returned and continued to lead me up this hall, where there were many rooms. He took me off to the side into another room, where I saw three of the gray beings standing there very still, but their eyes looked strange, like something was wrong with them. They looked milky gray like they had cataracts or something, so I asked the Elder what was wrong with their eyes. He replied, "They are here for new eyes (he called them biorbits or biorbics). Their eyes are no longer useful. They have to receive new ones." I was soon to realize that the strange creatures I had seen dwelling in the shimmering red atmosphere during my 1967 abduction were being raised for such a task.

In 1967 I was taken from my home by gray beings. At that time, two beings dressed in silver suits escorted me through a dark tunnel. They had black hoods on their heads, and as we were moving along a track, we entered through a shiny mirrorlike glass door into a world of shimmering red atmosphere. Within this atmosphere, there were these strange red creatures. They had very big, round, black eyes. Evidently the beings I was with did not care if I saw these odd creatures or not, for they did not provide a hood for me. Or perhaps they thought my long dark hair was enough covering. The gray beings and I continued to move along through the red atmosphere, but now, many years later, while I was within this elongated ship, these same red creatures that had been dwelling in the vibrating red area back then were shown to me once again while aboard this ship. There were quite a few of them, but they were not free here. Some of them were now in a room of red light, with one of the tall white Elders watching over them. Each red creature was very still and floating up to its neck in a liquid-filled glass tube. The Elder that had taken me in here lifted up the top part of the tube, reached in, and removed the red creature's eyes. There was no reaction from the red creature; it just stood there, did not seem to be in pain, and appeared to be more relaxed. The Elder placed the large black eyeballs on a plate close by and said the red creatures eyes would grow back again very shortly. At this point I could see that two of the other red beings were already starting to grow new eyeballs.

The Elder said to me that he could control or communicate to the grays through these eyes that never close; however, I didn't think all the gray beings needed new eyes, even though they are always open, always watching (evidently this is where they get their name, the watchers). Both parties, watcher and Elder, can send and receive messages and directions through the red creatures' eyes. What's strange is, in 1967, the two silver-suited watchers had black hoods over their heads while in the red area. Evidently they are not supposed to look upon the red creatures for some reason. Now back to the watchers. What about their gray skin? The pigmentation of the watcher's skin must be very strong to withstand or repel ultraviolet radiation. That must be why they seem to be extremely important to the Elders. What about the Elders' light skin? To me, their pale flesh, white hair, and light blue eyes could label them as albinos, which means they would have to be very careful around extreme forms of light, such as the sun. If the Elders who claim to be ambassadors of "OH" and masters of rings, cycles, and orbs lack enough pigmentation, they undoubtedly could suffer dire consequences; if so, this may be the reason the Elders have the grays as their servants, doing certain work for them. According to one of the Internet medical dictionaries, regarding pigmentation, it says, the color of people with light skin is determined mainly by the bluish-white connective tissue under the dermis and by the hemoglobin circulating in the veins of the dermis. One wonders if these angels—Elders—may even have blood like a human being has, for hemoglobin is a component of human blood.

The Elders said they were going to show me how biorbics work. And as I followed them down the long hallway, we stopped and entered a room where a gray being lay very still on an oddly shaped table. There were two similar beings standing by, as a third one was busy working up by the being's head. I could see that this third being had already removed both eyes from the patient's eye sockets. When the Elder drew closer to the subject on the table, the three watchers quickly left the table area and stood with their faces turned toward the wall. The two Elders began to work and quickly removed the black eyeballs from the plate. Somehow one of them was using an instrument with light as they somehow placed the new eyes into the empty sockets. As he did, he pressed his fingers against the head in different areas, and tiny light spots appeared inside the new set of eyeballs. The Elder kept pressing on different sections of the top of the being's head, and tiny pinpoints of different colored lights kept popping up in the eyes like it had hundreds of sections to it. It was amazing. The other Elder pulled some kind of machine out from the wall, and moved it closer to the back of the being's head. On the opposite side of the machine was a chair where the Elder sat with his head pressed backward. A glass hood from the machine was placed over the gray patient's head, and again, the Elder pressed his head backward as if he was mentally transferring something to the gray being under the glass hood, who had just received new eyes. These eyes would now be used to remotely send information directly to the Elder, and the Elders' commands would be received and understood within the gray being's eyes and mind. The other three beings came back to the watcher on the table and lifted the round glass hood off the gray watcher's head. The Elder pushed the chair back into place by the wall. The job of biorbics was completed by inserting the new eyes and the Elders' commands.

After the operations were completed, one of the Elders told me to come along with him. As we walked down the hall, I could see out of a large window the darkened sky with a multitude of stars. We continued to move along the hall, and I could see the many rooms in this ship, and as I listened, I began to hear a tinkling sound, like music. The Elder was so much taller than I that it became hard for me to keep up with him, and he kept saying, "Come along; come along." While I followed, I continued to hear a tinkling sound of music. We entered another room where another Elder was standing by the wall. And next to him was a rounded inset shelf that had many small stemlike things that looked like *Y*s coming out of its base. He seemed to be touching different stems with the stroke of his fingers. While in midair, there were different-size brightly glowing colored crystals. He was making music as he stroked the bottom stems and moved his right hand over the floating pyramid-shaped gems. It was a soft and beautiful sound. Besides the wondrous sounds, there were small solid balls of colored lights like marbles flying past the Elder from the music and landing in a liquid-filled basin that had risen up from the floor.

The Elder with me moved to the basin containing small orbs and liquid. It appeared he was washing his hands. He then scooped the objects up and put them somewhere in his robe. The music and magical experience was breathtakingly beautiful. The Elder came toward me and said, "We must go, for someone wants to see you." We entered the long hallway once again. I could see way down one end and way up in the opposite direction. The Elder and I were patiently standing there, while I wondered why we weren't moving. Suddenly I could see why. Some distance ahead of us, there were three very old men in black robes who had entered the hallway escorted by three gray watchers. They looked like the same people I had accidentally peeked in on earlier. The strange thing was, beside each one of those very old men was a hovering ball of red glowing light. That's why the Elder had stopped. We watched from a distance as they disappeared down a set of stairs. The Elder said, "Come along now," and once again we continued our walk. As we moved forward, we stopped to enter another extremely large rounded room through an invisible door. We passed through it.

Once inside, I was brought before another Elder, and while standing before him, I asked, "Are there any other ladies on this ship? Are there any other women here besides me? All I see is men." He replied, "No. We are neither male nor female. Humans are male and female, and the male is the dominant one."

I asked, "And what am I doing here?"

He said, "Don't you remember your blessing?"

I said, "No, what blessing? What are you talking about?" He brought me into an unusual round room to show me what the blessing was all about. A glass-like platform extended out from a huge ball of rings. And as the rings began to swirl round and round, the scene suddenly changed to the exact time I was at the church in Ashburnham, Massachusetts, with my mother and father. This experience had happened many years ago, and the Elders wanted to refresh my memory concerning my blessing. This blessing refers to the experience I'd had so long ago when the two angels, unknown to me, had appeared. They said I would be blessed above women. If you remember reading about it earlier, that blessing was something more than the genealogy of being male or female. It was the reason I was aboard this huge ship and being shown their craft, machines, and physical evidence of higher powers that exist and assist the needs of the human race.

Again it brings me to wonder, was this what the One had meant when he told me, "I have chosen you to show the world?" Or was it to let the world know we are not alone and are not the only ones who occupy this earthly and heavenly realm? If it wasn't any of the explanations or possibilities I just spoke of, then I am at a loss for words. After seeing and going through the experience again, I was flabbergasted. Why was I going through such extraordinary and unbelievable things that I could not quite understand?

Three other tall Elders entered the room and walked over to a round design upon the craft's floor. Within the circle, there were six designs, like six divided places or pieces of a pie. The three Elders each stood in a separate triangulated section of the interior design and spread their arms to touch the right to the left of one another's hand, so that their palms were flat and their fingers were pointing upward. They bowed their heads. A beam of light shot forth from one side of each forehead and touched one another's heads, forming a triangle of light between them; out of thin air, a ring of light formed at the very center between them. It was beautiful. Three other Elders came forward and stood in the three remaining triangles on the floor. They quickly put their right arms under each of the first three Elders' joined arms. And then they continued on the other side to put their left arms over them. And all three of the second group of Elders did the same as the first three Elders, connecting the palms of their hands together with their fingers pointing upward. They also bowed their heads, and a beam of light streaked out of each forehead and created another triangle of light. As they bowed their heads, a circular rim of light surrounded all six Elders, and they began chanting in low voices, "OoooooooH...OoooooooH..."

As they repeated the chant, the two triangular lights on each Elder's forehead seemed to join closer together between the center of their eyebrow area, and the light of the double triangle made a six-pointed star appear with a smaller interior circle of light. The Elders kept repeating a long, low "OoooooooH." The H sound at the end was like a release of power from the mouth. I had no idea what these Elders were doing. The other Elder and I just stood there watching the amazing ceremonial scene taking place before us. The larger ring of light started to rise and grew smaller as it continued above their heads. The light lowered itself even more and joined the small, round bar of light between the six Elders. The streams of light coming from each Elder's forehead disappeared, and they were letting go of their hands. They raised their arms and hands in the air, still chanting. The two central rings of light joined together between the Elders' outstretched arms, as the rings kept swirling around one another, causing a bluish-purple light to appear. The rings began to solidify into a ball of light. All the Elders stopped, and one of them grasped the unusual ball of light and quickly carried it to the Elder standing beside me, while the other Elders began to depart. The ball looked like something was moving around inside it, and the Elder took it over to a stand close by, which had a single pedestal with four prongs that held the ball of light securely within it. Close to this pedestal was another round, triangular design on the floor that looked identical to the one the six Elders had used earlier. But close beside the floor design was a large doorway with what looked like vibrating water within it. Off to the left was a huge window looking out into the darkness of space and thousands of stars, while beside that was another large slanted tube with balls of light going up and down inside it. I had seen this same kind of huge tube in the room where the Elder had retrieved some small orbs of light created by the tinkling music. As I stood in this area of the large room, near the glass platform, I noticed four glass-like chairs in a row, and the Elder told me to sit down.

At this time in my hypnosis, the hypnotist asked if the large purple orb was the same as the orbs I had seen before I'd been taken aboard this elongated craft. I knew the purple orb was not the same as the clear orbs, which were record keepers of knowledge and intelligence. The hypnotist asked about the orbs again; this time he wanted to know if I had asked the gray beings any questions about them, but the gray beings were not there at this time, only the Elders, who revealed that they are the ambassadors of OH, which was the internal, external, and eternal presence.

About that time, the Elder approached me and said, "We are now going on a journey to Earth." He told me I would have to disrobe. As soon as he said that, I was amazed, for suddenly I lifted out of my body and was in two places at once. I looked back in wonder at my lifeless form, as the Elder immediately handed me the beautiful purple ball of light and told me to hold on to it. We moved to the large doorway that looked like vibrating waves of water. The Elder placed his hand on my shoulder, and we silently entered a strange location of moving waves of light. It became dark, and I could see some people who looked like homeless men, lying down, sleeping in a wooded area. One of the men awoke, stood up, and started to glow as he came toward us. The Elder withdrew some small colored balls of light from his robe and slipped them onto the fingers of his left hand, like rings, and he stretched out his hand to the glowing young man. The young man reached out and took some of the rings, which appeared to return as small orbs. As I held the large purple orb, I could see and sense something was definitely moving inside this strange ball of light. There were rolling purple waves of moving energy, like smoke. The Elder said we must go to another place now, and he touched my shoulder once again; there appeared to be bright light, and we were in another place that looked like a hospital room. The room held a bed that contained a very elderly man who looked very ill. There was also a black woman sitting beside the bed, evidently watching over the man. Her head was bowed as in prayer. There was something very strange going on, as I could see there were two black, thin creatures floating in midair while tugging away at the old man's head. It was like they were trying to pull that man's soul or spirit out of his body. Down by his chest, there was a being of light trying to hold him and pull him back. I could tell there was a life-and-death struggle going on between the unusual creatures. The tall Elder drew two small balls of light from his robe and cast them at the ugly black creatures; as the light struck them, they immediately flew away.

The Elder once again placed his hand on my shoulder, and as he did so, the purple ball of light suddenly turned a brilliant green, while the substance within the orb continued to move. The Elder then said to me, "We must go again," as the bright white light appeared, and we were back in the woods. It was as if either the Elder or the ball of light had the ability to change the light force of an environment, and we were somehow being instantly transported by the white flash of light from one place to another. The Elder walked ahead of me, and the interior of the ball of light, still resting in my arms and hands, began to turn into a swirling blue. I wanted to keep this awesome light orb, because something about it seemed to be so powerful. We continued to move along this forest to where two gray beings in blue suits stood beside a silver craft. It appeared that they had been waiting for us, and as we both drew closer, the blue ball began to turn into a lighter blue and then turned into a white light. I wondered what had happened, as we entered the craft and were brought into another room. The beings left the room, and only the tall Elder and I were standing there. I was unable to tell if the ship had lifted off the ground.

This room was very empty but brightly lit, when suddenly the purple color returned to the beautiful ball of light resting in my arms. I could still see its energy that was revolving around inside the beautiful orb. The Elder and I just stood there waiting, and I asked him, "Where are we going now?"

The answer surprised me, as he said, "We're going to see the One."

"The One?" I asked fearfully. This meant it would be the third time I would be brought before the all-knowing One. So many times I had tried to remember, to verbally relate and understand what was being revealed to me, but I had been unable to emotionally, intellectually, or physically de scribe the presence of such words of power and light or the inaudible mys teries that surrounded the indescribable One's being—that is, the highest station of light. It was not possible for me to comprehend such power. Why, oh why, was I being put through this strange initiation of his will? What was I supposed to do? He would have to help *me* understand, if I was supposed to show the world. I stood there, gently rubbing the orb's surface and looking at the beautiful purple depth of color in wonder. *If only you could help me understand*, I thought.

One of the blue-suited gray watchers entered the very room where the Elder and I were standing and asked me for the magnificent orb. I didn't want to give the orb to him and asked, "Why do I have to give it to you?" The Elder said not a word but gave me a displeased look. I quickly—re luctantly, but without another word—handed the watcher the purple orb, and he left the room. The Elder silently put his hands on my shoulders once again, as if he understood my feelings, for I had been the keeper for a while of that mysterious orb, which had been created through the six Elders' praise to OH. It looked like light was all around us as the craft came to a stop. The door opened, and one of the blue-suited beings came in for us. We moved out of the silver craft into the brightest light shining everywhere. *Whoa*, I thought, *it is so bright here*. We were at the great door.

The gray watcher stood back, as though he could not enter the door. The Elder went to his side and was touching him on the shoulder, while speaking to him through the mind or eyes.

Then both of them returned. The Elder, followed by the gray watcher, came over to me and asked, "Are you ready?"

"Yes," I said, sighing, for I was going to see the One. We turned and ran toward the overwhelming light. Suddenly the Elder's form changed into a body of white light, just as a blue shining light suddenly covered the being. We were filled with joy while running through the great open door, toward the brightest light of all. We were going to see the One. I glanced down at my arms and body, for I could see I had also changed into a golden light form. I felt his love, as I breathed in and out a deep sense of joy and peace within. There was glowing white light everywhere. I could barely breathe for the possibility of missing one measure of the presence of his love, for somehow I was engulfed in true light and blended into its supreme oneness. Words of praise for the presence of such peace were inadequate. The soft and lovely sounds of beautiful singing and music within the light permeated every portion of being, like everything was alive.

There was so much love there. I didn't want to leave, but something was pulling me back from this wonderful joy of being. I thought, *I don't want to go; I don't want to go back. I want to stay. Please, I want to stay.* The light was everywhere. It's impossible to explain the wonder, beauty, love, and peace that are present in the One's world of light. As the three of us moved closer to the door, I could see the white light disappear from the Elder's form, and the blue light faded from the gray being. Then I no longer was bathed in the golden light that had permeated my body. Once again my mind could not fathom what happened. The Elder had said we were going to see the One. Where was he? When I'd been taken from my home many years ago and brought before the One, I'd heard his voice. Even then, though, I could not remember seeing him, only supremely bright light. Why had I gone through all this wonder, only to be unable to remember and understand the appearance of the One? Once outside the great door, floating lights from colored orbs appeared, making lovely music. The four of us were mesmerized by their unusual rhythmic sounds, but they also moved away, back into the great door to the world of light, into the One's domain. I could see the gray being walking to the silver craft, and the Elder and I followed close behind him. Right away the gray being started to board the craft. I stood beside the Elder, and he touched the top of my head and passed me three marble-size balls of light. I took them, and as I held them in my hand, I realized the Elder was not coming with us this time. He remained standing by the craft as I entered it. The gray being escorted me into another room, where there were instruments hanging on the wall.

We were taking off, and I could see out the ship's window a brightness surrounding the area; as we moved upward, it started to get dark. We continued to move along, and the being revealed to me that I would have to get into another transporter. The being escorted me into another room where a clear, bubble-like orb waited in the corner. I was told to step into it. When I entered, it didn't feel solid, and I walked right through it. The separation between room and orb seemed not to exist. I sat down in the center of the orb, and it shot out of the craft with me in it. It was like I was moving along in midair within a transparent ball of light. I could see the tops of trees below as the orb suddenly started to drop downward. As the orb drew level to some trees, I could see our trailer. The orb kept descending, lower and lower, until I could finally see the ground below me. The next thing I realized I was standing on our wooden platform, where the clear ball separated from me and took off toward the woods. I rushed to our trailer door, happy to be home, and headed for the bedroom, where Bob was still fast asleep. As I reached my side of the bed, I was shocked, for I saw myself just sitting there...yet I was standing there beside myself. I slipped back into my resting body.

Once again an odd feeling came over me, as though I needed to go outdoors. I got up, moved to the foot of the bed, and walked down toward the living-room area. I turned and moved past the kitchen table, as I struggled with the urge to go outside, yet kept telling myself, I'm not going to go out there. I climbed back into bed and looked out the window.

It was dead calm outside. There were no sounds of insects or birds, and I wondered what was going on. Then I heard something in the woods, like the loud sound of a falling tree, and I looked out there, wondering, *What is happening?* I was still feeling the need to go outdoors when I heard a second tree fall in the woods. It made a loud cracking noise and a heavy thump as it fell. I now got up, and moved down to the bottom of the bed. Bob was now awake, and he said, "Where are you going?"

I told him, "I have to go outside. Something is making me feel as if I have to go outdoors."

Bob immediately said, "You're not going anywhere."

I got into bed and told him I had this awful feeling that I had to go out. "I kept on fighting against it, and then I heard two trees fall. I heard two trees fall down in the woods," I said. Suddenly I felt exhausted and lay down. "Hon," I said. "We've got to look for those trees tomorrow." I didn't feel as if I had to go out anymore, and thankfully I fell asleep. The next day Bob and I took a walk down the campground road, where I had heard the two large trees fall to the ground. It was not very far from where our trailer was parked that we found two large, freshly split oak trees in the woods, just a few yards off the edge of the dirt road. Bob took pictures of both trees and removed some fibers from the split tree to be examined.

A botany teacher examined the piece of tree, saw that the wood was strong and healthy, and could not determine what might have caused two healthy oak trees to break and fall. There was another oddity present too: The tops of the trees' leaves seemed to be blistered. This was odd because I had experienced a similar encounter in this same campground, though we'd been in a different trailer, at an earlier time.

CHAPTER 22

The Call of the One

• • •

THE LAST AND VERY IMPORTANT UFO experience was in 1994. I had undergone an earlier hypnosis session concerning this encounter, but we had been able to only partially retrieve the memories of this particular experience, and they appeared to be in two separate parts of my memory that did not seem to connect to each other. It felt as though I *wanted* to remember, even though all the missing information had been held back; because of it, I was left with a feeling of anxiety and wonder. I definitely remembered the strange action of an Elder pulling a large, round, glass-like mask off my head, but I could not remember why. I remembered only having a feeling of alarm at the time. The memory haunted me, as it meant I would have to wait until the time was right to go any further. I was left with an unanswered question concerning the harsh action of one of the Elders. Almost two decades would pass before the rest of the experience was finally ready to be revealed. Rather than go through the hypnosis sessions, however, I will start off with what actually happened. It would be almost twenty years, from 1994 to 2014, for me to receive an answer and finally learn what had happened at that time.

SESSION L FOR THE 1994 EXPERIENCE: THE BEGINNING

The alarm went off, waking both Bob and me. Before we got out of bed, I purposely looked down toward the closet area and could see a dim projection of light in the left mirrored door. The quick flash sort of jogged my memory of a strange entrance I thought I had dreamed of during the night. I got up to examine it closer, and the soft light immediately vanished from my mind's eye. I opened and closed the door, half expecting something might be inside, but only our clothes hung there. I glanced over to the right at the second mirrored door and caught my breath. A very large and obvious mark was on the glass. I was surprised and wondered, *How did that get there?* I had washed these mirrors and had gone through our fifth-wheel trailer to make sure everything was fresh and clean. My daughter and grandchildren, who we had not seen for quite a while, were coming for a visit. And here was a large oily smudge on the mirror.

At first I thought Bob or I must have brushed against the mirror the night before going to bed, but as I looked at the smudge closer, I could see it was a three-fingered handprint. Bob examined it and was surprised as well. When my children arrived, my daughter also saw the strange image. Because our life has been a continual involvement with the UFO phenomenon, Bob said we'd better call Ray and see what we should do. I called Mr. Fowler, but he was in New Hampshire on vacation, so we were unable to contact him. We didn't know what to do or how to take the print from off the mirror. So to preserve the evidence, I quickly drew a picture of the print and wrote down all the details I saw in the hand and three fingers. Then Bob tried to take pictures of it with the camera, but with so many mirrors there, that did not work. Then I opened a charcoal capsule, and dusted the print with the dark powder. I pressed a white piece of paper against the mirror, hoping for some good results, but that didn't work either. I was frustrated and afraid the unusual mark was starting to dry up. I wondered, *What else could we possibly do to save this peculiar three-fingered handprint?*

Then we came up with one more idea. I had a sheet of protective covering, which Bob and I had bought to protect some important papers. I peeled the clear plastic away from the adjoining sheet of paper and carefully pressed its sticky side firmly against the print. Much to my surprise, it worked. The sticky substance had managed to capture the entire handprint from the mirror. I slowly and carefully reapplied the white paper, and the print was sealed. A few air bubbles developed between the paper and plastic. However, they were small, so thankfully, over a period of time, they flattened out without hurting the strange imprint. It was because of the obvious and unusual presence of three fingers that Bob decided to put me under hypnosis once again. He wanted to see just what had happened that evening.

There were a few other peculiarities we had both experienced days earlier and did not know why. For instance, I was standing at the sink doing dishes when I felt something very little tug strongly on my shirttail. When I turned to see what it was, there was nothing there. It felt like it was a child wanting my attention or wanting to play. Then there were a couple of nights while Bob and I lay in bed that a mischievous presence had pulled on both Bob's and my feet as if to play. During that time, my cat, Captain, refused to come into the trailer, and when he did come in, he would not stay. Animals seem to know when something unusual is around and happening. During this 1994 encounter, we were living in our trailer at the country campground. The first time Bob hypnotized me concerning the 1994 experience, I relayed what I remembered, but for a reason you will learn in this book, something had happened that was covered up; at that time, I was totally unaware that something more had happened. Late in the evening of July 20, 1994, I suddenly awoke. Bob was still sleeping, but I sat up, because I could see a bright

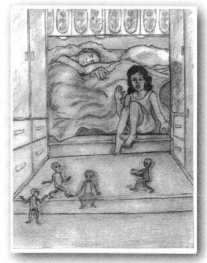

light in the closet area, which is the next level down from our bedroom. I moved closer to the foot of our bed and could not believe what was there. But first, let's get back to the next day, after we found the physical three-fingered handprint proof and realized the UFO phenomenon was still alive and kicking for us. Once again we began the hunt to find the truth of what had happened that night.

Here is what the first hypnosis session revealed once I was placed in a hypnotic trance. We taped it, which made it easier for Bob to refer back to the experience and zero in on anything that might need further or deeper investigation. Those present during the hypnosis included Bob, Becky, and me. Of course it takes a lot more time to put me under, but to save time, I will only give a few words that Bob uses that eventually put me in a deep hypnotic state.

Bob: I want you to relax. You are in complete control. Now, I want you to tell me what you saw and heard the late evening of July 20, 1994.

Betty: There's a bright light, and it's down by the closet area. It looks like a door, a rectangular door, and there's a hazy light inside it. I couldn't believe my eyes. There were very small, unusual little people that are sitting right by the door and step. And they are turning around and looking at me. They must be afraid because they jumped down from the step, ran past the bathroom level, and down toward the kitchen. I glanced back at the opening on the closet door where there was light. There's not supposed to be light there. That is odd.

Bob: Can you tell me what is odd?

Betty: There's that doorway right in the trailer, and it's against the closet doors, but it is inside the closet. There's an entrance to the inner part of it. Huh. It can't be that way. Its entrance and edges cut right through the mirror. At this point I turned to look at Bob, who was fast asleep. I wanted him to see what was going on. But he wasn't moving, just quietly lying on his side, sleeping. So while sitting on the side of the bed, I turned back again to watch what was happening. The little things, the little people, I can't see them anymore, so I decided to get up and go over to the peculiar lit entrance, and as I moved closer to the closet, I immediately put my hand through the door. This is odd. How can I possibly do this? My hand is going right through the door. But the closet mirror is there. That's impossible.

(My breathing gets heavy.)

Bob: Just relax.

Betty: The door is opening up wider and wider. I'm suddenly in a room. And it's big, very big, and bright. But there's mist all around. And a gray being dressed in a light-gray uniform is coming over to me. Off to the right-hand side of this area, I see groups of little, tiny children, like thin infant children, sitting around in a circle, looking at some kind of pillar of light in the center of them. They look just like the little ones  that went down to the kitchen earlier. These little ones seem to be concentrating on something in those towers of light, wide beams of light. The gray being is talking to me through my mind.

Bob: All right. I want you to stop for a moment. I want you to look at this room and fix it in your mind in great detail, so that later on you'll be able to draw it for me. The little beings, the tower of light, the gray being—just fix it in your mind and then move on, please.

Betty: I've seen him before, or others like him. He's a watcher. He's

standing before me and telling me to follow him, because I have to learn something. And it feels like he is probing my mind, almost like he's searching for something. I don't know what it is. And he says to follow him. I'm just moving along with him into another adjoining room, and I see one of those tall people in white. He is at some kind of machine that's against the wall. I think he is working, like directing or setting up something. In the middle of this room is an odd thing that comes out from inside the floor. I don't know what it is. It comes up out of the floor, and it looks like there is water around the bottom of the base. And there's a basin on the top. It has four points to the upper portion of the bowl.

Bob: I'd like you to stop again. Pause; fix this scene in your mind, almost like photographing it with your mind in detail. Later you will be able to draw what you have seen. You may go on when you have remembered that scene.

Betty: In the water, there are all sorts of movement, like something is alive in the water. There's like symbols of something moving. Strange, odd symbols moving in the basin water, and there's water moving around the stem below as well. At this point other things were happening in and around this pale whitish-blue, ceramic-like fountain with four hornlike handles. Two rings of lights appeared above the revolving water, and then small  holographic symbols, or hieroglyphs, started to come out of the rings of light. These unusual symbols were swirling around in a circle above, and suddenly a bright ball of light shot upward above the symbols and hovered in midair, above the two ringed lights. Close by on the floor, I could see a clear glass-like bowl-type container with a ceramic-type pedestal. The container was filled with clear glass balls. The tall Elder is working at all sorts of lights now. I don't know what they are. Things like balls of light popping out of the machine, as if he's playing something. I don't know what he's doing with them. Maybe it was the Elder who was making the floor machine to work? We're just standing there waiting and watching. I don't know why we have to wait so long, but he just keeps on doing something to the machine that's on the wall. We're just standing there watching him. He turned briefly and looked over at us, and then turned back to what he was doing. We're still waiting; I began to concentrate on the circulating symbols in the water, wondering what they were. They actually seemed like they were alive, like odd-shaped, skinny, thin, wiggly fish. But I knew they were not fish. They look like symbols moving around, almost like they're dancing in the moving water, and at the top of the basin filled with water, it seems as if two things are going on at the same time. I don't know what they are. The ball of light is still there, but the swirling symbols of light in the air are gone.

However, the two rings of light have changed into some odd wires. They are now two circles of what looks like thin wires. These wires looked like they were twisted together with gold, black, and silver material. There was a smaller inner ring of green- and orange-colored wire. This is a strange water machine. I wondered what it actually does and why I was being shown this odd thing. As we stood there, the hovering ball of light suddenly seemed to explode and began to expand into a large, clear bubble that settled over the fountain like a clear glass-like cap. Suddenly thin streaks of electricity seemed to be shooting out of the gold, black, and silver twisted wired ring and were bouncing against the glass-like cap. The

glass cap seemed to fit perfectly around the interior mouth and between the four horns on the fountain. The wires and cap suddenly
dissolved and disappeared, so now there was only the water and symbols that remained. The bottom lower circle of water around the base
of this machine was held in by a band of iridescent pearl-like material.
I looked down at the moving water and odd dark symbols within it. I
wondered how long we were going to have to stay here, as we were
still standing there waiting, and I can't seem to move. The watcher is
still beside me. We're just waiting—for what, I don't know, but I'm
getting really tired of the wait.

Bob: I'd like you to move ahead to the point where you are done
waiting. Tell me what happens.

Betty: There's a door of bright light, and another Elder is coming in. He is coming over to us. He stops and just looks at the
watcher and then me. Then he went over to the other Elder, and
I'm thinking, *What's going on here?* It looks like he is saying something to him. I think they are agreeing about something, but
apparently we were not meant to hear what was being communicated, and I am still just standing there waiting. Now the second
Elder is coming over to the gray watcher again and is conversing
with him somehow. But again, I don't know what he's saying,
because he's not opening his mouth at all. Oh, he is leaving now,
and going back out that same door that just lights up. Suddenly
he is gone. Then the watcher sort of signals me to follow him.
We're finally walking around the side of the basin with the water
and symbols in it, and we also are heading toward the same door
that the other Elder just went out of. It just lights up as we pass
through into another real brightly lit room. This room is interesting, very large and circular. It appears to have many, many
doorway openings going to other areas. I think some of them
look like small changing rooms. The floor is also very unusual
and makes you feel as if you are stepping on something moving.
It is lighted somehow with a series of outgoing lights appearing,

then disappearing, small to big and big to small, moving in constant cycles with circular bands of circles. It felt and looked something like what happens to a pool of water when a pebble or stone is thrown into the center of it: a circle occurs, causing a ripple after ripple to continually move. It was neat lighting but seemed peculiar to walk on, as it sort of makes you feel odd and a little dizzy. Whoa, the watcher is leading me to one of the openings on the side and tells me in my mind I am to go in, and he wants me to change. Oh no, not again. I reluctantly entered the well-lit room, where there was a white robe. I felt nervous. Evidently that was what I was supposed to wear. I quickly took off my nightgown and put on the robe.

Bob: How does the robe feel against your skin?

Betty: It's very smooth and soft. The outside material feels slippery like glass but very silky, and the inside is different. It's like fine, closely knit fabric that's buttery soft. I put it on and came out of the changing room, where the watcher was waiting for me. He started talking to me through the mind and said I was going to have to be examined again. Oh no, I don't want to be.

Bob: OK, I want you to stop, and from this point on, I want you to realize that it was all videotaped.

He was referring to the rest of my experience. Once he saw the discomfort on my face at the prospect of an examination, he decided to pull me away from the scene to become an observer, rather than a participant. Once again he put me into a deeper hypnotic trance, to relieve any anxiety I might feel.

Bob: Everything that happened can be seen on the television videotape…you may begin.

Betty: I see myself standing there with the watcher, and now I'm just following him. The big circular room felt unusual with so many small changing quarters. Plus the rings of moving light on the floor were odd but beautiful, if you don't look at it too long. Otherwise it can make you feel dizzy. I see him moving along with me in back of him. We're going into another area, and we stop. We're just standing there for some reason. I don't know if he is talking to me or not.

Bob: Turn the volume up just a little on the television. You will then be able to hear and see everything. Everything that has happened has been recorded.

Betty: I can hear a humming sound. Sounds like some kind of machine. We're just standing there. I can't hear him talking, but we're waiting, just standing to the side for some reason. Now I see us moving into another room. It's very bright and misty there as well. The door just goes *sfit*, like that, and we go in.

Bob: What shape are the doors?

Betty: These doors are not really a shape. They're visible only because of their light, which you go through, but they have no real form or shape like our doors. They quickly open, sort of like a zipper, or like a long, quick slice in taut fabric that briefly lights up and just suddenly opens as we walk through. Right now we're going into another brightly lit room.

Bob: Remember you are watching this on television. It's already happened. It's in your past. You are viewing this on television. You are not a participant.

I'm an emotional person, and in the past, I have slipped back into being there during hypnotic regressions. This occasionally happens when my experience becomes too traumatic for me, and I think that's what Bob was worried about.

Betty: I am standing there looking around, as the watcher leaves me and goes over to four other watchers that are standing by. I can tell by their actions that the watcher is communicating with them. I can see that this room is also very large and extremely bright. It looks like there is an upper part to this area, sort of like another landing or hallway. There is something big and dark to the left on the upstairs wall. From here it is difficult to make out everything in this room. It's so bright, and there is some mist in the air. Just a few yards ahead of me, I can see an odd, elongated shaped table off to the left, and I can see there is a smooth, curved walkway going to the second floor. It looks like there may be another lit entrance to the right side of that lower part, where the walkway wall is curved. The watcher is now coming back over to me. The others left and went up to the second floor, past the big, dark metallic thing on the wall. I think the watcher with me is trying to communicate, but I can't hear anything. I think I see one of the other watchers dressed in a silver suit at the big metallic machine. He is pulling something out of it. The other three watchers now have joined him and are taking something out of the machine as well. The watcher with me is looking right into my eyes. I think he is trying to tell me something, but I can't hear anything except the constant humming noise. The watcher leaves me again and goes over to the others, who are now down at that table, preparing those small things in their hands. I began to get very nervous and thought, *They must be getting ready to examine me.* I started to feel stressed, as I see one of the beings coming over after me. He leads me to the table where he quickly lifts or floats my body upward and is gently laying me down upon it. They are quickly fanning me with those handheld instruments and began to touch different parts of my body.

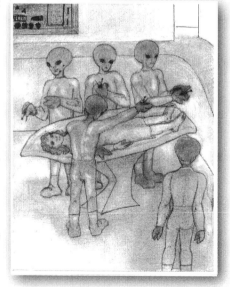

Bob: OK, I want you to pause and take a good look at this instrument, and you will be able to recall in detail and draw it. When it is in your memory, continue the videotape.

Betty: I see those small machines they're using to touch different parts of my body, and I'm all lit up, but I can still see my form and all. It doesn't seem to be hurting me in any way. I don't appear distressed. They just keep touching and fanning me all over my body with those things. They've finally stopped.

Bob: How many of them are there?

Betty: All together there are five, and now they're putting those hand machines away. I see a couple of the watchers coming back to me again and one of them is carrying a big, bulbous, glassy thing. It's big and rounded. I can see it. They're placing it over my entire head.

I started to feel distressed here, and Bob immediately pulled me back.

Bob: OK, OK, I want you to relax now. I want you to relax. I'm going to count to three, and you are going to come back to the present time.

After I came out of the hypnotic trance, I felt very tired. As recorded, Bob and Becky were the only two present during this first hypnosis session concerning my 1994 UFO experience. When the session was finally over, Becky asked me, "You didn't like that helmet, did you, Mar?" She was absolutely right.

The second part of the 1994 hypnotic regression would not take place until three years later, and then the recorded tapes sat dormant for almost fifteen years. I knew there was more that had happened, but I just wanted to get away from the phenomenon for a while, as it's been with me throughout my whole life; however, I have to admit, over the years I often wondered, *Why did the Elder yank the bulbous helmet off my face?* I remembered that happening, and it bothered me. As time moved on, I let it rest, because we got pretty busy doing our own thing. We bought a condo in Florida and enjoyed time spent basking in the sun, but after five years, we were ready for a house, a dog, and a place to garden. We finally decided to move to the beautiful state of Virginia. Then in 2013, after listening to the old tapes, we decided it was time to find out what else happened.

SESSION 2 FOR THE 1994 EXPERIENCE: AUGUST 13, 2013

Bob: We're going to pick up to where we stopped yesterday. I would like you to go back in life to where you were living in Higganum, Connecticut. I would like you to tell me what you saw and what you heard from this point on.

Betty: I'm lying on this long, odd-shaped table. I can't seem to move my body, only my neck and head is free to move. There are four watchers dressed in silver suits that have small metallic tools in their hands. Two watchers flank each side of the table, which I am laying on. They are waving small hand machines, which buzz and beep and light up as they move them across my body from top to bottom. They keep waving them over me, and it seems like my robe is brighter, like there's a bright light all around me. I feel all right as they continue to wave the small beeping machines over my head and feet. For some reason, they seemed to be checking certain parts of me. Occasionally they would stop and adjust their hand machine with a small tool magnetically attached to their suit and arm. Once again, they're touching my forehead and ears. One of them lifted the robe away from my shoulders, and I could feel a slight vibration from the machine as he passed it over me. This only happened whenever they touched my skin beneath the robe. One watcher stopped, moved away from me, and went up to the upper left level of this room. It looked like he was placing the hand machine away into the big machine that sticks out from the upper wall. A few minutes later, the three others finally finished and also moved to the second floor to put away their tools. I turned my head away and was able to glance down at myself and was stunned. I couldn't believe how much bright white light was coming from my whole body and the white robe I had on. I looked back toward the upper landing to see if they were aware of the light covering me or knew what was happening to me. I was unable to see where the beings were, except for one that looked like he was now going over by the side of the big wall machine and pulling something else out from the same area. I thought he was retrieving something from a wall opening, but it was difficult to see. It looked like he pulled something big and shiny out and was now carrying a rounded, glassy thing of some kind. He was moving down the sloping, curved floor and over to where I was. I could see that the object he was carrying was very big and looked like a rounded, half-bubble-type of glass or a crystal-type thing in his hands. It was very large, and he was bringing the thing over where I was, and…oh no. He's going to put that thing over my face, and I can't move or do anything to stop him. The light reflecting off my body and robe made the glass glisten as he drew it closer to my head. It's like a huge, rounded glass mask. As he placed it over my head, I could see this thing had an indented curve, with a strip of something dark, like a lining of some sort on the open edge of the crystal. He's making sure to securely adjust that opening area down by my neck for some reason. It feels like there's about three or four inches of breathing room inside, between my face and this thing. After he was finished, he pressed down hard on the center to secure the cover. Then suddenly, I could feel and hear a suction take place between the glass and table. It's like I was locked inside this hideous mask. I felt helpless. My body felt paralyzed. It's like there's not enough air. I can still move my head and can see some kind of shiny material embedded in the middle top of this crystal. As I took a deep breath, I managed to stretch my neck, to lift my head up as far as possible against the glass, and looked out. I could see the watchers standing on the curved walkway, just watching me. There were a lot of tiny lights going off and on in the center top and around the edges of this thing. It's starting to feel warm in here, like it's hard to breathe. The glass interior began to haze over from the warmth of my breath. I laid my head back down, realizing there was nothing I could possibly do but accept what was to be. Suddenly, I saw

something like big hands clasping the glass above me, pulling and yanking the heavy mask away from the table and off my head and face. The heat, blinking lights, and lack of sufficient air within the mask caused me to feel woozy and very dizzy. It took a while for my eyes to adjust, to see what was happening. I looked up and saw one of the tall beings standing over me. Ahhhh...I breathed in a deep breath of air. I'm shocked but thankful. It's one of the tall, white-haired Elders that must have yanked that crystal cover off my head. I can see the Elder carrying the crystal object over to the five watchers standing by on the curved walkway. He handed the thing to the watcher that had been with me earlier, who was dressed in a light-gray fitted suit. The watcher in turn passed the large mask to one of the other workers to take care of. I started to feel much better but was still amazed over the light covering me. The Elder drew the watcher aside and appeared to be conversing with him when suddenly the watcher jumped back, like he was surprised at something that was said. I thought, *That's strange. I wonder why he did that.* The white-haired Elder was now coming over toward me again, and he quickly laid his hand on my cheek, then both my cheeks, as well as on my forehead. I looked up at him and said, "I feel OK. I don't feel dizzy anymore." He then lifted me off the table, and we stood there briefly. I'm standing up and amazed at myself, because I look like a lightbulb. I'm all lit up, and I'm asking him, "What's going on? What's happening? What's the matter with me? I'm shining like light." And he said to me, "The One has called for you. The One has called and wants to speak to you." At this point, hearing his words did not help. It caused goose bumps to rise up all over my body. For some reason, I swallowed in fear. I guess it was because each time I had been before the One, I did not understand what was going on or what I was supposed to do. I've been taken to see the One three different times, and each time I stood before him, there was no physical form that I could see, only a beautiful, very vivid, bright white light. I've heard his voice before but could never make out a form. "It's been a long time since I've been involved with and going through these strange, unexplainable things that have happened to me. I'd like some solid answers. Like *why*. So tell me, what do you mean the One wants to speak to me? Why?" I asked. But the Elder would not tell me. He then said, "We have to go." And he reached out and took me by my arm, and I'm walking with him. He's so tall

that it's hard to keep up with him. Now he looked over at the gray watcher that was with me before, the one who had brought me here earlier. At least I think it is the same one, and he's coming over with us. The Elder took us out of this area and into a corridor. We are going down this big long, long corridor, and as we reached the end, it seemed like we were stepping outdoors. The Elder continued to lead us.

This area was beginning to feel cool and breezy, and it seemed dark here. But I didn't mind, even though all my body and the robe were still lit with an aura of bright light. Ahead, just a short distance away, we could see a large, round, shiny object. As we draw closer, I saw that it was an orb-like craft. When we reached the huge craft, the Elder made some kind of hand motions that automatically turned on the inside lights and opened the door. We were able to enter immediately. All three of us went into the brightly lit craft. Once inside, the interior appeared much smaller than the exterior. Close to the center, there were five seats. The Elder directed me to the middle of the row of five seats and told me to sit. The watcher sat to the left, and the Elder was seated to the right of me. At this time I sensed the watcher was reading my mind, which was racing with silent unanswered questions. He could tell I felt lost and uneasy, wondering how this thing was going to fly. *Where are all the instruments?* I thought. *Why are these seats just sitting in the middle of this glass floor?* Through my mind, he assured me that the orb was very capable and mentioned that all four seats have the ability to move or switch to other locations, into any direction, and that in this particular ship, they can even form a cross. I thought that was an odd thing for him to telepathically relate to me. I wondered if he was trying to comfort or reassure me by mentioning the cross. Evidently, without question, the watcher or Elder must know how to fly this thing. But the most amazing thing about this orb was, besides the outer glass exterior, the interior is all glass as well. Even though I could not see any engine or moving parts in between the separation of the two inner and outer glass shells, I could see right through them like a windowpane. There definitely wasn't any kind of mechanics or machinery in between the solid glass that I could see that would help fly this orb to get it off the ground. As I sat there, I thought, *Could the power be in the seats?* Maybe the center seat was the main control area. Oh, I hoped not, for that's exactly where the Elder told me to sit. Maybe the four seats that the watcher mentioned, which have the ability to move, have some kind of hidden, unseen power system below them. Probably the orb's interior is not just glass but crystal, which could be an electrical energy source supplying power to any technology possibly hidden under the seats. Beside the anxiety of the fact that I was actually being taken to see the One again and waiting for us to move, my mind was racing. I continued to mentally justify my curiosity about this glass ball I was sitting in. My thoughts quickly returned to the present, as I felt the craft suddenly lift and slowly move upward, then outward. We were finally on our way. I turned my head to check the gray area we had left behind and could see a dark open hole in the distance, where we came out of the big corridor before boarding the orb. Suddenly I felt the orb stop, then fall. My throat and stomach felt weird as I swallowed hard and braced myself against the seat, trying to understand what was happening. The orb had dropped downward into some dark water beneath us and was slowly moving across the bumpy surface. It was extremely windy there, and white foam and heavy waves were smashing against the outer shell of the glass orb. The craft began to slowly submerge into the surrounding rough water. We were definitely going down. I quickly clutched the side of the seat, whispered a silent prayer, and held my breath. Much to my relief, the Elder knew my thoughts and

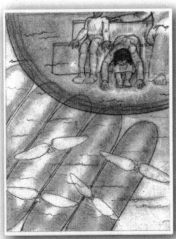 assured me we would not drown. The deeper we went, the calmer the waters became, and I breathed a big sigh of relief. As we moved along, it seemed a little bit dark here, but there was light inside the orb, and I was still glowing from the light upon me and the robe. The three of us remained sitting and silent as the craft continued to move smoothly along. We could now feel the orb slowing down and

shifting its direction when once again, it began to move upward. Water was rushing away from the body of the craft as it continued to slowly emerge and finally broke free from the water's hold. We remained sitting as the orb lifted off the surface and into a beautiful light-green atmosphere. We moved through this unusual green area for quite a while. Its reflection in the orb was eerie. The orb began to descend again as a second wave of energy appeared and forced the orb downward. Once again we splashed into the deep, only this time it was green water that was covering the crystal glass orb. Another underwater energy field managed to push the craft even deeper. These energy waves were extremely powerful, and we were now caught in, and being forced along by, an aggressive current into deeper deep-green water. Somehow the orb managed to break free from the current's control and moved us deeper into this dark-green realm below. The Elder reached over and touched my forehead again. I told him I was all right, but I think he knew better. Like a broken record, I asked him once again, "Will you please tell me why the One wants to speak with me?" I could tell he was a little annoyed with my constant questioning, because he finally said to me, "You will have an answer soon enough. It must come from the One." I thought, *Oh no, the answer he gave me was not what I wanted to hear*. I sighed and sat back. The orb finally stopped going down and leveled off. We were once again moving slowly along. The water was still a beautiful green color. To get my mind off his answer, I bent forward in my seat and looked down into the beautiful green water below to see if there were any fish in here. As we moved along, I could see a number of odd, very long, grayish objects way beneath the water. They were perfectly lined in rows below us and appeared to be enormous, bulging tubes side by side. Then I saw these really white things that looked like birds moving in the water. *There can't be birds flying in water; they must be some kind of unusual fish that looks like a bird*, I told myself. They had long fins that looked more like wings, with a small head and a fanlike tail, and there were about three or four of them, just freely swimming around, over these huge tubes that we were crossing over. What's really strange is, they are extremely white, and the green water does not change their color. Plus, as I mentioned before, the more I looked at them, the more they looked like flying birds than fish. As we continue to move on, they seem to be keeping the same pace as the craft. This orb was so wide open because of the glass all around us that I can see anything above or below, plus anything around it. It feels strange.

Bob: Just relax. You are perfectly safe in there.

Betty: We seem to be going deeper and deeper in this green water, and I still see a lot of those white things swimming around. They definitely look like birds, but I know they can't be. They have to be fish. We just keep moving along in the orb when I happen to look down again and saw more of those huge, huge tubes. Even bigger and more than the last ones. They look as if they are lying on the very bottom floor of this green water. There are rows and rows of these things. I thought, *Maybe they're cigar-type craft or large water pipes?* They are right underneath the orb. Wow. I can't believe there are so many of them, all lined up in rows. The fluttery bird-fish are all around the area as well. We're now moving away from where all those things were parked. *The tubes must have been parked there for a reason*, I thought. I breathed in deeply and sighed, and the Elder said to me, "Be still, please; be very still." *Now what?* I thought. I'm trying to be still, but I can't see what is around here unless I move a little. The water seems to be so deep here. I sat back and quietly watched, to see just what was up ahead. I'm starting to feel upset, realizing we are probably getting closer to our destination. I began to wonder what the One might want to speak to me about.

Bob: You're very safe; just relax. Relax; this is within your past. You're very, very safe. I want you to relax and continue on your journey. OK, go ahead.

Betty: We're just moving along in the dark-green water, and I can see up ahead. There appears to be bright lights shining down through the water. I can feel the orb is starting to climb upward again. As we continue to move, the dark-green water seems to be changing into a much lighter green color. We're still traveling upward in this glass orb with five seats. So far, I have not seen any of the seats move away into a different direction or area within the craft, like the watcher said they were able to do. Oh well, I'm kind of glad they didn't move while in the deep water, anyway. As we moved upward, there were more and more streaks and flashes of light that appeared from above, shooting down into the water below. As the orb moved higher and higher, the increase of light flashes were turning the water into a very soft light green. The orb then started to level off and slowly move along, while light flashes were still striking the surface above. After a while, because of the light, the water seemed to be changing into a pale, light-blue color. Oh, something beautiful is up ahead. I can see some colors of lights penetrating through the blue water, and it is absolutely breathtaking. Oh, it's so beautiful, and it is getting brighter. Then real

bright. Oh, wow. I can feel the orb lifting upward and moving faster. I can see dazzling lights, as the orb is coming up really quick now. I see lights like rainbows up above the blue water. I breathed in a deep breath of air to try to relax, for my body felt tense, as the orb lifted gently out of the water, suddenly stopped, and hovered in midair. The falling streams of foam and water rolling off the craft returned to the water below, as the orb continued to hover in place. I could see scattered water drops still clinging to the glass exterior and catching a spray of light, causing thousands of tiny reflections to glow into multiple sparkles of brilliant colors, covering the outer shell. I held my breath as the spectacular show got even better. There just before us was a fantastic array of glowing lights. Just a small distance beyond us, we could see massive groups of fantastically beautiful floating crystals, causing bright rainbows to appear throughout the area. The silent orb continued to hover, as if it was allowing us to observe the beauty and majestic presence of such unusual light, colors, and crystals. Whoa, wow, unbelievable. Just too beautiful to behold, or take in, and believe with our eyes and mind that they are real and truly there, but they are. Crystals of all shapes, sizes, and colors. Small and large glistening glass forms and some even bearing unusual structures, just hanging in midair. This is awesome. Many looked like fabulous cut and uncut jewels radiating and glistening with different bright colors of shining light. So beautiful. There appeared to be a few open spaces between some clusters of crystals that seemed to be moving; I could see these crystals slowly move away as they began to separate and create a narrow open door of extreme white light. The orb suddenly started to move forward. It seemed attracted to the narrow area and was heading toward the strange separation and bright light, almost like the entrance was opening a gate, like a doorway into space. The rainbows of color flashing everywhere were magnificent. The orb quickly moved in, and along, the narrow passage, which seemed to cause the crystals on each side to sway even more. Wow.

Bob: Just relax.

Betty: We're going through this bright area, with swaying crystals on both sides of the orb, and I hear tinkling like glass, as the crystals managed to touch one another. It's so bright and beautiful here.

Bob: Relax. Relax and enjoy it.

Betty: There are flashing rainbows all over the place, along with sparkling colored lights everywhere. Now as we moved forward between these sparkling crystals, I'm hearing wonderful musical sounds, as well as chimes. Oh, how wonderful. The harmonic sounds blend so perfectly beautiful. It's almost like a strange, un-believable, orchestrated, symphony happening. The whole orb also seems to be vibrating with so many unusual tones. It's amaz-ing. All the musical sounds seem to blend together in such a beau-tiful way. Wow. Off and on I'm also hearing soft, lovely singing voices with the music. It's as if the sparkling, jewel-like crystals are alive. Once again, I felt goose bumps all over me. This place feels like a piece of heaven; it's so beautiful and awesome. The orb was still slowly moving in and out and in between these shining crys-tals that continued to lightly sway back and forth. To my surprise, a large swinging gem actually struck another crystal very hard, causing it to ring and a massive blue flash of light to occur. The ring of the crystal was so loud and long that when the noise finally stopped, the musical tempo from the crystals had switched into a new direction of sound. It was almost as if a new orchestrated piece was being performed as we pressed onward. It seemed to me that certain colored crystals possessed a different note, having a high- or low-pitched sound, and their timing ability definitely comple-mented one another's sound. The whole crystal experience felt like a living treasure. They possessed a mystical presence of light, beauty, and sound, a melody that I shall never forget. Oh, it's just so beautiful here. The orb continued its course, moving freely in

and out from among the living crystals and stunning rainbows. Suddenly, an extremely bright flash of white light washed against the orb, causing the entire craft to be-come enveloped by intense light. It began to get warm inside. I leaned toward the Elder and asked, "What happened? We can't see outside." He remained calm and silent, as if he knew and was not concerned. Meanwhile, I wondered, could that intense bright light have something to do with the One? If so, maybe that's why the Elder was not at all troubled. My mind was still spinning, trying to understand and figure out how this glass ball we were sitting in could fly on its own without any mechanical devices like an engine. Maybe that light was from the One, checking on the orb's progress? Maybe that's why there doesn't seem to be anything visibly flying this craft. Oh, too many questions, and not enough answers. We continued on as the light began to slowly fade off the craft's outer shell, allowing us to see outside once again. I turned around to check the crystals. There in the distant background were the wonderful floating crystal gems, with shining, multicolored light flashing everywhere, while inside the orb, it began to get even warmer. It was very bright in this area, and as the orb continued to move onward, the further we traveled, the warmer and brighter it got. I could feel the heat inside the craft.

Bob: I want you to relax. Just relax. You will not feel any excessive heat. You will enjoy the very beauty of the place.

Betty: It is beautiful. Oh, but the light seems to be strange and unusually bright. It had gotten warmer since we moved further away from the field of crystals and seemed to be brighter. Something up ahead in the bright atmosphere is beginning to form. It looked like a huge white veil or sheet. I don't know; I guess it was like a shield of some kind. Even though we're moving further away from the crystals, I could still hear and enjoy a little of their music and see their awesome reflections, reflections that now appear to be bouncing against peculiar dancing light waves that stretched across the sheet. The orb is now moving into and through the unusual sheet of odd, soft folds of energy, which continually lift up and down and away. Once again I braced myself against my seat, for I could see the peculiar waves were now directly in front of the orb and were creating something outside like sparks of static to occur. The glass orb continued to enter into and slowly pass through this odd energy, which to me looked something like Earth's aurora borealis, but not quite. I think it was actually the reflection of the distant crystals' light that made it look like the waves were colored. The craft finally managed to escape the waves without any danger to the ship or us. But now we've entered another space that is all lit up with a very bright light again. And there, a short distance ahead of us, was a second sheet of light energy. We are starting to slow down, for this sheet appears almost like a smooth vibrating mirror, with waves of energy running through it. This time there were no colors present; however, the waves seemed more active. Why I thought there was static involved was because of my hair. I briefly brushed my hair back, since it felt like it was standing on end. The orb continued to move through and past this second field of energy waves with no problem. As we moved along, outside began to get brighter and brighter, and the orb started to slow way down. I could see up ahead of us, there was the brightest light I had ever seen. I sighed a deep sigh of relief, for although it was extremely bright, a feeling of euphoria embraced me. The brightness of the white light was absolutely beautiful. Even though it was so bright, I felt calm and at peace as we moved above an area that appeared to be like an edge of a cliff of solid white glass or ice sticking out, with mist and light below us. Some heavy mist was lifting and swirling upward as the craft swept across the unusual plain. The orb slowed down, for it was causing the heavy mist to drag and

follow the craft. While traveling over this area, I could see ground in front of us that looked like solid white glass or stone with veins and spots of gold color running through it. The craft was automatically moving toward the left and began to slow down from an accumulation of heavy mist. Finally, it came to a complete stop. The Elder stood up and approached the watcher sitting on the other side of me. I knew he must have been leaving instructions for him in his mind. The gray watcher and I were still just sitting there, as the Elder moved in front of me and reached out his hand for me to get up and motioned for me to follow him. As I stood up, I glanced back at the watcher, who was now holding a very small object in his hand. The door swiftly opened, and we step out into the beautiful bright white light surrounding us. I hesitated and glanced back at the orb that looked like a mirrored ball. We were now walking on a glowing surface of white and crystal glass, with shiny, wide veins that looked like gold running through it. A soft mist is moving about us, as we continue to walk toward the brightest white light up ahead. The Elder is telling me to stop, that he must tell me what to do. *Finally*, I thought, *he is going to tell me where we are and what this place is.* But instead he is telling me that I will have to go on by myself for a short distance. "What?" I said. "What? I can't believe it. You're going to leave me alone here." He could definitely see and feel my anxiety. I thought, *This must be where I'm supposed to see the One.*

He answered, "Yes; this is why you've been brought here. Make sure you bow your head before him when you get to the place."

And I asked him, "What place? I don't even know where I am."

"You will definitely know where and when you have reached the area," he replied. "The path is over there." He pointed.

"Where are you going to be?" I asked.

"I will wait and come back to get you," he said.

"Do I have to go by myself?" I asked.

He replied, "Yes. You must go now. The One awaits your presence."

I turned and watched as the Elder moved away and disappeared into the mist. I fell to the mist-covered ground and wanted to cry. After a few moments, I reluctantly stood up and started walking toward the center path, where the beaming bright light was glowing up ahead. The light was so very bright. I'm all alone walking on the path, and I'm wondering if I will be able to find where the certain place is. The surface below my feet looks like crystal at times, and with the moving mist all around me, it was

difficult to see. I kept walking closer to the brightest, most beautiful light up ahead. Suddenly, without warning, my knees gave way, and I fell to the ground. I bowed my head, for I remembered what the Elder had told me to do. I wiped my eyes and remained on my knees waiting, and then I heard a loving voice call my name. "Betty, stand on your feet before me." Chills rushed through my body, for fear of the voice of the One. Tears rolled down my cheeks. I felt alone and not able to know what I should do or where I was.

Bob: Relax. Just relax. This is all in your past. Relax; you're all right. You've been to see the One before. Continue, please.
Betty: When I heard his voice, I tried to be strong and quickly rose to my feet, but my mind refused to let me raise my head. I stood there shaking, too afraid to look upon the One. His presence and voice was overwhelming. My soul listened intently, as he spoke, "I have called you forth for a reason. Fear not. I am with you." I trembled at his words and immediately tried to hold back more tears.

Seeing my emotional situation was out of control, Bob immediately pulled me out of hypnosis and back to August 13, 2013, in our Virginia living room.

Session 3 for the 1994 Experience

Bob: You are in a very comfortable state of relaxation. You are going to return to your last known experience while you are under hypnosis. Relax; you are at the beach. It's a perfect, re-laxed day. All the background noises are fading away. It is as if you have not a care in the world. You're perfectly comfortable and know you are in complete control. You have already experi-

enced what you will be seeing today. You will remember it as a pleasant experience, a relaxing experience, and as I touch your shoulder, you will go even deeper into this restful state. You will return to a time where you went to see the One. You knelt down and bowed your head at a certain place. When the One ap-peared, he called your name and told you to stand. What happened after he told you to stand?"

Betty: My head was still bowed, and I could see below me but dared not lift my head. Suddenly I felt a cooling mist circle my feet, and I closed my eyes, waiting and longing to hear the One speak. His light was overwhelming. I stood there not knowing what to say or do, when suddenly I felt his love surrounding me. I could not see a person, form, or being, but I knew his love and light was sweeping over me. My body, mind, and spirit felt comfortable and relaxed. I suddenly heard the One's voice say to me, "Fear not, child. I have called you forth for a reason. I will never hurt you." As I am standing there, I'm beginning to feel safe and realize that there is nothing to fear, that I am protected. At that moment, I could feel strong vibrations, like my mind and nervous system was being washed and cleansed in light. An extreme amount of radiating en-ergy swept over my body and entered my total being. I caught my breath, as if I was taking in life's living essence. Rolling waves sur-rounded my whole being. I glanced downward at the moving vapor below, where heavy mist whirled around my feet. I felt dizzy and could no longer see the bottom of the floor. The mist continued to circle my lower extremities and started to climb upward. My whole being was starting to tremble, as the circling energy continued to move higher and higher above my waist. The glowing light within began to take form. A soft, white cloud suddenly enveloped my whole being, and as it circled me, I automatically raised my hands with joy. I felt an omnipresence within and around me. I still dared not lift my head to look up. The cloud's intense energy started to make me feel shaky, and once again, I heard the voice of the One address me. "Betty, be still now. I am here placing spirit language, knowledge, and directions within your mind. Be still." I'm trying to be still, but I'm feeling the strong vibrations, which are now making me feel like I am floating. The brightness within the cloud is holding and comforting me somehow. I feel something is over my head, like a covering. The One continued to speak and once again said, "Listen well. The spirit language, knowledge, and directions I have now placed in your mind will be opened when it is time for them, and not before." His powerful living words swept through me. I felt weak, and I wondered how and why this was happening to me. What did it mean? Was his message for me alone? Or was it for the world to know?

Bob: You're doing fine. Relax. Just relax.

Betty: I could hear his wonderful, loving words speaking from the cloud of light. "Fear not, child; I have placed this within your mind. You will understand when the time is ready." The overwhelming energy before me started to dissipate into the surrounding mist. My head still fixed in a bowed position, I dared not look up, afraid of what I might see, as there was still an extremely powerful, glowing white light shining in front of me. The entire cloud finally spread out and settled down into the mist below, and I could now see parts of the floor again. The One continued to speak. "That which I have given you will come out in time. You will not remember what I have spoken to you now until you are ready to receive it again. For now you will have a time of waiting and rest. Over two decades of life shall pass before you learn and know why I have done this for you. As you rest and wait, you shall do as you please. You will not recall our meeting during that time, for I have allowed you to rest and wait. You will not remember." I felt shaken from his fateful words—*I will not remember*—and briefly kept hearing them, echoing through my mind. The intense light within the cloud and mist surrounding me suddenly made a loud noise like a great rush of wind, as it whirled above and beyond me. There was silence. I wondered what had happened. Was the One still there with me? Should I dare raise my head and open my eyes to check? Still, I dared not take the chance to see.

Bob: Relax. Just relax; relax.

CHAPTER 23

The Mystic Returns

• • •

Betty: I thought, *What was that strong wind I heard?* I could sense a strange stillness, where even the mist settled down and seemed to move very little. There was still a very bright light within the entire area. Much to my surprise, the strong vibrations I had experienced began to rapidly diminish. It felt as if something had changed and was very different. It seemed quiet, like I was standing there all alone with my head still bowed. I waited to hear his voice when suddenly someone touched my shoulder. I was shocked. Could it be the One? Should I open my eyes? I bravely lifted my head and forced my eyes to a squint. A huge sigh of relief washed over my whole being. It was the Elder, who came back for me, as he promised. Evidently because he surprised me, he thought I should rest for a moment. Then once again he placed his arm on my shoulder and said to follow him. We moved through the thick mist that covered the floor of gold, white, and crystal. The whole area was still bathed in the awesome white light. I followed the Elder as we move to the side and then downward. It is still so bright and beautiful here. I'm defiantly starting to lose the shakes I had earlier and began to feel better about this strange and unusual encounter.

Bob: Just relax. Just relax. You're fine.

Betty: I'm following the Elder, who once again turned toward me and put his hand upon my shoulder in a gesture for me to keep up with him. I pulled in some deep breaths of air to catch my breath. I thought how much I appreciated the majestic energy of such beautiful light all around us. It was as if it had its own living presence that goes on forever. It is spirit. Oh, how beautiful life really is. There is so much to be thankful for. I was amazed, for I was truly seeing and feeling, beyond my physical senses, the incomparable beauty of light. Its warmth and shining brightness bestows so many blessings. After a while, the Elder stopped and purposely pointed to the orb for me to see that it wasn't much further. I was happy the craft that we had come here with was still there. *Now maybe we could slow down a bit*, I thought. I could see the mist surrounding some of the orb, and the watcher who stayed behind was standing by the open entrance, patiently waiting for our return. As we reached the orb, the watcher at the door signaled something to the Elder with his hand and entered the craft. The Elder and I then entered, and I saw the watcher, who was now settled in one of the seats, which he had somehow moved out of the original five-seated line, over to the right side of this rounded room. He was touching and concentrating on some type of small panel in his hand. The craft's door suddenly sealed shut. It was a little difficult to walk on this see-through, slightly slanted floor, which I did not notice before. The Elder then directed me to a front seat, turned toward the watcher, nodded, and sat down beside me. From what I could surmise from coming and going in this perfectly round orb, the interior and exterior of this machine seemed like the walls, were just all window. The smooth, rounded interior of crystallized glass material had no visible seams, no metallic joints, or paneled sections to hold it together. It was like we were sitting in a solid rounded layer of glass, with seats and a few other small metallic objects attached to the interior. It's strange, because I didn't take note of the small wall objects before. Once seated, we automatically lifted off the mist-covered unusual floor stationed below us. As usual, the orb moved along smoothly, and I thought to myself, *This machine must be a ball floating, or moving within a ball, for it to be so stable. Or maybe it's the distribution of weight that keeps it steady.*

At times the light outside was so extreme reflecting through the glass it was difficult to see. I spoke too soon. We were moving closer to something that was lifting the orb upward and causing sparks of light to roll along the smooth outer edge of the craft. The orb seemed to sway a little as we turned toward an area that spread out like an immensely expanded sheet of moving energy, which felt warm. Once again we had reached and entered the second energy field we had come through before, but it seemed as if we came upon it a lot faster than the first time. It began to get very warm while traveling through this blanket of rotating waves. Static electricity continued to bounce off the orb's shield of glass, and my hair felt odd. Finally the craft managed to cross the erratic stream of moving energy into a calm sea of nothing but white light. It was obvious we had reached and entered the wide expanse of sky that lay between the two very active sheets of electrical power. It became much warmer and quite impossible to see what was up ahead, for everything was white. We sat back in silence, knowing that sooner or later we would once again enter the second field of energy. The craft continued to move through the snow-white sky. There in front of us, just a short distance away, it suddenly cleared. We were moving toward and into the first sheet of moving rolls of energy again. It was scary. I braced myself in the seat, for although there was no static going on inside the craft, while moving through these strange rolling waves, its peculiar electrical charge created a shower of strange crackling sparks to bounce off the orb's exterior. I was thankful the heat inside managed to dry my hair. I closed my eyes, hoping we would quickly pass through the rest of the rolling waves of power. The static electricity in this area continued to dance over the orb's outer shell but did not hurt the craft or us in any way, except it was very warm and made loud, annoying crackling sounds. Once again it began to feel even warmer. We were almost through the second energy field when the Elder gently shook my shoulder for me to open my eyes and see what lay beyond. Flashes of white and sparkling lights were sweeping away some heavy pockets of mist, and in the distance, a spectacular array of colored beams of light could be seen, as we finally left the huge double field of energy. Once again our journey was bringing us closer and closer to the wondrous floating crystals. I could hardly wait. In the distance, up ahead, I could see the multicolored sprays of vivid rainbows as we moved further and further away from the energy field and closer to the wondrous lights. Bursts of colors and sparks of light were floating and flashing throughout the air and patches of mist. The orb was headed toward the awesome living presence of the fantastic field of crystals, and I thought, *This has to be the One's heavenly garden in space.* As we moved closer, I could hear the sound of softly ringing bells. I strained to listen to the unusual melodies, as if the beauty of the magnificent hanging crystals were not enough glory. Once again, the fantastic crystals were making beautiful sounds of unusual music, as they continued to rhythmically sway back and forth. I breathed in deep to catch my breath and release the pure joy I was feeling. The miraculous vision of such exquisite beauty left me weak. We had finally reached the enormous spread of glowing, living stones. Crystals of all shapes, sizes, and colors were floating in midair and stretched outward like a field of color. Some clusters moved about making glorious musical sounds as they gently touched one another, and then, with the soft music, to my surprise, I began to hear singing like voices as well. Once again the orb maneuvered within and between the opening spaces and suddenly had to stop. We were now surrounded and setting in the middle of a spectacular circle of beautiful, glowing colored crystals. We could not move. I turned to the Elder and asked him what happened. "How can we move from here? There's no opening. It's absolutely beautiful, but we can't stay here, right?" Suddenly a flock of large white birds appeared that flew upward from below the center area of the crystals and briefly circled the orb. "Look. Look," I said to the Elder. "I was right. I knew it. When you were taking me to see the One, those were the birds I saw in the green water, not fish. Why didn't you tell me? What is this place, where birds can swim underwater?" The Elder sat still, as if he was listening to the unusual music surrounding us. He was definitely not talkative. It seemed like he was not interested, nor concerned about what I thought, had to say, or what was happening. I suppose he was not happy with all the questions I had asked him. My attention turned back to the beautiful, exceptionally large birds settled on the top of some moving crystals close by, which allowed me to take a real good, close-up look at them. I was astonished, because the constant bright flashes of colored lights from the moving crystals did not reflect nor change the white color of the birds' feathers. They remained completely stark white all the time. These unusual birds had very small, rounded heads, with big eyes, sort of like doves' eyes. But the strange thing was they didn't seem to have a beak. I thought it may have been buried in the feathered neck area but wasn't sure. I could still hear the unusual, yet beautiful sounds of music. Only now, there was a blend of extremely soft singing voices as well. When I had first heard the singing, I thought the voices were coming from the crystal stones. But now I began to wonder, could it be that the pure white birds were doing the singing? Was it possible that they might be some type of feathery angel? They looked different than

most birds, with such small heads and long, wide wingspans and tails. The singing suddenly stopped, as the birds lifted off the crystals and began to circle the orb once again. They definitely had an impressive presence, as they stretched out their beautiful wide, flat wings and flew downward. Suddenly, I felt the orb plunge downward as well. It was as if we were following them. Or were they somehow carrying us along with them? For above, beside, and below the craft were these large flying white birds. One way or another, the orb was definitely going their way. It appeared as if the craft had a mind of its own and instinctively knew to follow the birds' flight downward, as we passed through an opened area below. The birds' outstretched wings gave them overwhelming control of their journey as they glided well past the craft and crystals into the now pale-green atmosphere. I glanced at the Elder and in my mind said, "We made it." To my surprise, he actually nodded his head to me. We were now moving along in the beautiful light-green sky. I glanced back at the flashing crystals and rainbows still hanging in air and wondered what happened to the birds. The orb continued to move onward, and once again I searched the sky, but they were not there. I glanced down into the water below, hoping to see them. The birds had somehow disappeared. I looked all around and concentrated on the waters below, yet as far as I could see, there were no birds or fish to be seen, only a gentle vast sea of green water. The orb was moving quickly across the calm waters. There were no heavy winds to push the craft around, as it did before, when we first had started out to see the One. I was thankful for that blessing. I did not relish the thought of the orb becoming a bouncing submarine again. However, while flying across the deep-green water for quite a while, the area seemed very calm and deserted. I sat there looking out at the emerald-green sea and atmosphere, thinking I was so happy to be heading home. As usual the Elder and watcher were quietly sitting at attention, waiting for us to arrive back to the landing area, so they could secure the glass orb. The Elder drew my attention, as he pointed to some land in the distance. As we continued flying, I could now see it was the same wide-mouthed opening of the corridor we had come out of. The self-sustaining orb swung over the landing area, hovered briefly, and settled down to park. The door opened, and we all rose to our feet. I was ready to go home. The Elder escorted me up the corridor, as the watcher trailed behind. We approached the door up ahead, stopped in front of it, and it opened with a flash of light as we passed through. I could see the long odd-shaped examining table was still there, but the room was empty. We all moved across the floor toward another adjoining room. I'm thinking, *They must be bringing me to the changing rooms, so I can get out of this robe and go*

home. I was surprised as I looked down at myself and the robe. I was still glowing with light. I had grown so used to the extreme glowing light while standing before the One that I had not thought of the light that was still covering me. The watcher stood by as the Elder took me by the arm and asked if I would please follow him. We went through the lighted door and entered another extremely bright room.

Bob: I want you to pause and look around in this room. Is there anyone in there?

Betty: Yes, there are Elders and other people, and they're all dressed in a robe like I have on. I'm still glowing. I can see like a glow coming out of my whole body. I'm amazed, and the people over there are looking at me. There are three other Elders; actually, there are four Elders, the one that just brought me in here and three others. There's a group of eight strangers standing to the right-hand side. Each one of them is dressed in a robe like I have on. The Elders were waving their hands over the heads of each person. The people were staring at me. I turned to the Elder that had brought me here, who was standing in back of me, and asked, "What are they doing?" As usual he did not answer. I could see two of the three Elders over by the group of people fanning their hands over the tops of their heads. I kept asking the Elder with me, "What are they doing that for? Why are they doing that?" I noticed that both the woman and men were patiently standing there as the Elders continued to wave their hands repeatedly over each one of their heads. It seemed like the people and their robes then started to glow. Something unusual was happening, because they were all starting to glow, exactly like I was glowing. There were eight people, but I didn't recognize any of them. They looked sort of ghostly. I held out my hands to check my light, to see if I was still as white as them, and I was. A partially bald, husky man came over to me and put out his hand to greet me. "Hello." I reached to shake his hand, when suddenly—wow—I saw and felt a bright-blue streak of electricity zap between both our hands. The touch went through me. "This is so strange. Am I dreaming?" he said.

"No, you're not dreaming."

"Then am I dead?" He reached out and touched my hand again. "Whoa, I can't be dead. Why am I feeling such a shock?"

I kept asking the Elders questions, but didn't seem to get any answers: Where is this place anyway? Where are we? What is this place? Why have you taken me here? In back of me I could hear an Elder ask, "Should we tell her?"

The Elder who had brought me there answered, "No, it is not the time. She must wait and rest. Eventually she will remember." I felt upset as he led me out of the room to the same gray-suited watcher standing by. He said something to the watcher and immediately returned to the same room we came out of. The watcher told me to follow him. We went into an empty room, through another doorway of light. I can still see my skin is glowing white light and wondered if I was going to stay this way or not. We passed through the lighted door into the large round room, where the moving floor design was still spreading out wave after wave of bands of light. The watcher led me to the same changing room for my clothes. As I removed and hung up the robe, the strange light disappeared from both the garment and my body. I quickly put on my nightgown and thought, *Finally I'll be able to go home.* I felt very tired. I rushed out to the waiting watcher. We immediately moved across the floor to the same entrance, which I recognized as the same door that opened quickly with light when we first came in here. Once we were in the room where the Elder had been working before, I could see the bunch of lights, unusual designs, and button-like switches on the wall. Also there was the stemmed basin still there, with the water still circling at the bottom and the moving water in the basin. Both waters carried something like moving symbols within them.

For the time being, Bob feeling we both needed a time of rest, decided to end this hypnosis session. We would return at a later date to see and record anything else that may have happened. I was happy to call it a day, but at the same time, I knew there was more to be addressed. There was still the matter of the three-fingered handprint to deal with.

SESSION 4 FOR THE 1994 EXPERIENCE: NOVEMBER 11 AND 12, 2013

Bob: When I press your shoulder, you will go deeper and deeper and become more relaxed. You are totally relaxed, in control, and perfectly safe, as you return to the time within a brightly lit room, before something that looks like a birdbath. There is water with some unusual moving symbols in it. You are waiting for something. Now, what I would like you to do is to tell me what has happened from that point on. What happened while you were standing by that birdbath? You can see it clearly in your mind's eye.

Betty: I'm just standing there with one of the gray watchers look-ing at the basin of water, with those strange little black things moving in there. They look like symbols, and there are some at the bottom stem, as well as the top bowl of the basin, where there is water rushing and swirling around. We're just standing there wait-ing and watching when all of a sudden I see something slowly ris-ing out of that water basin-like fountain…I don't know what it is.

It looks like thin wire. I don't know if it is actually wire or what. It doesn't look like what I saw the first time I was here, but something is coming up through the water to the top of the basin. It's now up above the surface of the water. I don't know what the things are. It's odd and different from the wire rings and lights we saw appear in there the last time. The thing looks like a whole bunch of different wires strung together in a peculiar shape. They must have come up from the bottom stem of the basin again. Earlier they looked much different. They are not the same. Some of them seem to light up. OHH. One of the tall Elders is coming in. He must be the Elder we saw stationed at the lights on the wall across from us. He's coming over to us; oh, and he's going on the other side where the watcher is. The watcher is looking up at him, and it seems as if they may be talking to each other through the mind. I don't know what they are communicating, as I can't hear anything. I'm tired. I'd like to go home. The watcher looked over at me and then back at the Elder. Then the Elder returned back to the lights on the wall and pushed some of the button-like things, and the wall lit up. Some lights were white, and others blinked on and off with multiple colors. We're still just standing there watching the lights as the Elder turns and goes past us and leaves our area. He heads way over toward the left. I turned to look once again at the

strange basin's wire machine still sticking out of the water. Then I heard the watcher talking to me in my mind. He said, "We have to go. Follow me." He moves around me, and I'm just automatically following, just moving forward. Oh, we're going in the same direction as the Elder went. We are also passing the area where that huge, wide beam of bright white light is, where all those little childlike beings were when I first came in here. They are not there now, but the beam of intense light is still vibrating with light energy. We continued to move on past this area and into another room, where a door of bright light just opens. We entered the room, and as I looked across the room, I could see three beings of light sitting very still. Their legs are crossed, and in their laps are their folded arms with open hands and palms exposed. They're not moving, just sitting very still. There is another Elder standing there with them. The other Elder, which must be the one who was with us at the lights and peculiar water basin, tells me to come over and sit down on the seat that's there. It was some kind of weird-looking chair. As I sat down, I glanced over at the light beings and noticed the other elder raising his arms and hands up and moving his fingers up and down. The three light beings quickly stood up. Amazingly, as they stood up, they turned into normal people. There was a woman and two men. They were dressed in nightclothes. The woman wore a nightgown, one man had pajamas, and the other had a white T-shirt and boxer shorts on. Suddenly I got a rush of chills and stood up. The short, husky, partially bald-headed man deliberately turned to face me and revealed a look of astonishment on his face, as if he knew me. I thought to myself, *That man looks very familiar. I think he is the same man that shook my hand when we were all in white robes.* The Elder continued to move the three people along, and they went out through another brightly lit doorway. Wow. That was something, wow. That had to be the same man that shook my hand hello and caused me to feel a jolt of electricity go through me. I think he recognized me as well, and that's why he turned and looked straight at me.

CHAPTER 24

The Forgotten
Job Revealed

• • •

AND NOW THE OTHER ELDER, who was with me and the watcher, is once
again telling me to be seated. The gray watcher is right next to me now,
just standing there at attention. As I sat down, the Elder stood in front
of me and said, "Betty. Betty, listen to me wisely, and understand." I was
listening, but wondering what's going on here. The Elder said to me, "Do
you remember when you were a child, and you were taken to see the One?"

And I said, "Yeah, I remember. That was when those small beings
told me they were taking me to see my father, and I knew they couldn't be
telling me the truth, because my father was at home. I remember, because
that's when they picked me up with that moonlike craft, when I was going
up to the field and woods."

Then the Elder said, "Was it not then that they also told you that the
One wanted to see you?"

I said, "Yes, but they also said at the time that they were taking me to
see my father."

The Elder said to me, "All children are from the one Father."

And I thought out loud, "What?"

The Elder then repeated, "The Creator, the One, is the father of everyone and everything."

"Well, this is an odd and strange conversation we're having. I never
thought of it that way before."

The Elder continued, "Do you remember as a child, when you were before the One? Do you recall seeing and hearing him?"

And I answered and said, "No, I don't remember. There was so much bright white light, shining everywhere, all the time I was in there, and I was afraid, for I was young when they took me there."

The Elder continued to inform me, "Well, the One gave you some work to do."

I said, "Work? What kind of work did I do?"

He said, "The One put the work within your mind and gave you a blessed gift to be able to do it."

And I said, "What? Why am I now being told?"

The Elder continued, "Because you didn't do the work right away, until you were older. You then did some of it. That work was to show the power of the Word, because he wanted the world to see and believe."

I said to the Elder, "What are you talking about? I don't understand this. I don't remember the work you are talking about."

He said to me, "You were given an assignment to do, to show the power. Pictures are powerful words."

I'm thinking, *What?* "What is this? What is going on? This is odd to me." I was bewildered. "Are you saying the One had actually given me a job to do at thirteen years old?" I asked again, "What kind of a job was that?" In my mind I tried to recall what happened back then. I remember that I had a difficult time understanding each time I was before the One, for all I could see was bright white light. I just didn't understand what was being said to me and what was going on. "Anyway," I said to the Elder, "at thirteen years old, I was too young to have a job."

"Well," he continued, "you managed to complete most of the work as you grew older. But after you finished the task for him, you never released it."

I then repeated, "Well, what do you mean? What are you talking about? I still don't understand. Don't forget; I was still little. I was a young person when I first went to see the One, and I really didn't know who the One was or what was happening. It was bright and absolutely beautiful when I was taken through the great door into the world of light. But, right now, I can't remember talking with anyone or what the One had spoken to me about. Don't forget, that happened to me many, many years ago. You said I finished the job. How did I finish something that I can't remember?"

The Elder finally said, "As you grew older, your soul and spirit understood. You felt and took the power from the Word and put it into picture to help people see and understand."

"Are you talking about the book of Revelation?" I asked.

"Yes," he answered, "The Creator's important messages to humankind. You studied, drew, and then painted pictures of the prophetic words and descriptions of things to come. But you didn't release it. You didn't complete the entire job that way."

"Is that why I'm here in this place today?" I asked.

"Yes, that and to receive another task to come in the near future."

Betty, being a little upset that she didn't understand what she was supposed to have done, begins to breathe heavy, and said to the Elder, "I tried to get the paintings of the Word to the people. I showed the pictures on slides, to two different congregations, and they seemed to understand and enjoy them."

"Yes, but it was not enough," the Elder replied. "It has to be shown to the world. It is time for the world to awake, before it's too late."

"How am I supposed to do this? There is so much controversy going on all the time...especially if people think it's something religious, and I'm just one person."

"Betty, listen well," the Elder said. "It will not be you that shall lift the veil covering the truth. It is the One that opens the mind, heart, and eyes from blindness. So all that truly seek is able to see the light, freedom, and joy."

Bob: Relax. Just try to relax. Relax.
Betty: The Elder continued to say, "Power will be given, and a way will be made. For it is time for that work to be done. It must go out. But for now, you have to return." The Elder moved over to the gray

watcher, as if to briefly communicate with him, before leaving. As the watcher drew closer to me, I stood up to follow him toward the brightly lit door we had passed through. Once again I could see the location of the large beam of light from floor to ceiling, which now seemed to have grown very dim. Thankfully, we were still able to see, for there was just enough light in this area, above the gathered low-hanging mist on the floor. Some yards ahead of us was another brightly lit doorway. As we moved closer to that door—oh. Whoa. We were completely taken by surprise and suddenly stopped and

stood still. There was another gray watcher rushing in through that door, moving very quickly toward us. He had something moving about in his hands. We waited as he drew closer and were able to see he was carrying something in each hand. It looked like it was two of those little beings I had seen much earlier in the trailer, and like those who were seated around the large beam of light much earlier. He was carrying them like a cat would carry a kitten, by pinching the nape of their necks, and they're squirming around, trying to get loose. The watcher put them down, and they immediately scurried off to the side and disappeared in the mist. The same watcher quickly turned and went right back out the door once again. "What's going on? What's going on?" I asked. Again the watcher with me was silent. "How come I can't get any answers from you watchers?" I blurted out. "I am tired of being ignored."

He just repeated, "Follow me, please." And again we started to move toward the lit doorway. Suddenly, once again, without warning the same gray watcher appeared at the entrance, carrying two more little beings, holding them like a cat with her kittens. He put them down, and like the first two, they quickly disappeared into the low, misty atmosphere. The watcher silently communicated to the watcher who I was with and then hastily moved away behind us. The guardian watcher motioned for me to follow him, and we both headed for the lit doorway, wondering if anyone else might be coming through. As we stepped out through the door, I'm surprised yet happy at what I see. I'm home and in familiar surroundings. We are standing right next to the bedroom closets in our fifth-wheel trailer. He's telling me through the mind, "You must return to bed now." I'm so happy to be home. And I started moving slowly to my side of the bed. I am passing him and stepping up to the bedroom floor. I can see Bob is still fast asleep. If only he knew what I've had to go through this night. I'm getting into bed, and as I looked down toward the lower level of the room, I can see the gray watcher going through the lit closet door as I lay back against my soft pillow, and quickly fall to sleep.

Bob: OK. Relax. Relax. I'm going to count three…two…one…to bring you home.

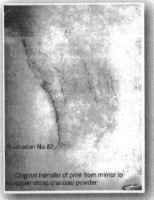

Illustration No. 82

Original transfer of print from mirror to paper using charcoal powder

Bob quickly pulled me back to our reality. Home, sweet home—or so I thought. The very next day, we discovered the watchers' calling card. The fact remains that an unusual three-fingered handprint left on the mirrored closet door became another hidden mystery in my life that would haunt, and conceal, an extremely important personal alien encounter that lasted almost two decades, before it was completely remembered and now, finally, released.

CHAPTER 25

A Signal in the Night

• • •

On August 12 or 14, 2011, I had a very unusual dream—one that I feel I should definitely relate to you in closing. In the dream, I was sitting beside an endless body of clear water. I was totally relaxed and enjoying the refreshing presence of sunlight now resting upon the still water. As I glanced across its silvery surface and looked deeper within the water, I could see thousands of shiny fish. They were all the same size, about five inches long. Some were golden, others were silver or white, and still others were shades of pearl or pale peach. Their bodies were not moving but were lined up in row after row in the water, and they remained stationary, as if waiting for something.

As I looked closer, I could see that they had side fins and a dorsal fin, but there were no tails. I remember saying, "Dear God, they have no tails. They need tails." At that moment, a canister of water appeared beside me with wiggling, live fishtails moving about. Although I did not see him, I knew he had heard me and supplied the living tails. Now it was up to me to get the tails to the fish. I reached for a living tail from the canister and plunged my hand into the water just to the rear of a fish. The tail swooped on to its back end. The fish immediately moved away, as if filled with joy, since it could finally swim. Again, I grabbed another living tail and plunged my arm into the water, and the second tail connected to a waiting fish. I continued the process over and over as each little fish worked its way into line for a tail. All night I plunged my arm in and out of the water to give each fish a living tail. I was not tired, just delighted that thousands of fish could now swim. As the last few fish received their tails, I awoke refreshed and satisfied; I had been part of providing them some direction.

But why in the first place had the small fish needed tails, and why did the Father give them one? Is it because the fish is the symbol for Christ, and these fish are his chosen ones? Later, I mentioned to Becky the unusual dream I'd had concerning the fish, and she said, "Mom, those fish sound like the one hundred and forty-four thousand sealed souls (in Revelations 7:4) that faithfully serve God—how they patiently waited in the water for the Father's direction and did not move until then." I was shocked at her revelation. Is it possible? Could the Father, who is the only one who knows when the end will happen, be giving his children special directions or specific instructions to know what to do when that unknown time arrives? My dream made a huge impact on me. For many days, I wondered, *What does this mean? Is the spirit trying to tell me something? If so, what is the message? Why did I feel it had something very important to reveal?*

I knew that eventually, through prayer and research, I would find the answer. I went to the Bible first. Jesus said to his disciples, "I will make you fishers of men." I knew the symbol for the ocean represented the world, so that had to mean the disciples were fishermen, and the ocean was the world. Those fishermen who baited their hooks with love, truth, and forgiveness have caught many chosen men and women for the eternal kingdom. I then considered the fish graphic that represents Christ. We know that Jesus said just before he died, "It is finished." The graphic symbolic body is finished, but the fishtail at the end has no closure; two sides of the tail are wide open on the fish graphic. This must mean there is still time for others to decide, or might it mean that humanity has no idea what will happen at the end and is sorely in need of spiritual understanding? Why not be ready? The Word speaks of the end and says in the King James Bible, Matthew 24:36, "But of that day and hour knoweth no man, no, not the angels of heaven, but my Father only."

I pondered on my unusual prophetic dream of small fish in need of living tails. What could it possibly mean? I soon realized and understood. These 140,000 fish are the children of Christ, a symbol of true and faithful believers who are waiting and trusting in the Father's Word. May your soul and spirit understand, and be blessed as well, with his Word of love and care. Thank you, dear reader, for your interest in our unusual life experiences. May they help in some way to strengthen your soul.

BOB'S NOTE:

Over the years, a number of people have asked if a movie would be done of our experiences. Well, for over thirty years, Universal Studios has owned the rights to this story, and they have shelved the project. To the best of our knowledge, they have no intention of doing a movie. The frustrating thing is that there have been others interested in doing this movie, but even though Universal purchased these rights years ago for a small amount of cash, they now want over $1 million to sell the rights to anyone interested in doing this film. Did Universal do this on purpose to keep our story from becoming even more public? Were we just taken advantage of because of our lack of understanding in how to deal with entertainment companies? Or is the problem rooted in some other reason? I can relate only the circumstances, so readers can decide for themselves if Universal has treated us fairly.

Also, we have mentioned a number of times in this book that for further or more specific details of one encounter or another, it would be necessary to refer to one of the previous books about our story. These are *The Andreasson Affair*, *The Andreasson Affair, Phase Two*, *The Watchers*, *The Watchers Two*, and *The Andreasson Legacy*. We are fully aware that books cost money, and in today's times, we don't expect people to run out and buy all of these books. Check your local library! Most should have copies of these on hand, for those of you who are interested.

Made in the USA
Columbia, SC
20 June 2020